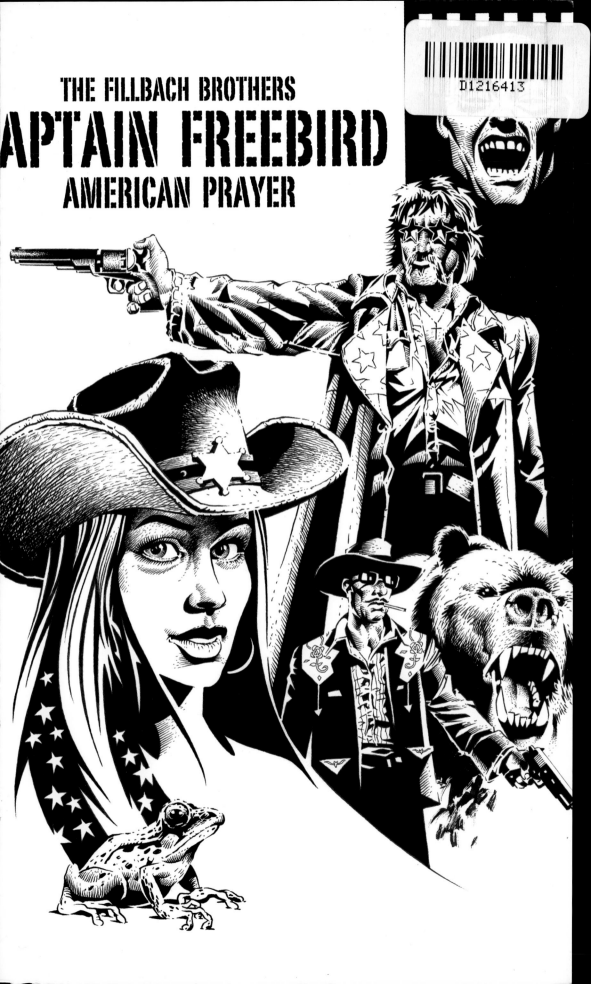

THE FILLBACH BROTHERS

APTAIN FREEBIRD

AMERICAN PRAYER

THERE WILL COME A TIME WHEN YOU
BELIEVE EVERYTHING IS FINISHED.

THAT WILL BE THE BEGINNING.

—LOUIS L'AMOUR
(LONELY ON THE MOUNTAIN)

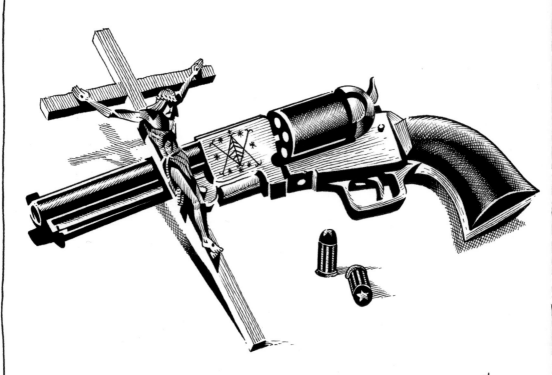

FILLBÄCH
BROTHERS

1

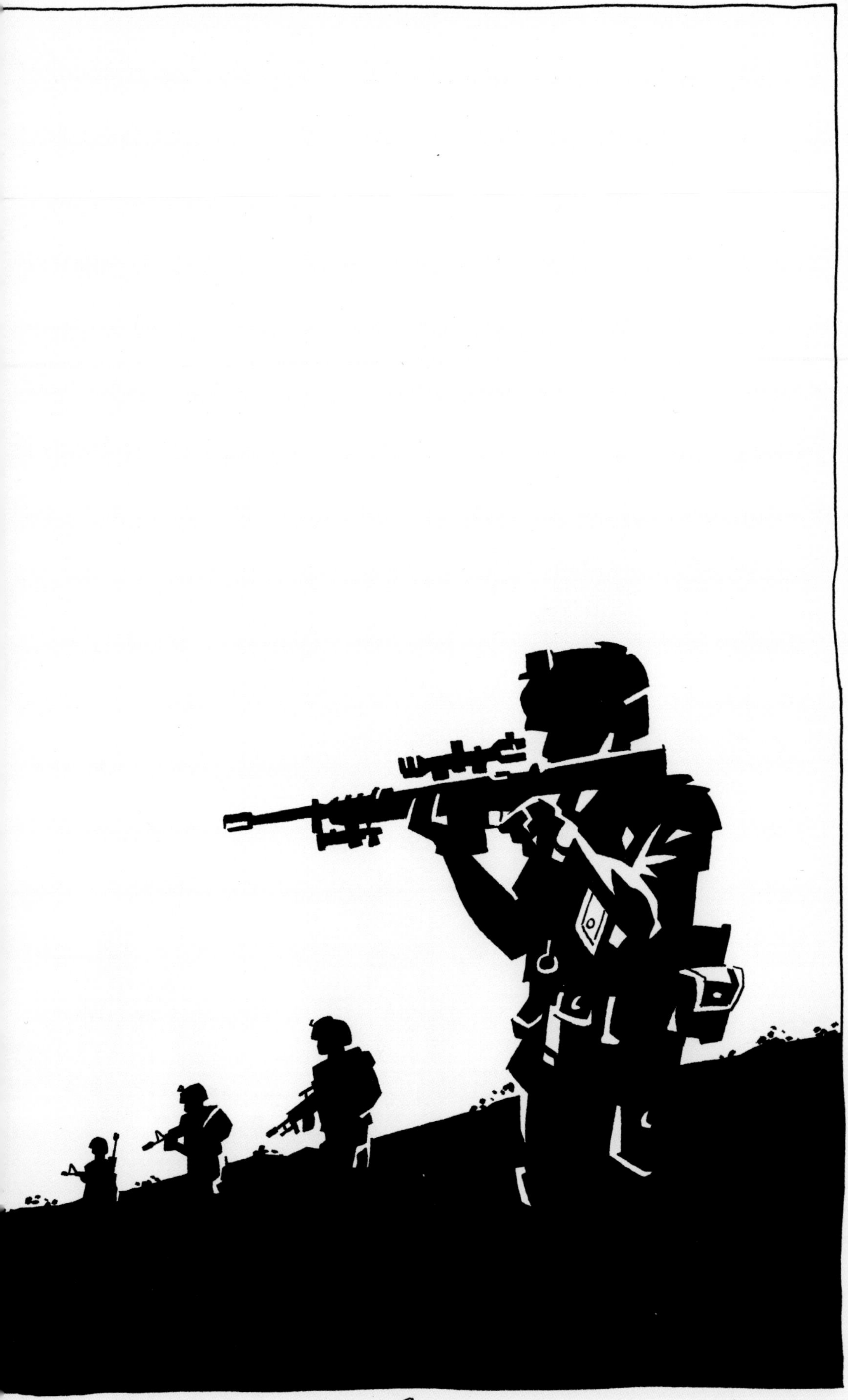

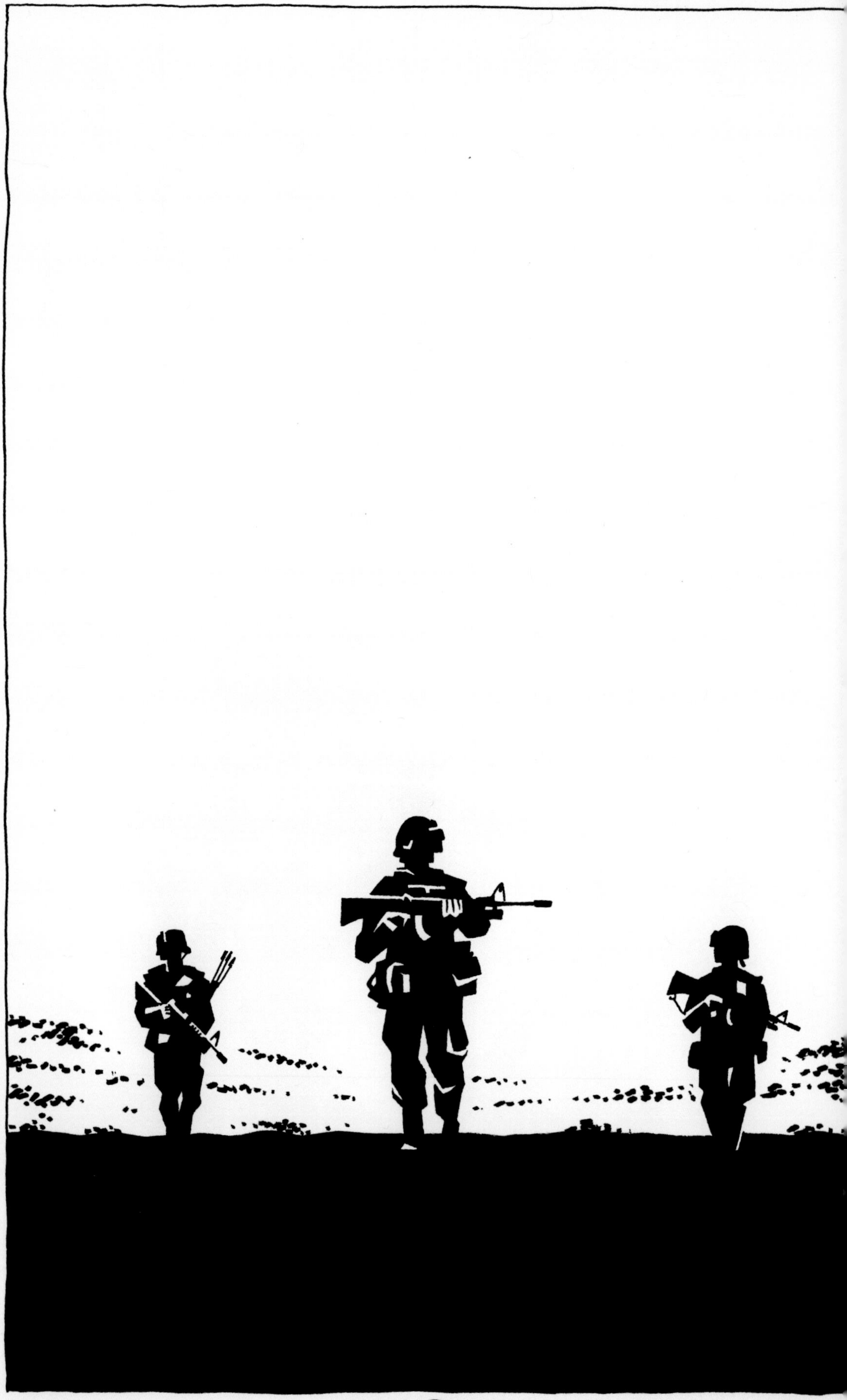

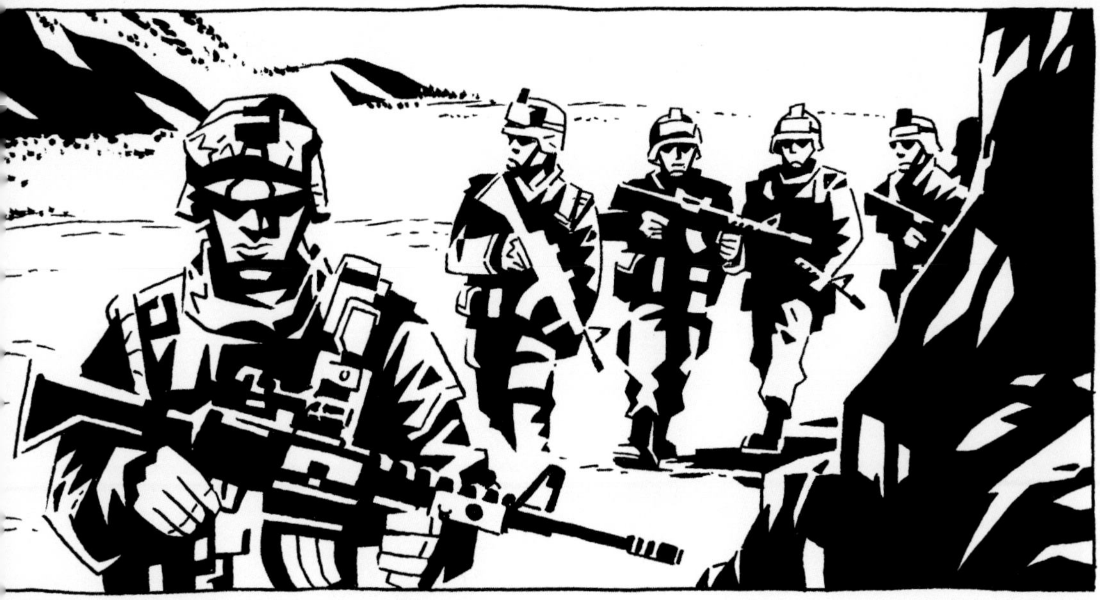

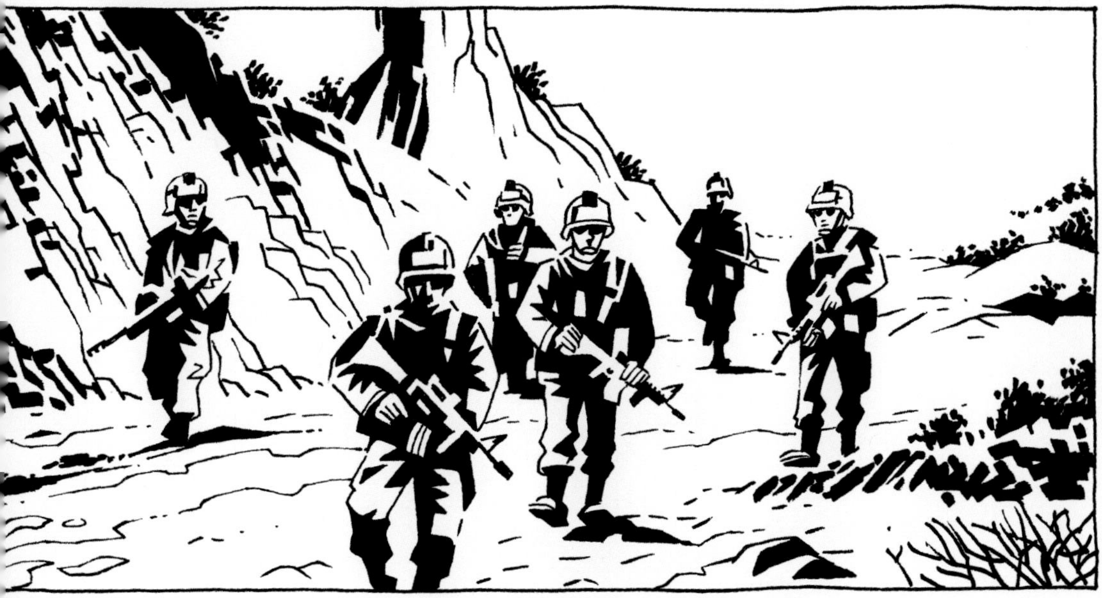

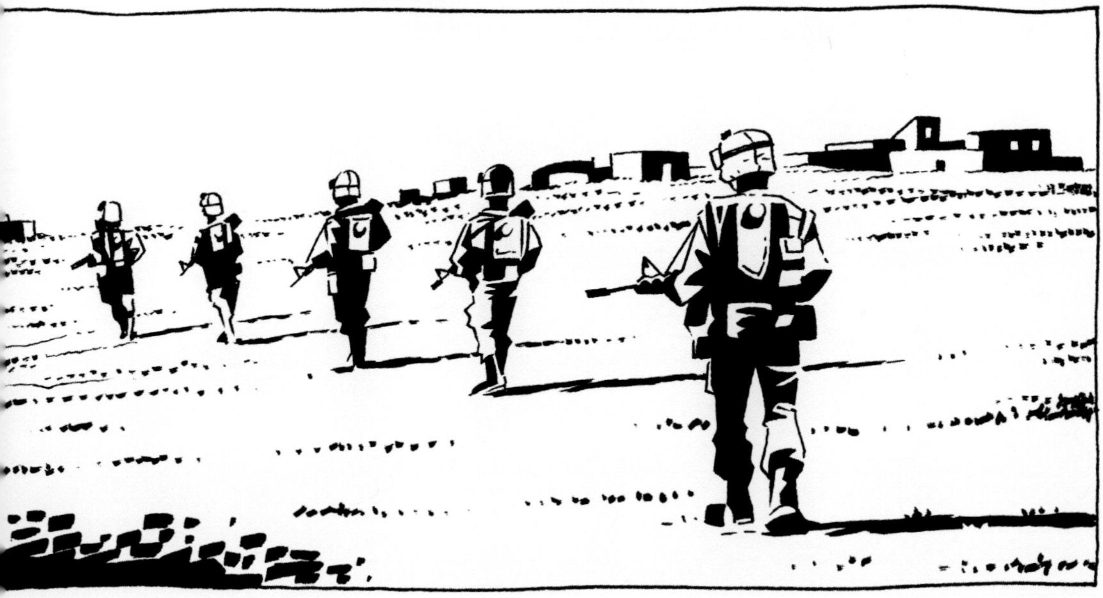

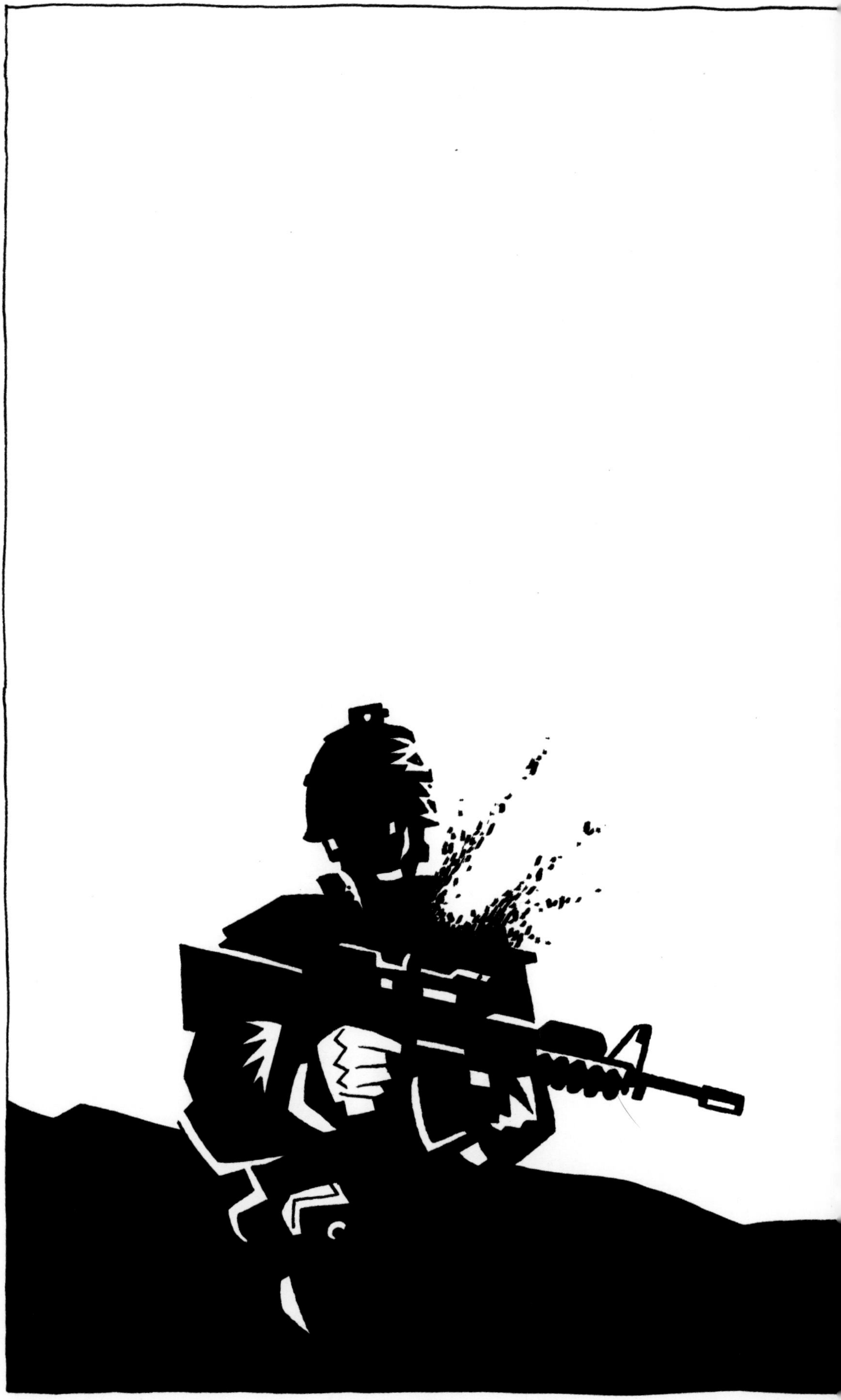

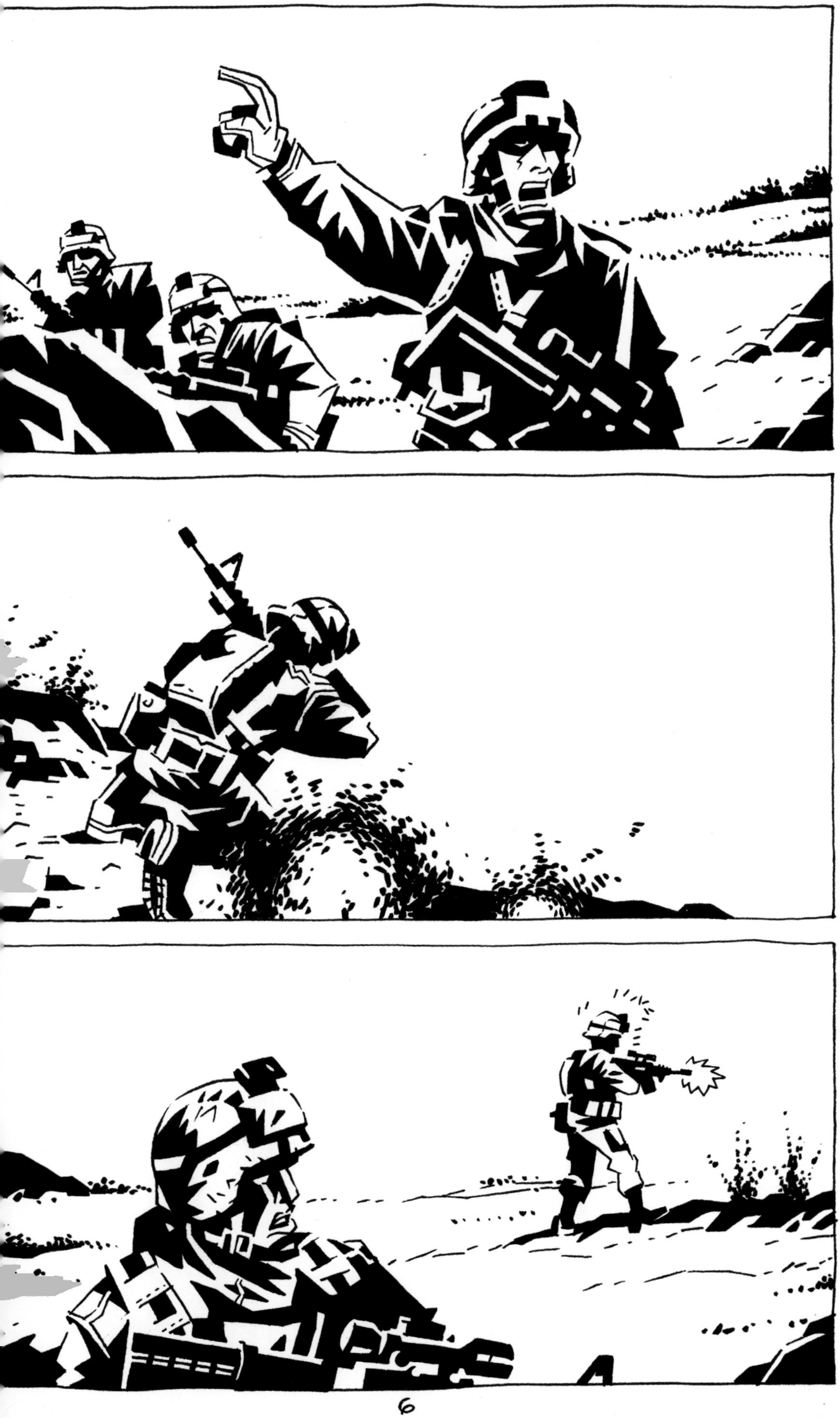

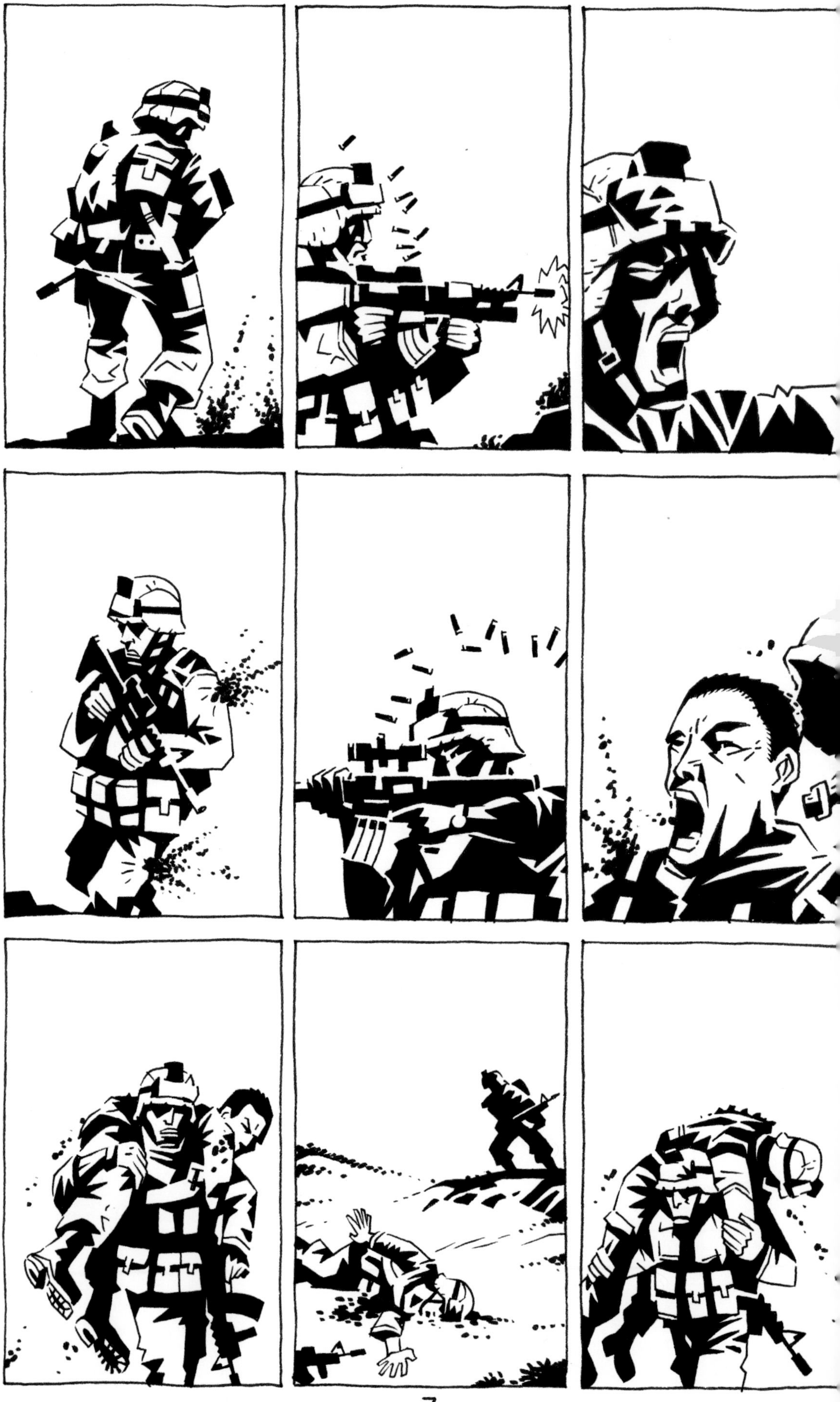

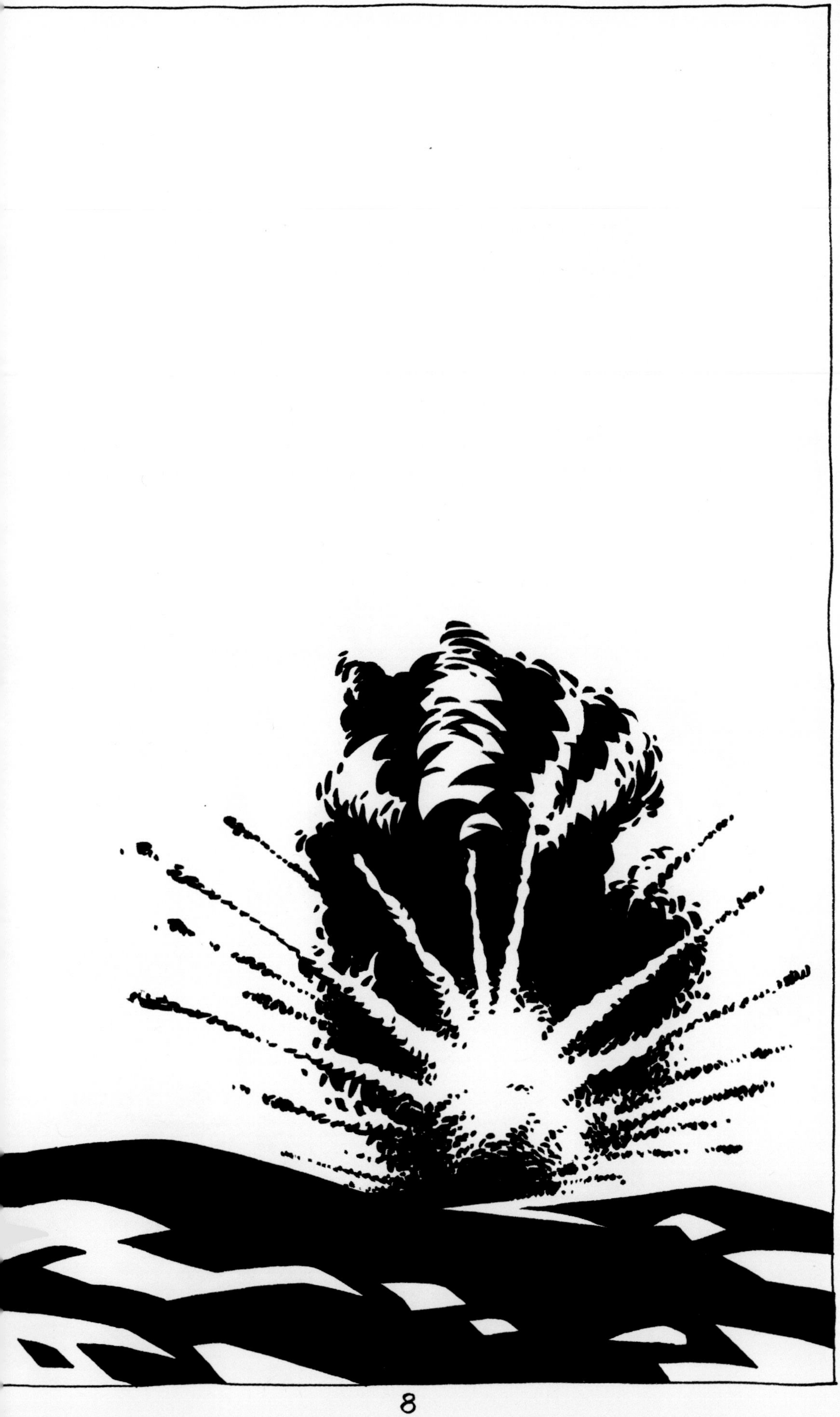

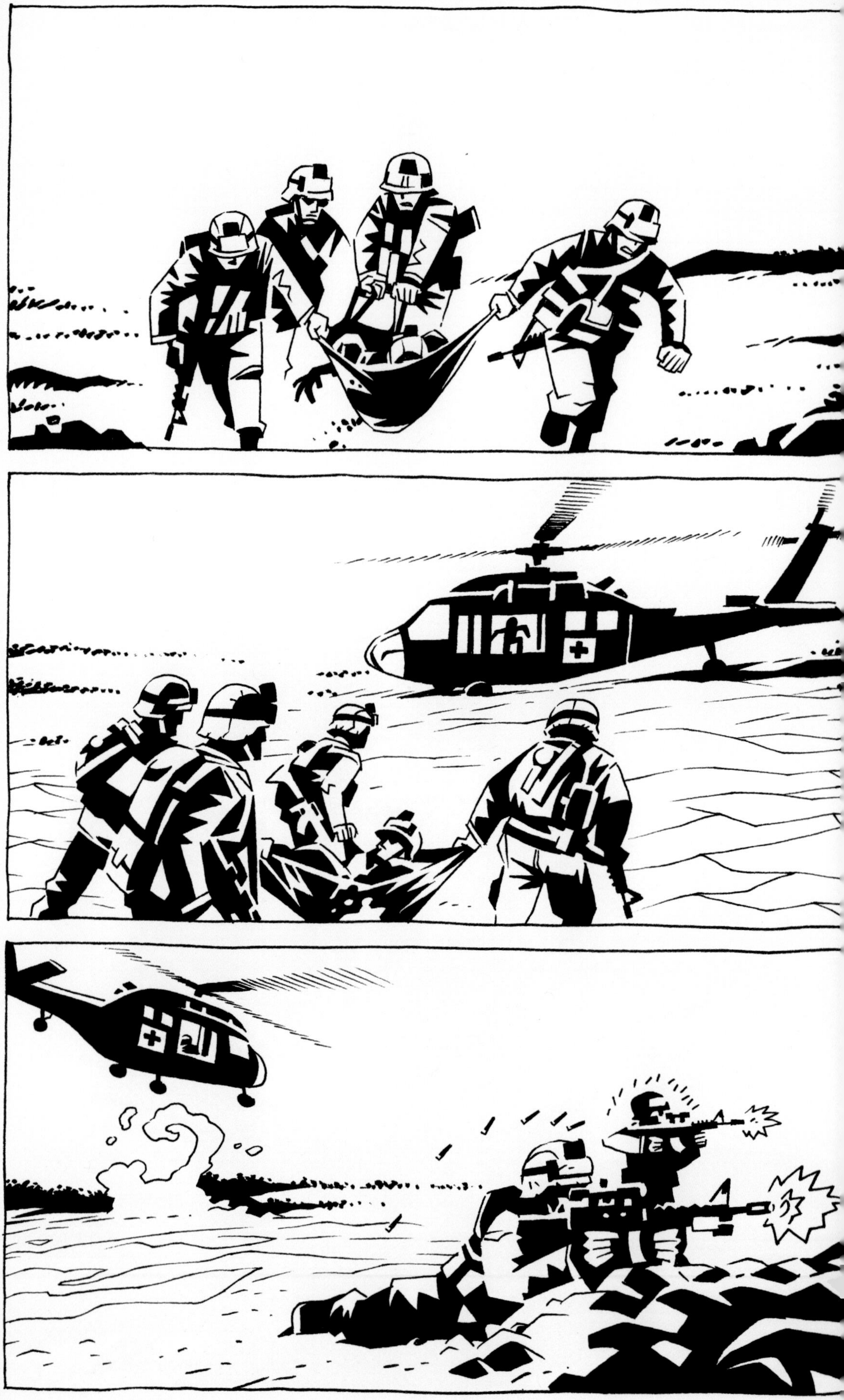

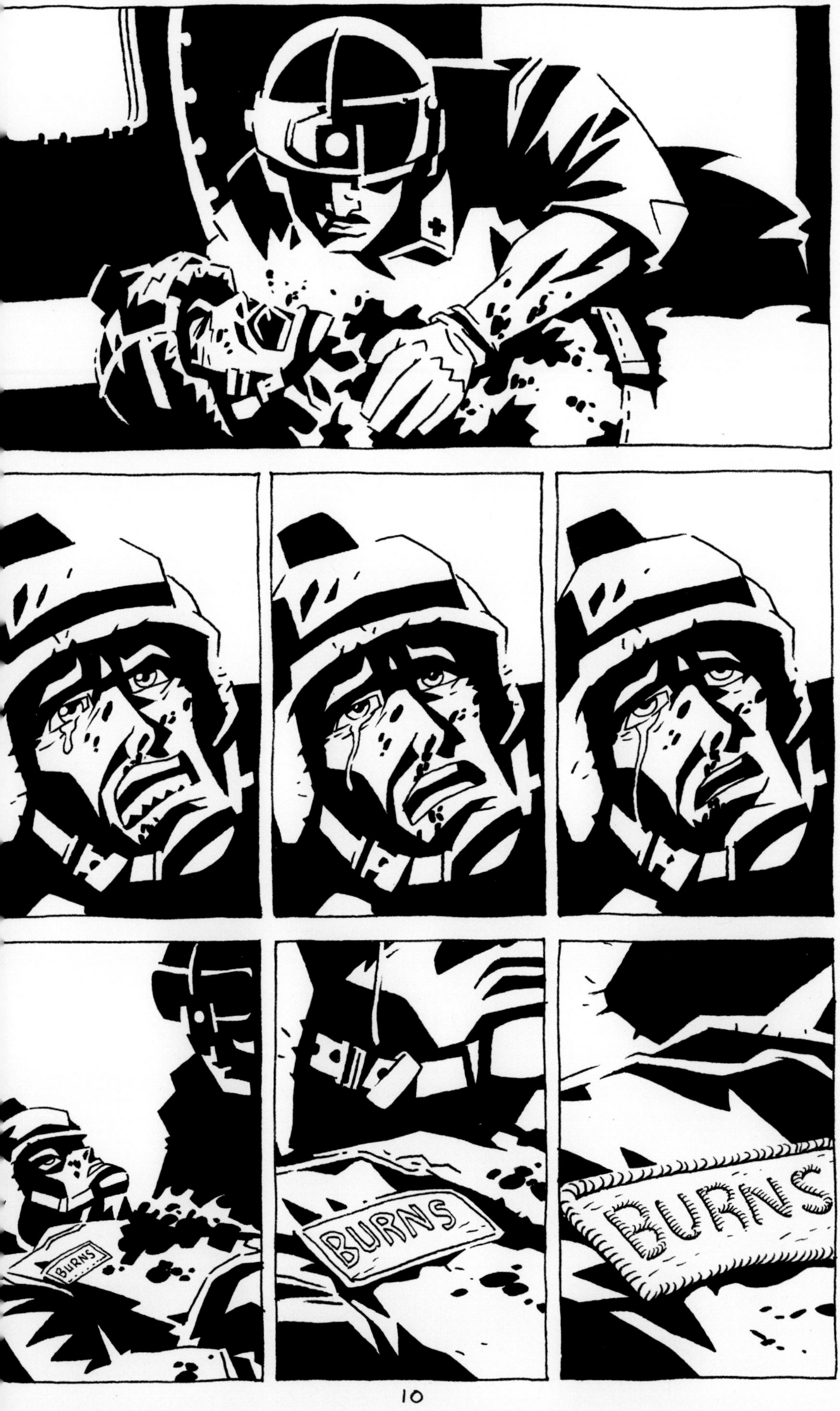
BURNS
BURNS
BURNS

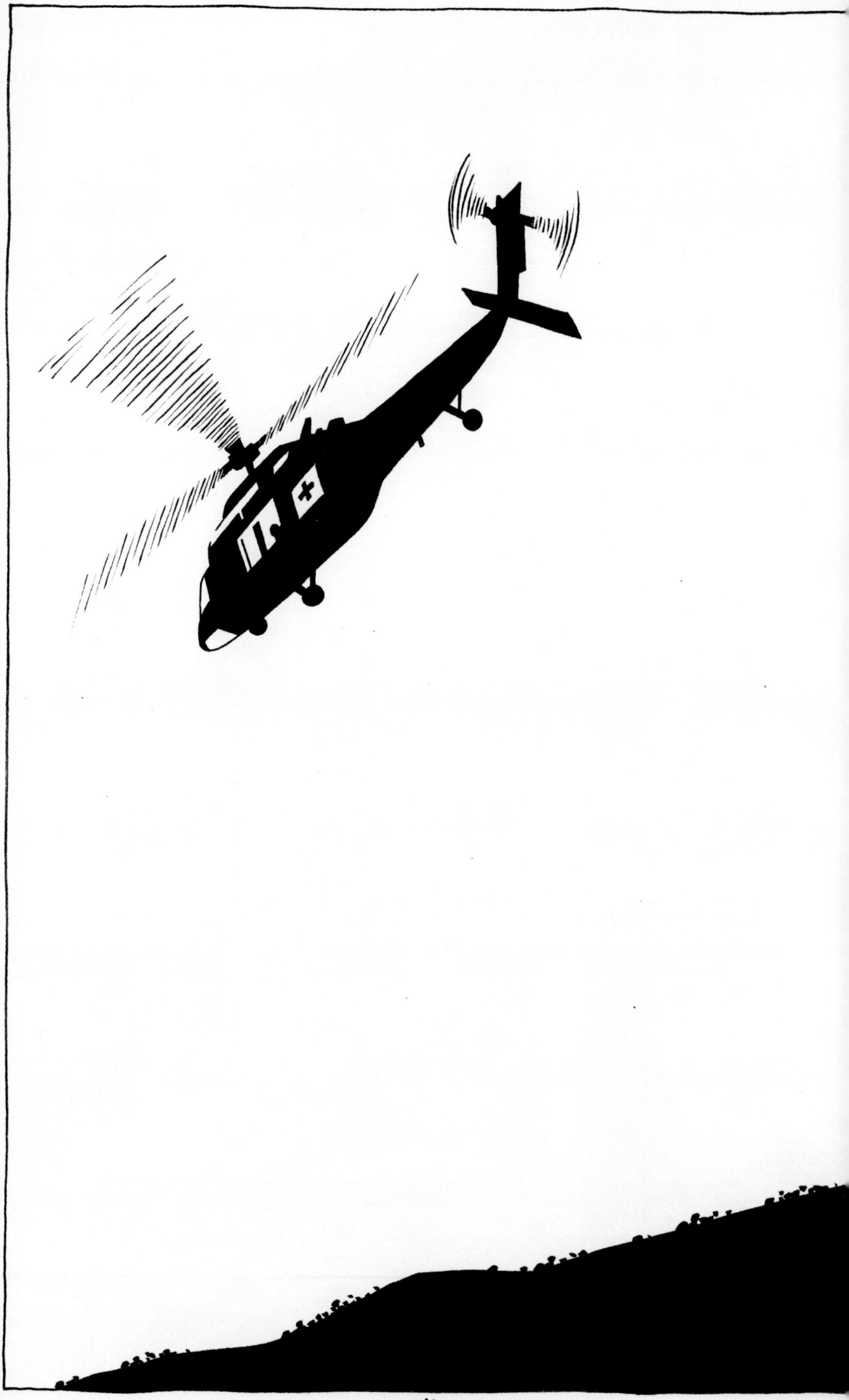

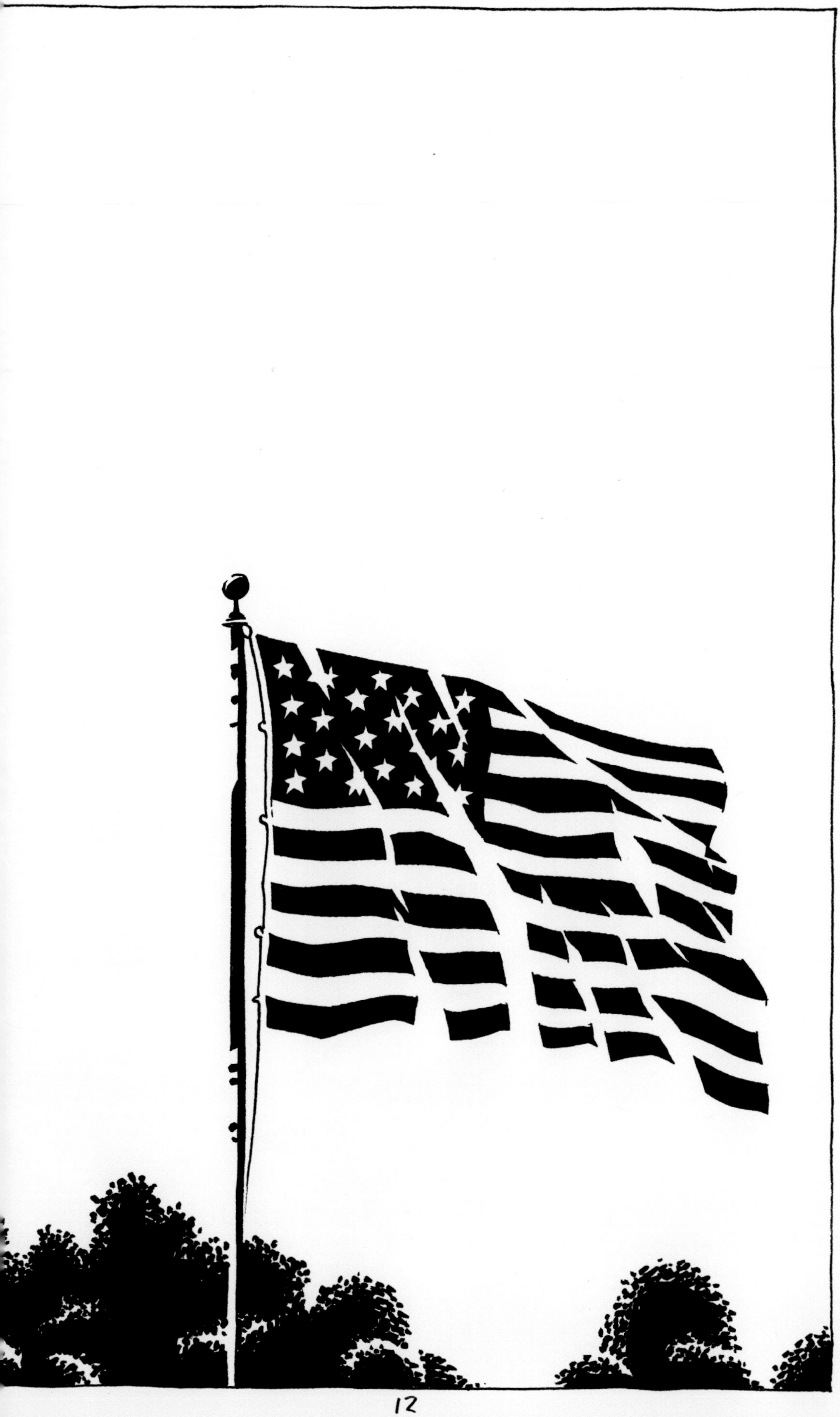

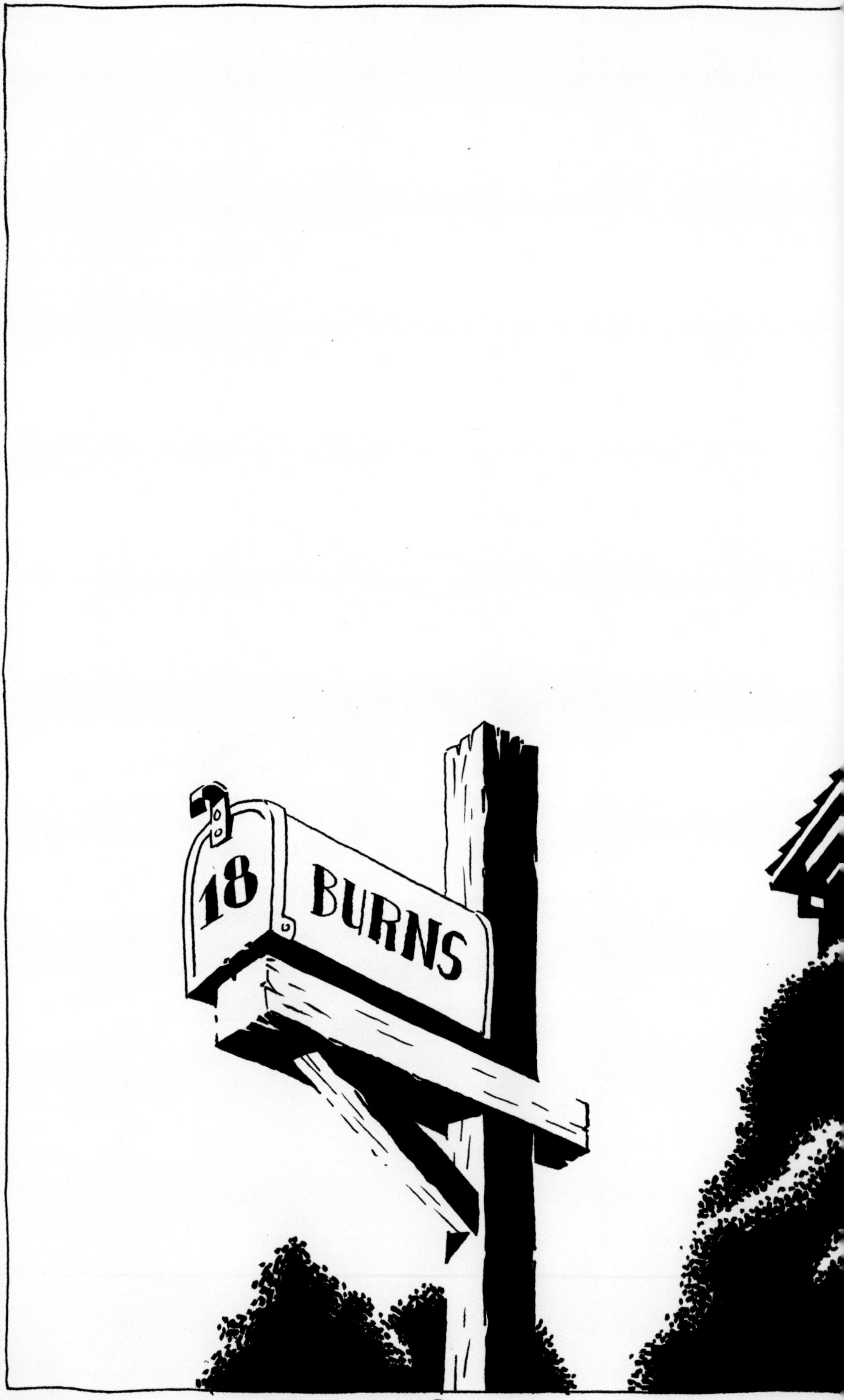
18
BURNS

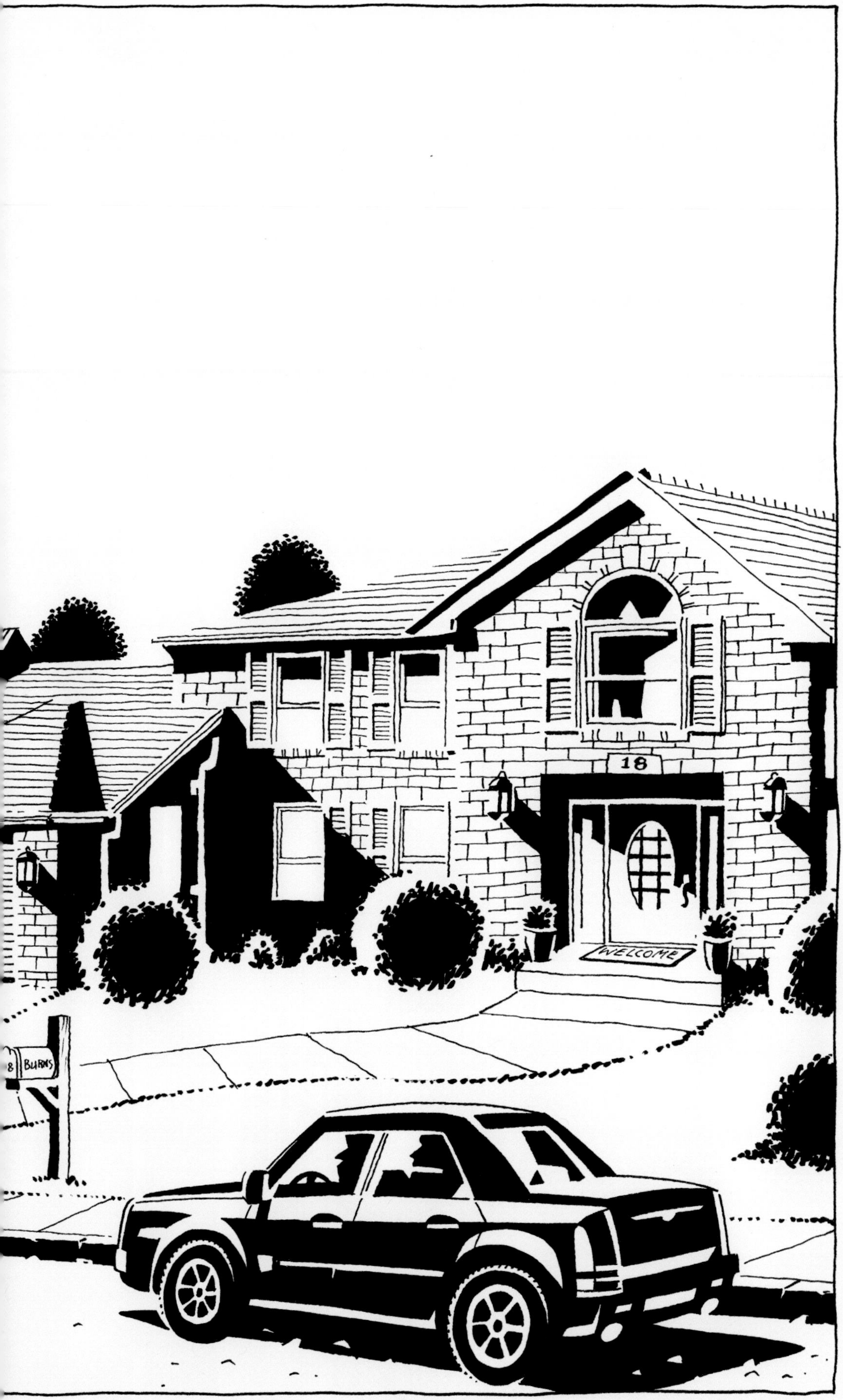
18
WELCOME

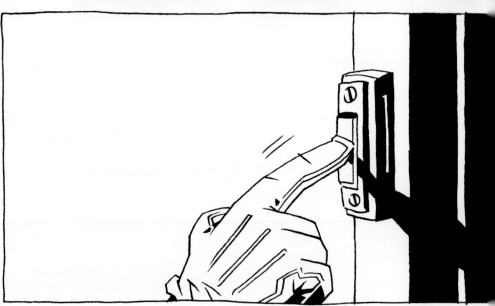

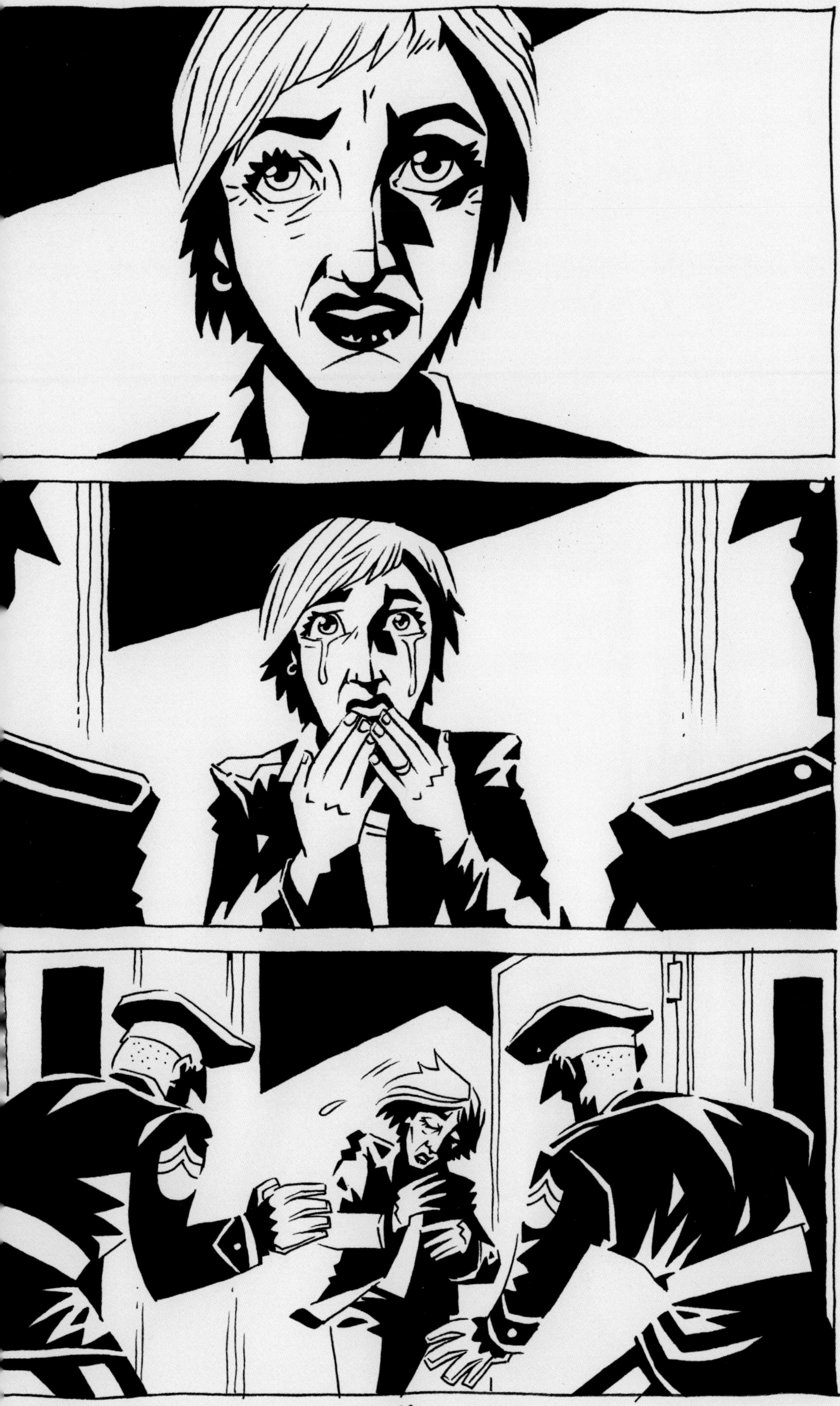

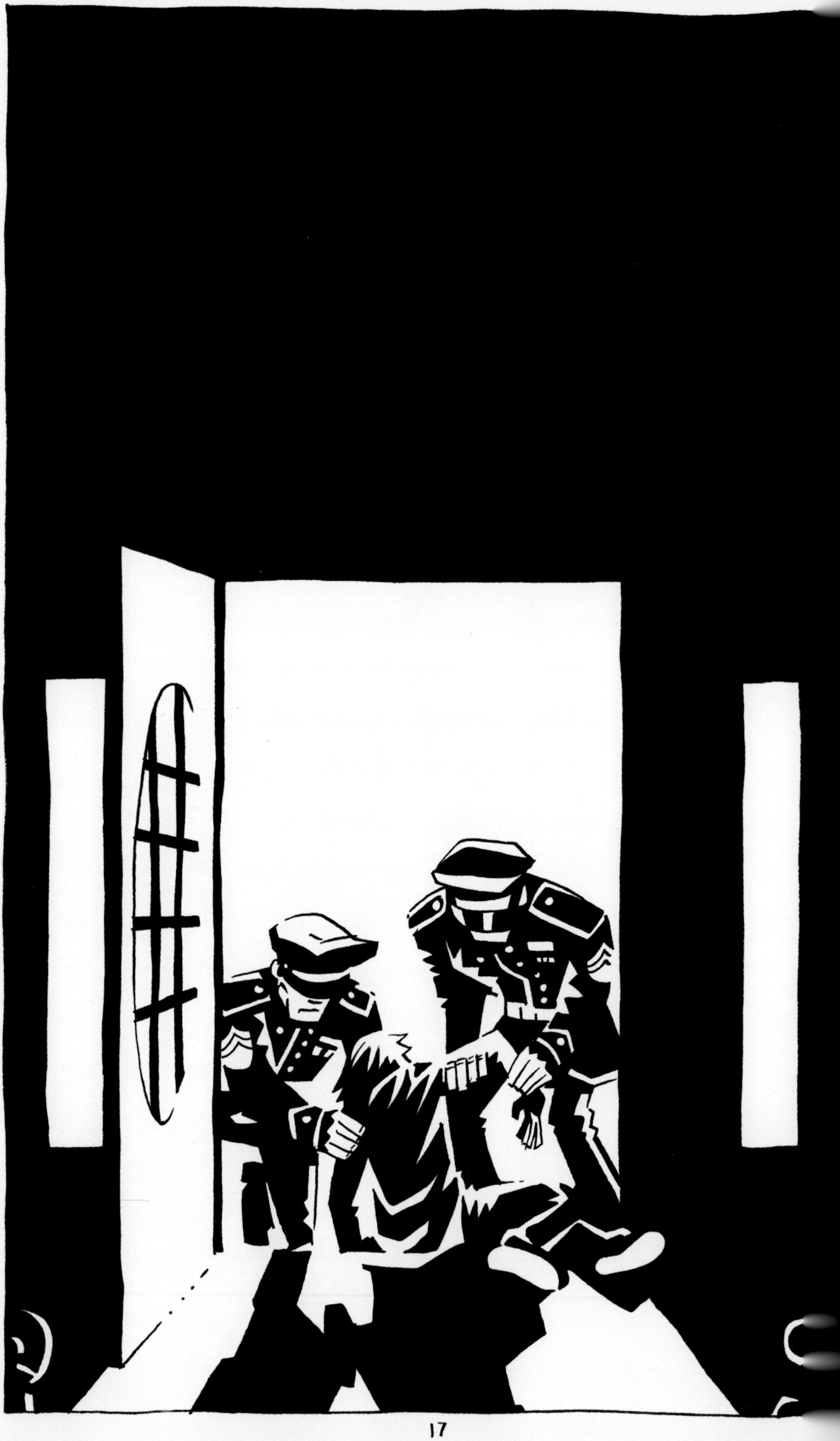

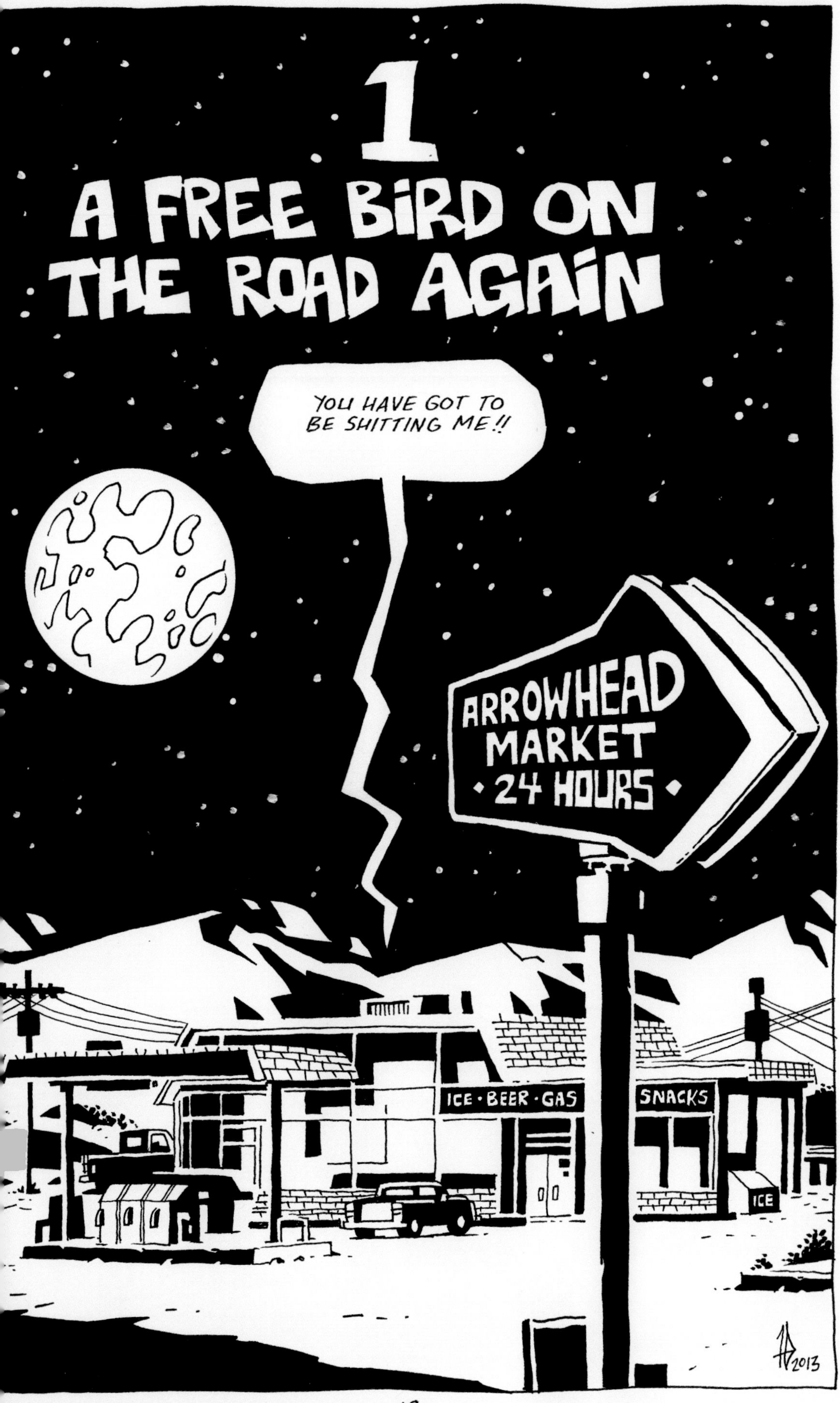
1
A FREE BIRD ON THE ROAD AGAIN
YOU HAVE GOT TO BE SHITTING ME!!
ARROWHEAD MARKET
• 24 HOURS •
ICE • BEER • GAS
SNACKS
ICE

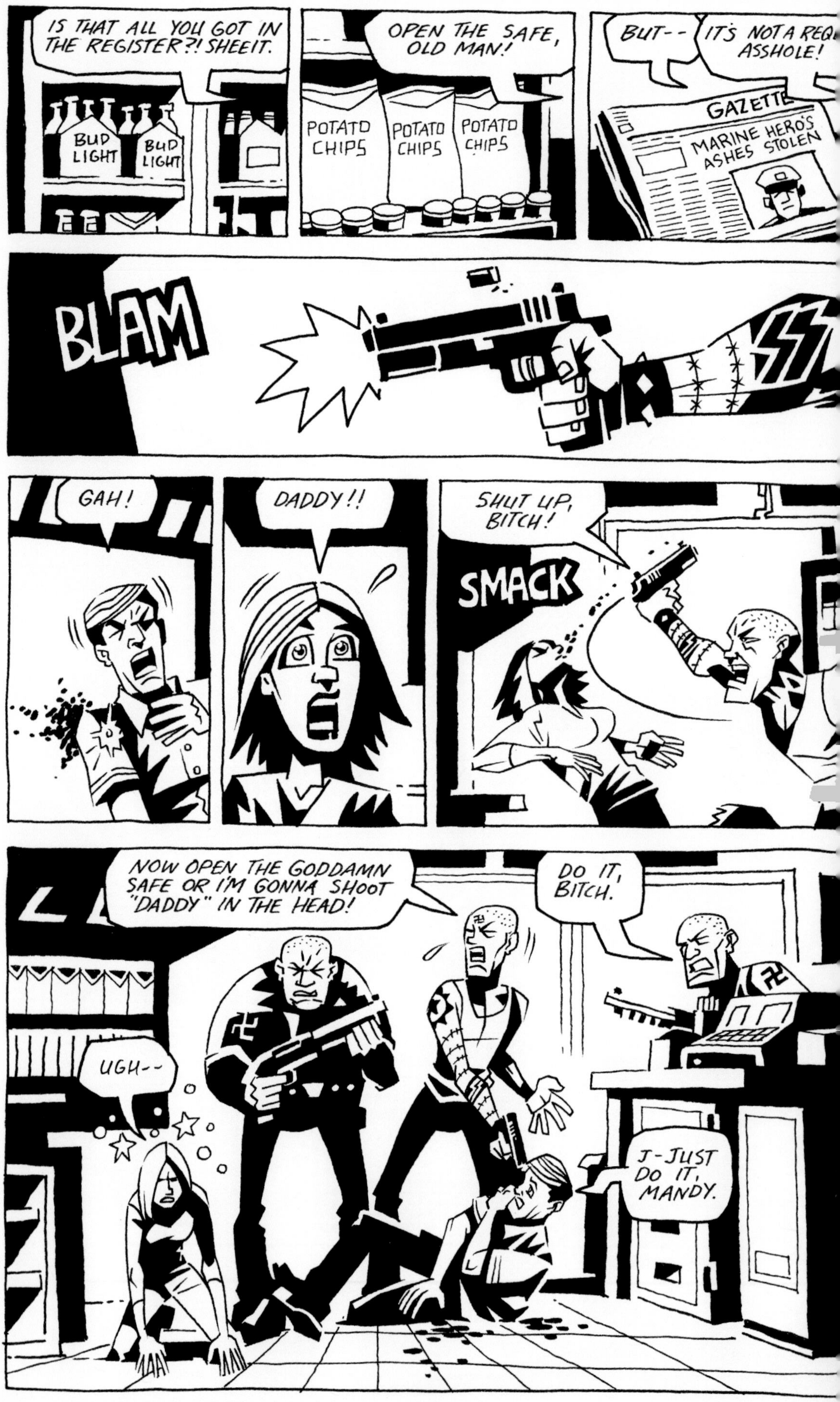
IS THAT ALL YOU GOT IN THE REGISTER?! SHEEIT.
BUD LIGHT
BUD LIGHT
OPEN THE SAFE, OLD MAN!
POTATO CHIPS
POTATO CHIPS
POTATO CHIPS
BUT--
IT'S NOT A REQ
ASSHOLE!
GAZETTE
MARINE HERO'S ASHES STOLEN
BLAM
GAH!
DADDY!!
SHUT UP, BITCH!
SMACK
NOW OPEN THE GODDAMN SAFE OR I'M GONNA SHOOT "DADDY" IN THE HEAD!
DO IT, BITCH.
UGH--
J-JUST DO IT, MANDY.

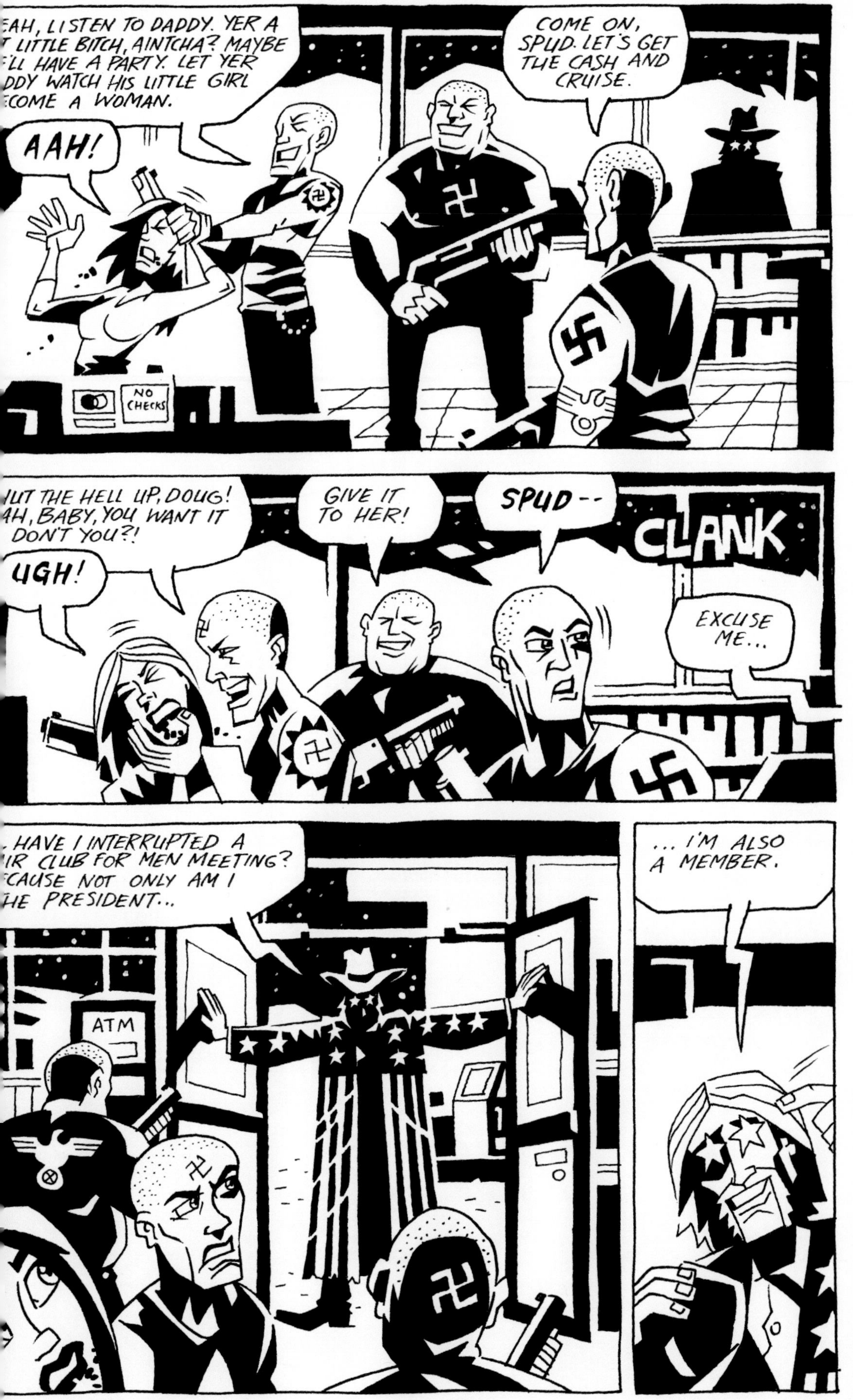
AH, LISTEN TO DADDY. YER A LITTLE BITCH, AINTCHA? MAYBE 'LL HAVE A PARTY. LET YER DDY WATCH HIS LITTLE GIRL COME A WOMAN.
AAH!
COME ON, SPUD. LET'S GET THE CASH AND CRUISE.
NO CHECKS
UT THE HELL UP, DOUG! AH, BABY, YOU WANT IT DON'T YOU?!
UGH!
GIVE IT TO HER!
SPUD--
CLANK
EXCUSE ME...
HAVE I INTERRUPTED A IR CLUB FOR MEN MEETING? CAUSE NOT ONLY AM I HE PRESIDENT...
ATM
...I'M ALSO A MEMBER.

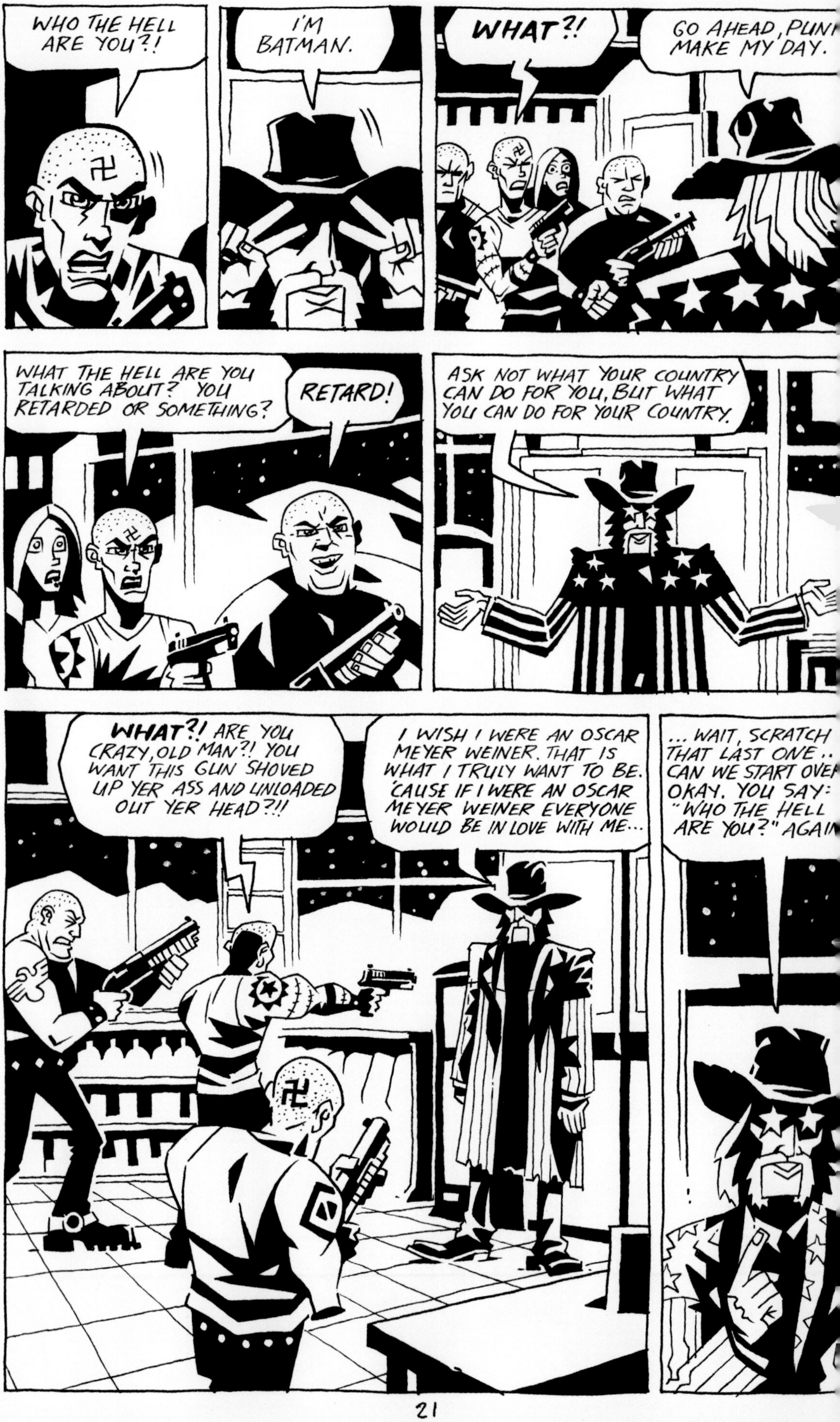
WHO THE HELL ARE YOU?!
I'M BATMAN.
WHAT?!
GO AHEAD, PUN
MAKE MY DAY.
WHAT THE HELL ARE YOU TALKING ABOUT? YOU RETARDED OR SOMETHING?
RETARD!
ASK NOT WHAT YOUR COUNTRY CAN DO FOR YOU, BUT WHAT YOU CAN DO FOR YOUR COUNTRY.
WHAT?! ARE YOU CRAZY, OLD MAN?! YOU WANT THIS GUN SHOVED UP YER ASS AND UNLOADED OUT YER HEAD?!!
I WISH I WERE AN OSCAR MEYER WEINER. THAT IS WHAT I TRULY WANT TO BE. 'CAUSE IF I WERE AN OSCAR MEYER WEINER EVERYONE WOULD BE IN LOVE WITH ME...
... WAIT, SCRATCH THAT LAST ONE.. CAN WE START OVE OKAY. YOU SAY: "WHO THE HELL ARE YOU?" AGAI

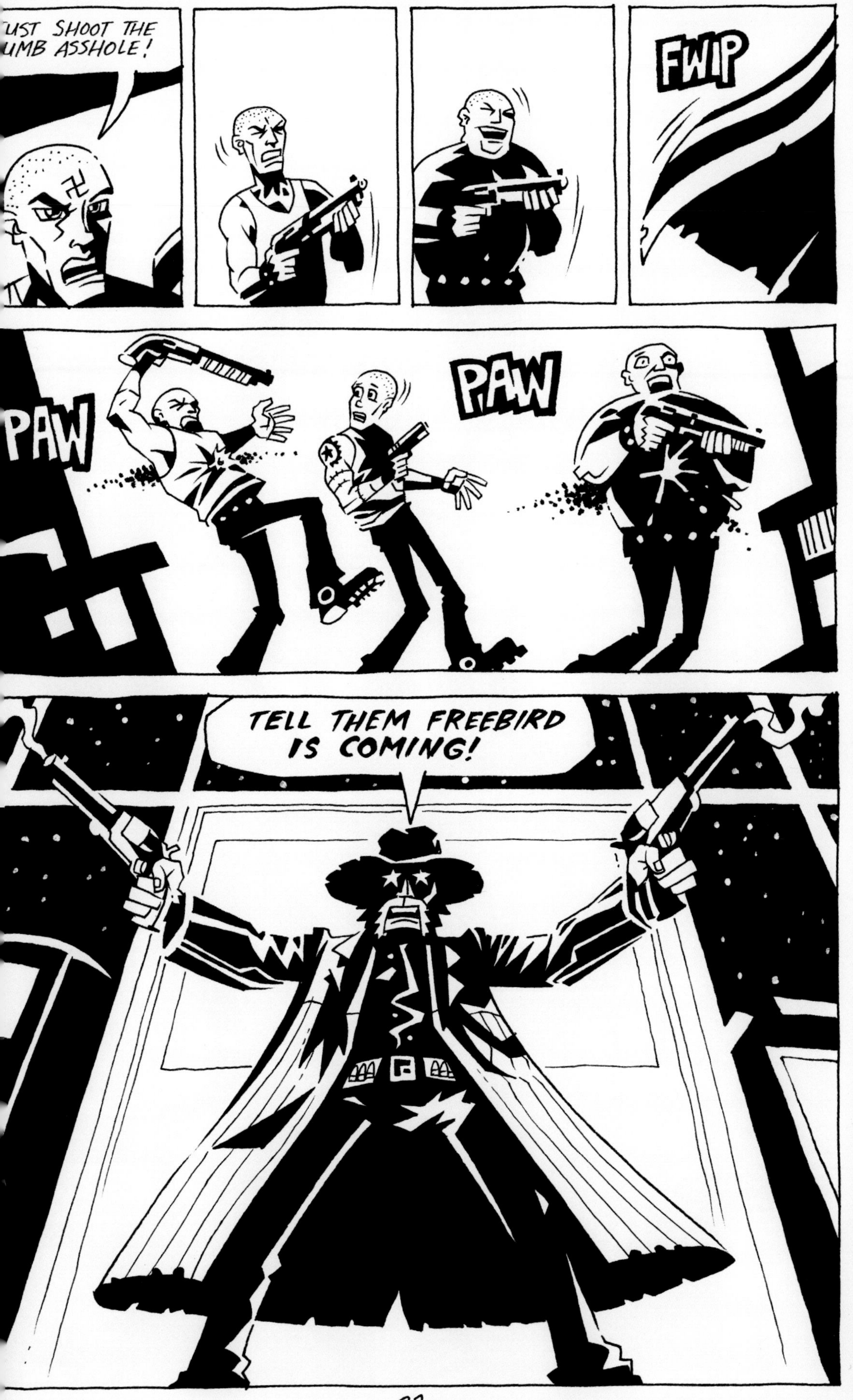

JUST SHOOT THE DUMB ASSHOLE!
FWIP
PAW
PAW
TELL THEM FREEBIRD IS COMING!

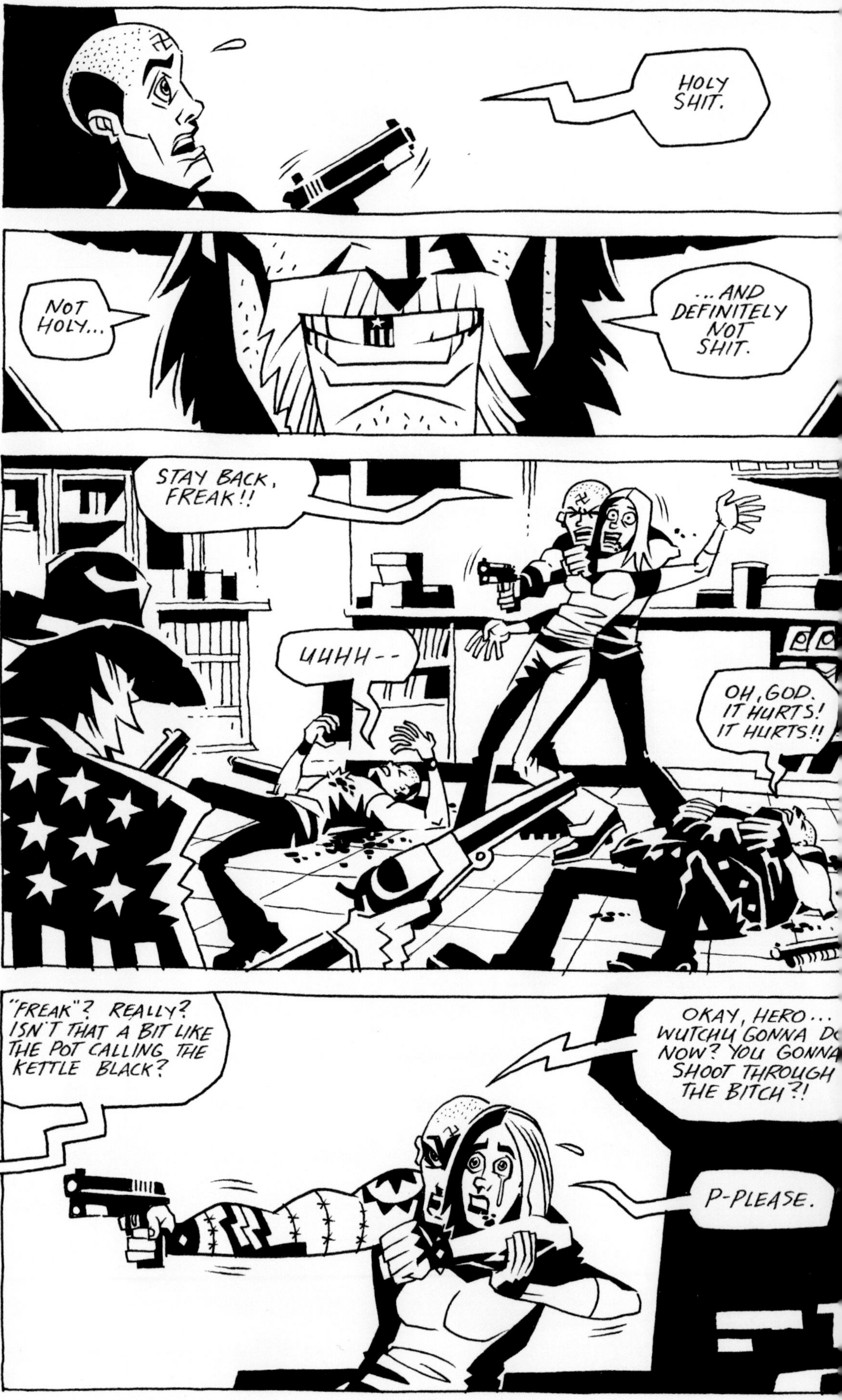
HOLY SHIT.
NOT HOLY...
...AND DEFINITELY NOT SHIT.
STAY BACK, FREAK!!
UUHH--
OH, GOD. IT HURTS! IT HURTS!!
"FREAK"? REALLY? ISN'T THAT A BIT LIKE THE POT CALLING THE KETTLE BLACK?
OKAY, HERO... WUTCHU GONNA DO NOW? YOU GONNA SHOOT THROUGH THE BITCH?!
P-PLEASE.

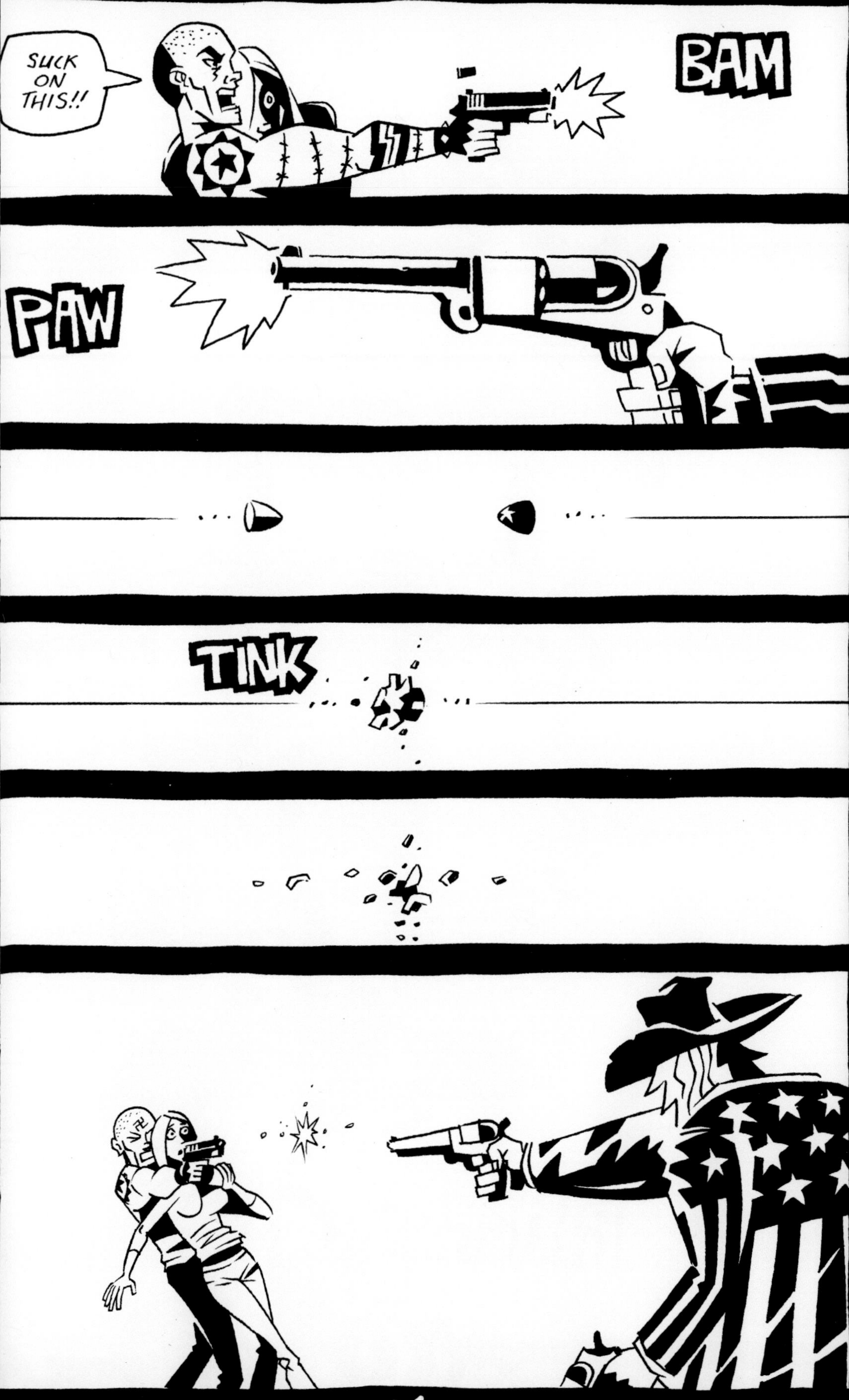
SUCK ON THIS!!
BAM
PAW
TINK

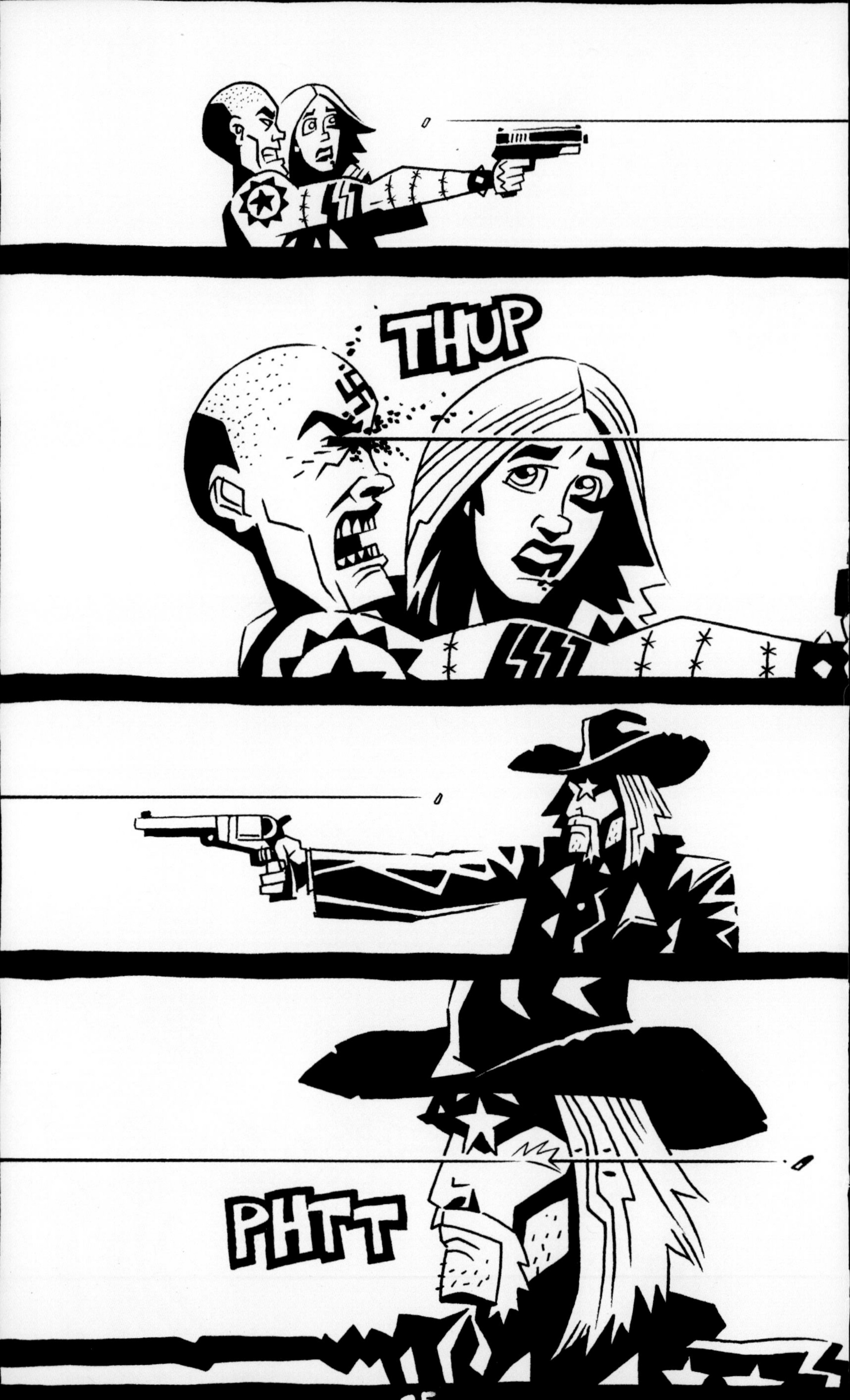
THUP
PHTT

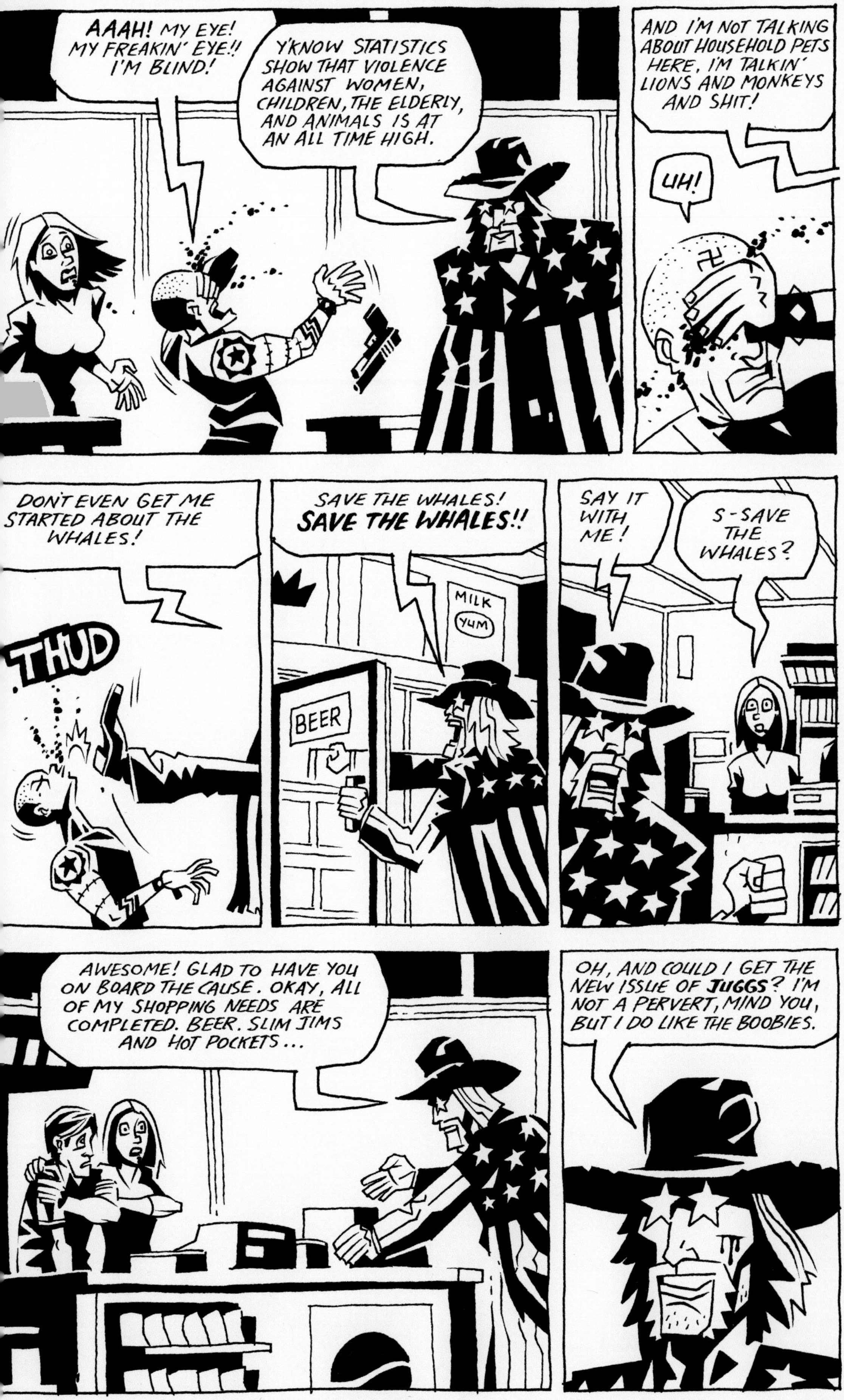
AAAH! MY EYE! MY FREAKIN' EYE!! I'M BLIND!
Y'KNOW STATISTICS SHOW THAT VIOLENCE AGAINST WOMEN, CHILDREN, THE ELDERLY, AND ANIMALS IS AT AN ALL TIME HIGH.
AND I'M NOT TALKING ABOUT HOUSEHOLD PETS HERE, I'M TALKIN' LIONS AND MONKEYS AND SHIT!
UH!
DON'T EVEN GET ME STARTED ABOUT THE WHALES!
THUD
SAVE THE WHALES! SAVE THE WHALES!!
MILK
YUM
BEER
SAY IT WITH ME!
S-SAVE THE WHALES?
AWESOME! GLAD TO HAVE YOU ON BOARD THE CAUSE. OKAY, ALL OF MY SHOPPING NEEDS ARE COMPLETED. BEER. SLIM JIMS AND HOT POCKETS...
OH, AND COULD I GET THE NEW ISSUE OF JUGGS? I'M NOT A PERVERT, MIND YOU, BUT I DO LIKE THE BOOBIES.

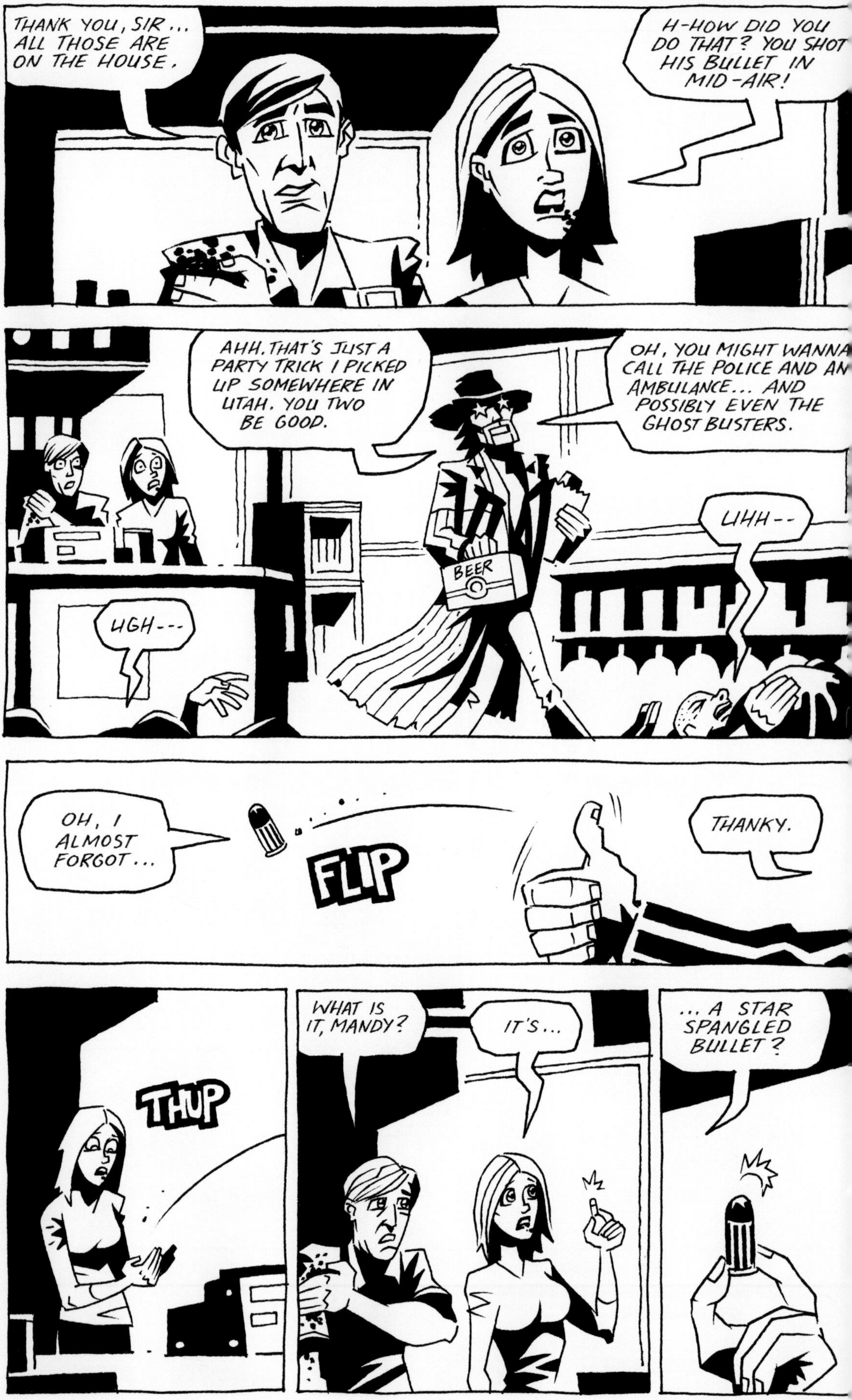
THANK YOU, SIR... ALL THOSE ARE ON THE HOUSE.
H-HOW DID YOU DO THAT? YOU SHOT HIS BULLET IN MID-AIR!
AHH. THAT'S JUST A PARTY TRICK I PICKED UP SOMEWHERE IN UTAH. YOU TWO BE GOOD.
OH, YOU MIGHT WANNA CALL THE POLICE AND AN AMBULANCE... AND POSSIBLY EVEN THE GHOST BUSTERS.
BEER
UHH--
UGH---
OH, I ALMOST FORGOT...
FLIP
THANKY.
THUP
WHAT IS IT, MANDY?
IT'S...
...A STAR SPANGLED BULLET?

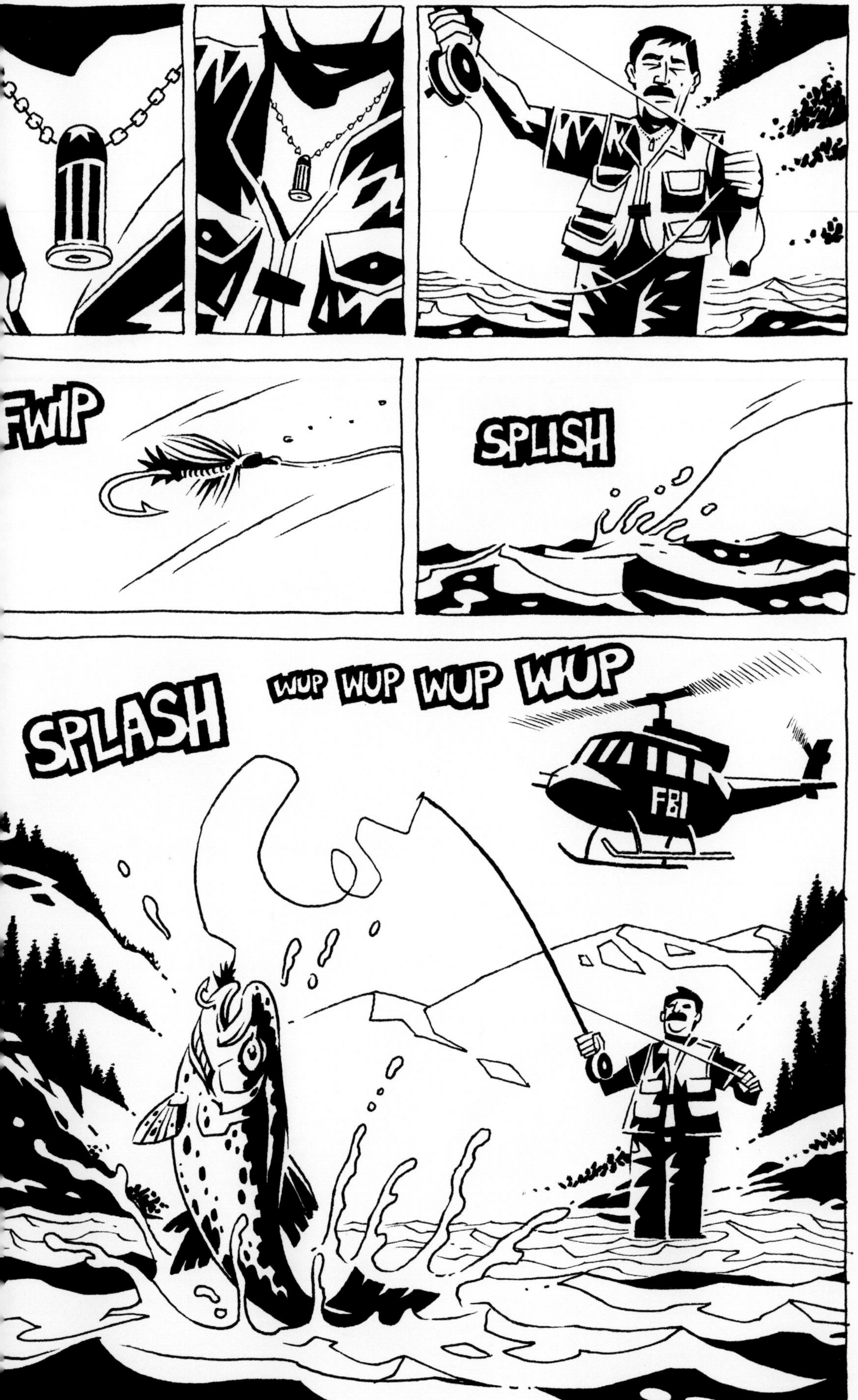
FWIP
SPLISH
SPLASH
WUP WUP WUP WUP
FBI

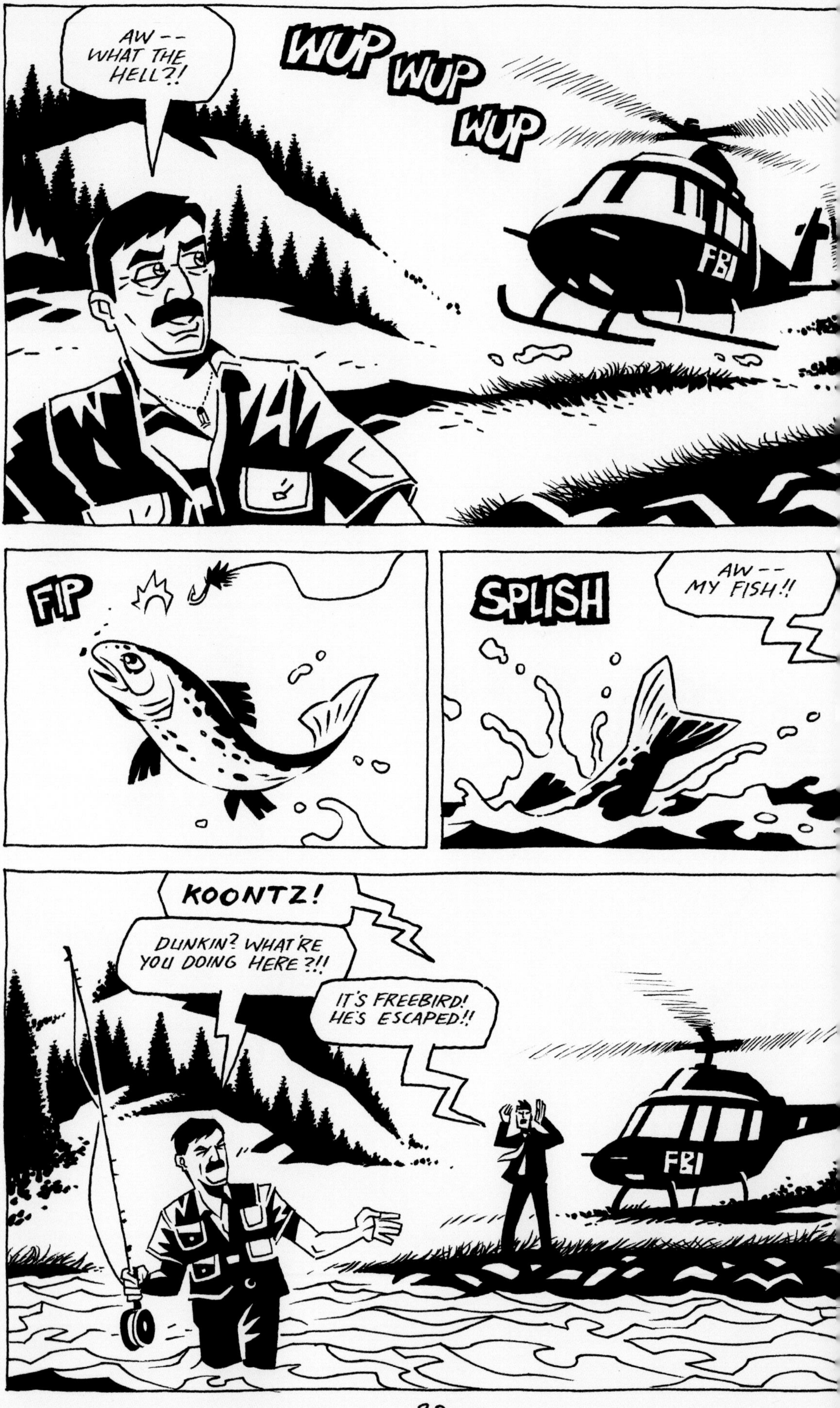
AW -- WHAT THE HELL?!
WUP WUP WUP
FBI
FIP
SPLISH
AW -- MY FISH!!
KOONTZ!
DUNKIN? WHAT'RE YOU DOING HERE?!!
IT'S FREEBIRD! HE'S ESCAPED!!
FBI

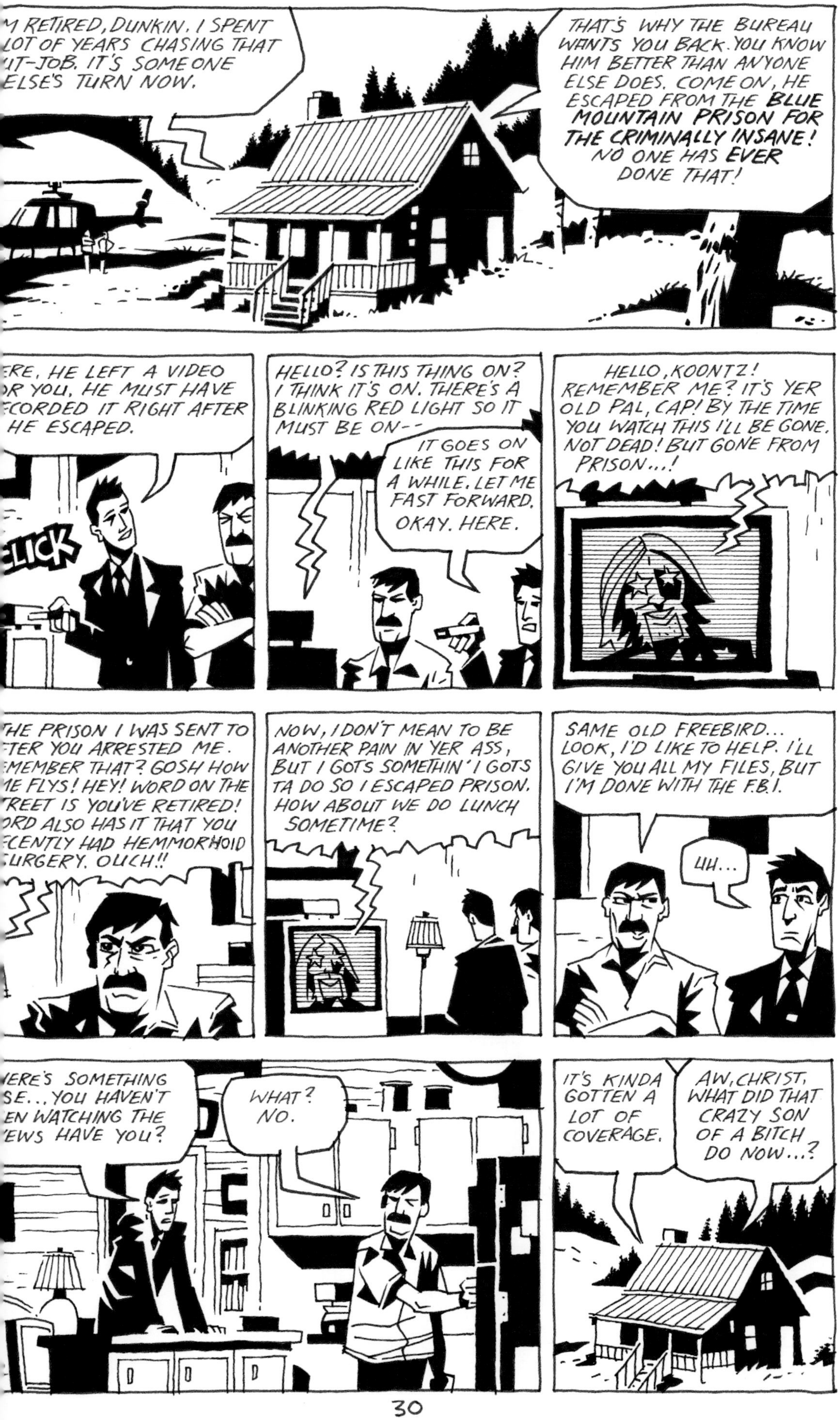

M RETIRED, DUNKIN. I SPENT LOT OF YEARS CHASING THAT UT-JOB. IT'S SOME ONE ELSE'S TURN NOW.
THAT'S WHY THE BUREAU WANTS YOU BACK. YOU KNOW HIM BETTER THAN ANYONE ELSE DOES. COME ON, HE ESCAPED FROM THE BLUE MOUNTAIN PRISON FOR THE CRIMINALLY INSANE! NO ONE HAS EVER DONE THAT!
ERE, HE LEFT A VIDEO OR YOU. HE MUST HAVE ECORDED IT RIGHT AFTER HE ESCAPED.
LICK
HELLO? IS THIS THING ON? I THINK IT'S ON. THERE'S A BLINKING RED LIGHT SO IT MUST BE ON--
IT GOES ON LIKE THIS FOR A WHILE. LET ME FAST FORWARD. OKAY. HERE.
HELLO, KOONTZ! REMEMBER ME? IT'S YER OLD PAL, CAP! BY THE TIME YOU WATCH THIS I'LL BE GONE. NOT DEAD! BUT GONE FROM PRISON...!
THE PRISON I WAS SENT TO TER YOU ARRESTED ME. EMEMBER THAT? GOSH HOW ME FLYS! HEY! WORD ON THE TREET IS YOU'VE RETIRED! ORD ALSO HAS IT THAT YOU ECENTLY HAD HEMMORHOID URGERY. OUCH!!
NOW, I DON'T MEAN TO BE ANOTHER PAIN IN YER ASS, BUT I GOTS SOMETHIN' I GOTS TA DO SO I ESCAPED PRISON. HOW ABOUT WE DO LUNCH SOMETIME?
SAME OLD FREEBIRD... LOOK, I'D LIKE TO HELP. I'LL GIVE YOU ALL MY FILES, BUT I'M DONE WITH THE F.B.I.
UH...
ERE'S SOMETHING SE... YOU HAVEN'T EN WATCHING THE EWS HAVE YOU?
WHAT? NO.
IT'S KINDA GOTTEN A LOT OF COVERAGE.
AW, CHRIST, WHAT DID THAT CRAZY SON OF A BITCH DO NOW...?

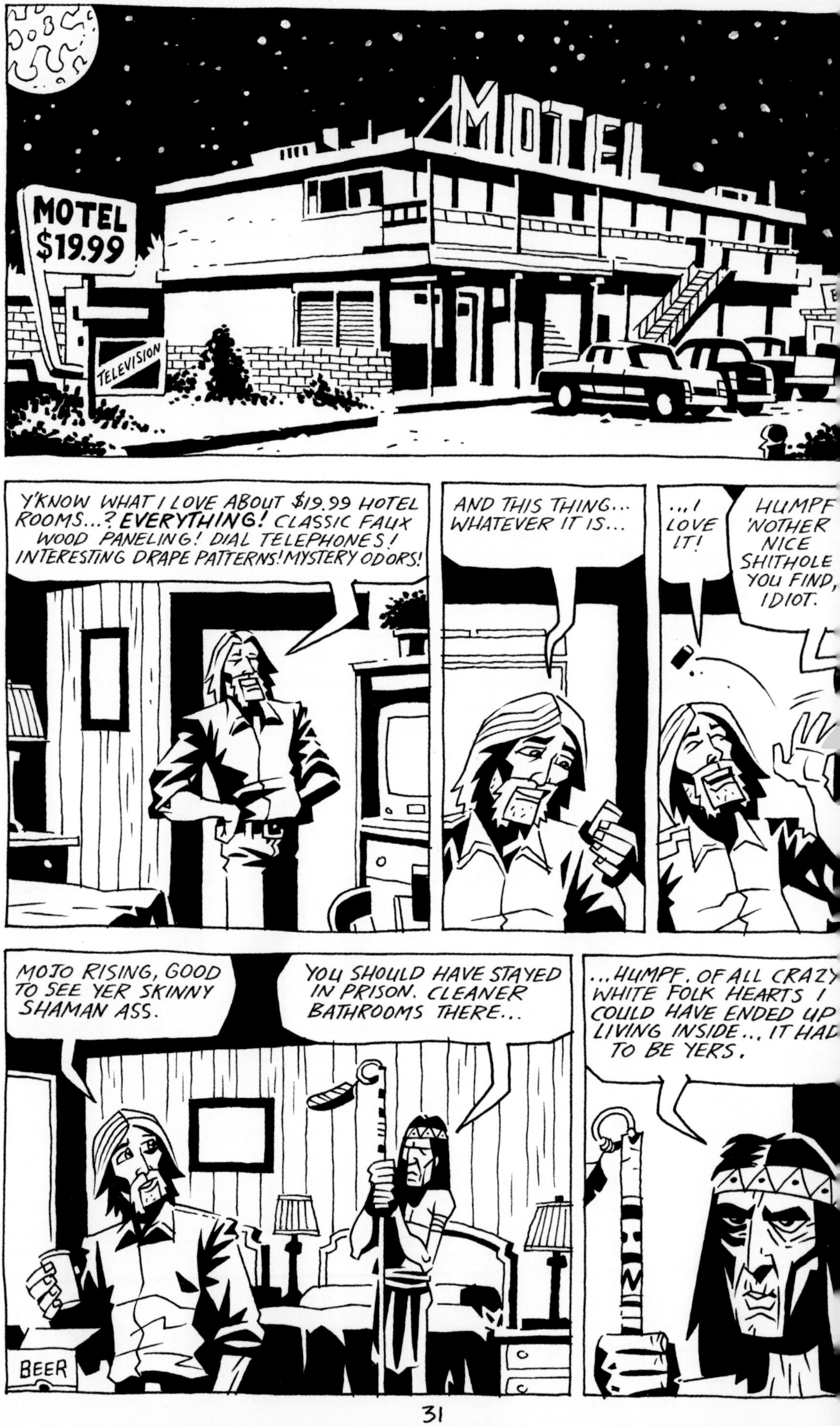
MOTEL
MOTEL $19.99
TELEVISION
Y'KNOW WHAT I LOVE ABOUT $19.99 HOTEL ROOMS...? EVERYTHING! CLASSIC FAUX WOOD PANELING! DIAL TELEPHONES! INTERESTING DRAPE PATTERNS! MYSTERY ODORS!
AND THIS THING... WHATEVER IT IS...
...I LOVE IT!
HUMPF 'NOTHER NICE SHITHOLE YOU FIND, IDIOT.
MOJO RISING, GOOD TO SEE YER SKINNY SHAMAN ASS.
YOU SHOULD HAVE STAYED IN PRISON. CLEANER BATHROOMS THERE...
BEER
...HUMPF. OF ALL CRAZY WHITE FOLK HEARTS I COULD HAVE ENDED UP LIVING INSIDE..., IT HAD TO BE YERS.

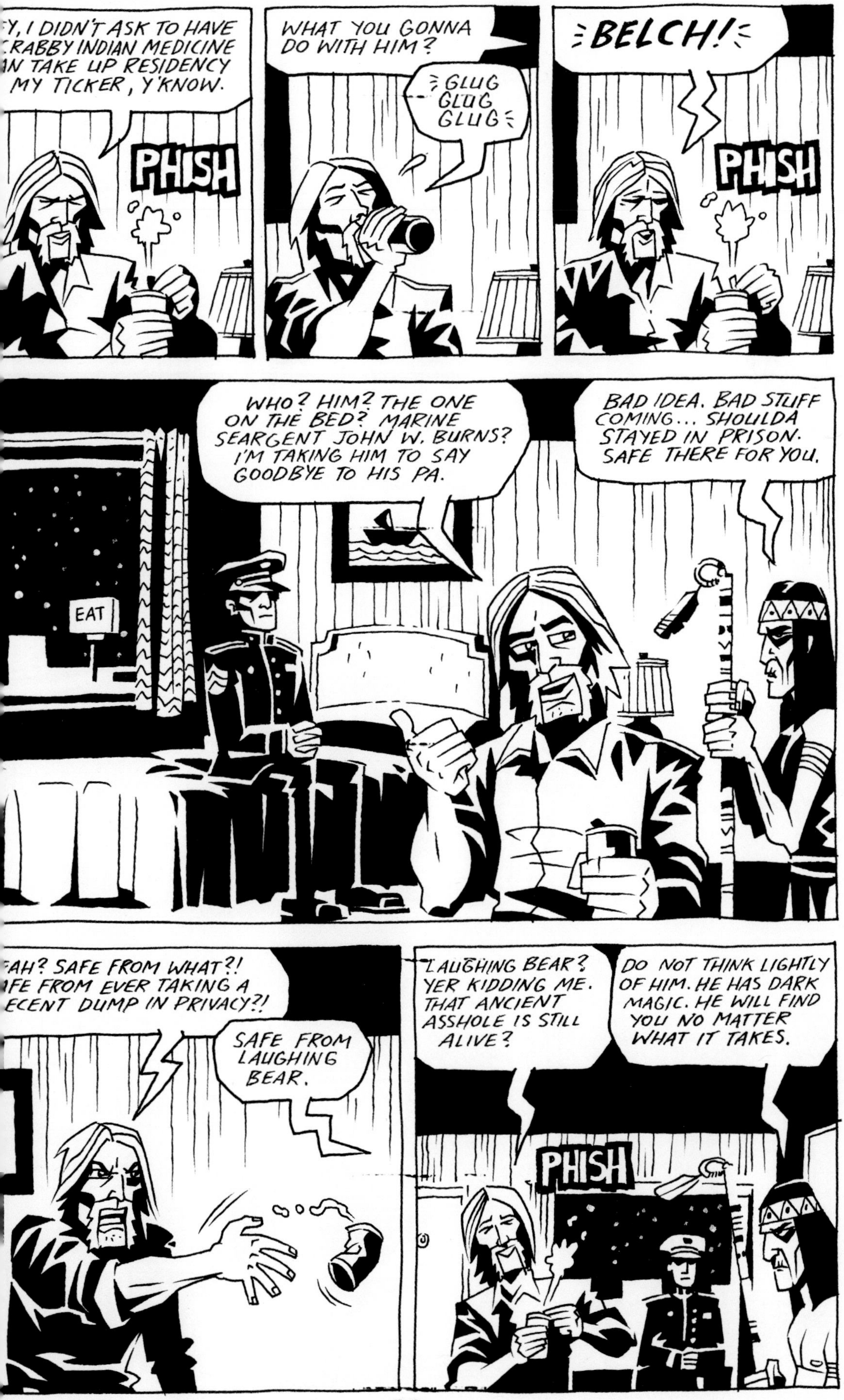

Y, I DIDN'T ASK TO HAVE
CRABBY INDIAN MEDICINE
AN TAKE UP RESIDENCY
MY TICKER, Y'KNOW.
PHISH
WHAT YOU GONNA DO WITH HIM?
GLUG GLUG GLUG
BELCH!
PHISH
WHO? HIM? THE ONE ON THE BED? MARINE SEARGENT JOHN W. BURNS? I'M TAKING HIM TO SAY GOODBYE TO HIS PA.
BAD IDEA. BAD STUFF COMING... SHOULDA STAYED IN PRISON. SAFE THERE FOR YOU.
EAT
AH? SAFE FROM WHAT?!
FE FROM EVER TAKING A
ECENT DUMP IN PRIVACY?!
SAFE FROM LAUGHING BEAR.
LAUGHING BEAR? YER KIDDING ME. THAT ANCIENT ASSHOLE IS STILL ALIVE?
DO NOT THINK LIGHTLY OF HIM. HE HAS DARK MAGIC. HE WILL FIND YOU NO MATTER WHAT IT TAKES.
PHISH

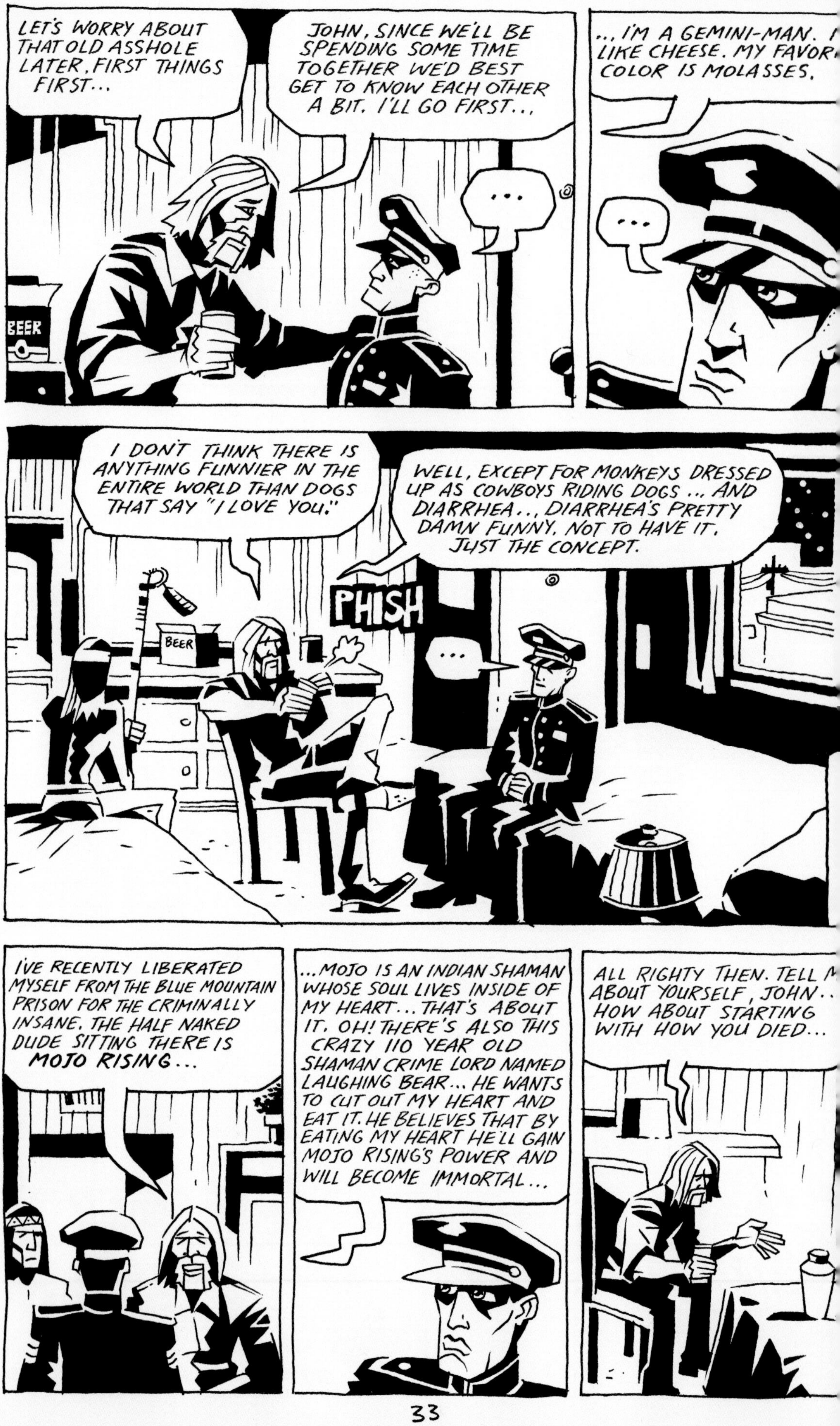
LET'S WORRY ABOUT THAT OLD ASSHOLE LATER. FIRST THINGS FIRST...
JOHN, SINCE WE'LL BE SPENDING SOME TIME TOGETHER WE'D BEST GET TO KNOW EACH OTHER A BIT. I'LL GO FIRST...
...
..., I'M A GEMINI-MAN. I LIKE CHEESE. MY FAVOR COLOR IS MOLASSES.
...
I DON'T THINK THERE IS ANYTHING FUNNIER IN THE ENTIRE WORLD THAN DOGS THAT SAY "I LOVE YOU."
WELL, EXCEPT FOR MONKEYS DRESSED UP AS COWBOYS RIDING DOGS ... AND DIARRHEA..., DIARRHEA'S PRETTY DAMN FUNNY. NOT TO HAVE IT. JUST THE CONCEPT.
PHISH
BEER
...
I'VE RECENTLY LIBERATED MYSELF FROM THE BLUE MOUNTAIN PRISON FOR THE CRIMINALLY INSANE. THE HALF NAKED DUDE SITTING THERE IS MOJO RISING...
...MOJO IS AN INDIAN SHAMAN WHOSE SOUL LIVES INSIDE OF MY HEART... THAT'S ABOUT IT. OH! THERE'S ALSO THIS CRAZY 110 YEAR OLD SHAMAN CRIME LORD NAMED LAUGHING BEAR... HE WANTS TO CUT OUT MY HEART AND EAT IT. HE BELIEVES THAT BY EATING MY HEART HE'LL GAIN MOJO RISING'S POWER AND WILL BECOME IMMORTAL...
ALL RIGHTY THEN. TELL M ABOUT YOURSELF, JOHN... HOW ABOUT STARTING WITH HOW YOU DIED...

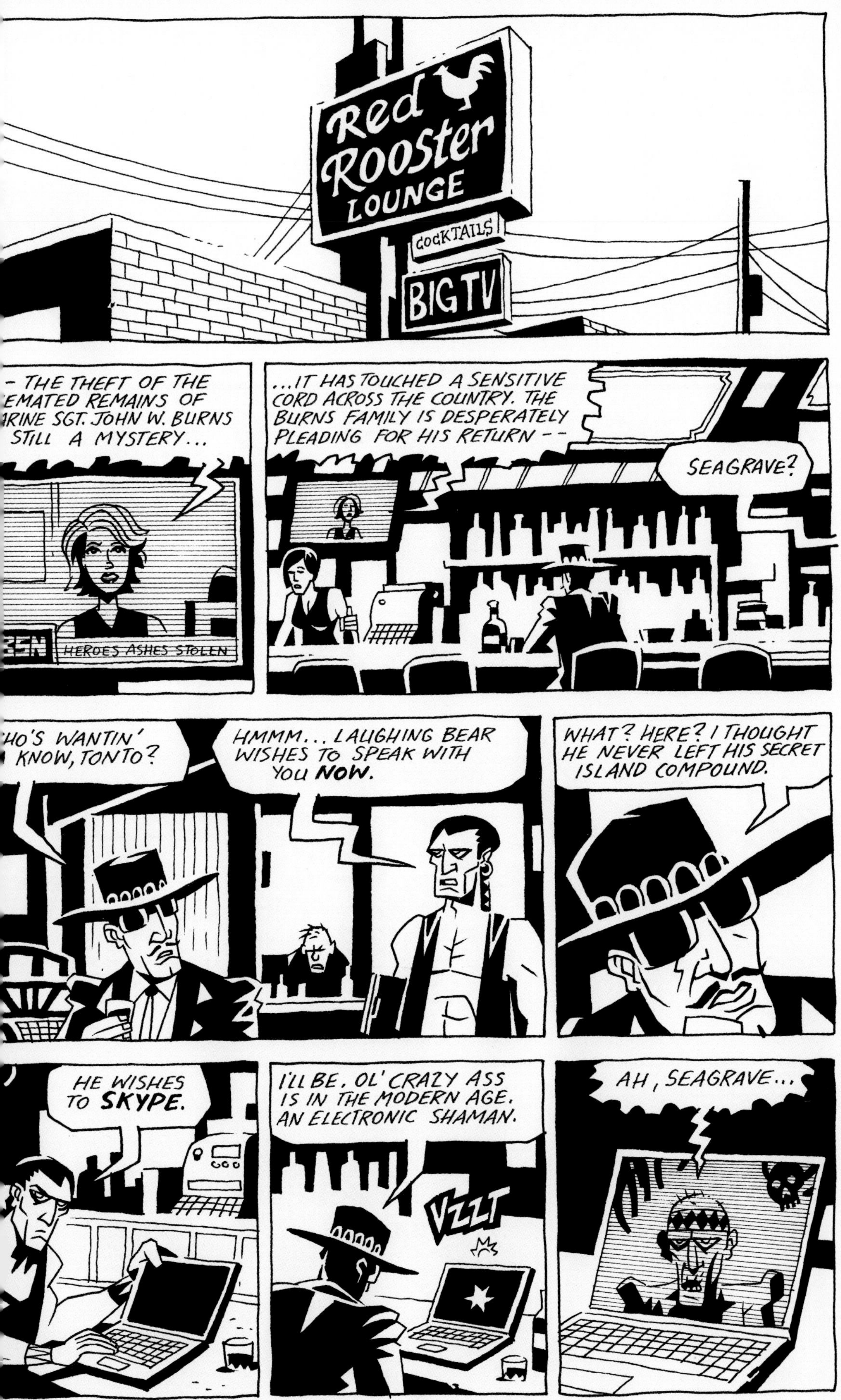
Red Rooster Lounge
COCKTAILS
BIG TV
- THE THEFT OF THE EMATED REMAINS OF ARINE SGT. JOHN W. BURNS STILL A MYSTERY...
HEROES ASHES STOLEN
...IT HAS TOUCHED A SENSITIVE CORD ACROSS THE COUNTRY. THE BURNS FAMILY IS DESPERATELY PLEADING FOR HIS RETURN --
SEAGRAVE?
HO'S WANTIN' KNOW, TONTO?
HMMM... LAUGHING BEAR WISHES TO SPEAK WITH YOU NOW.
WHAT? HERE? I THOUGHT HE NEVER LEFT HIS SECRET ISLAND COMPOUND.
HE WISHES TO SKYPE.
I'LL BE. OL' CRAZY ASS IS IN THE MODERN AGE. AN ELECTRONIC SHAMAN.
VZZT
AH, SEAGRAVE...

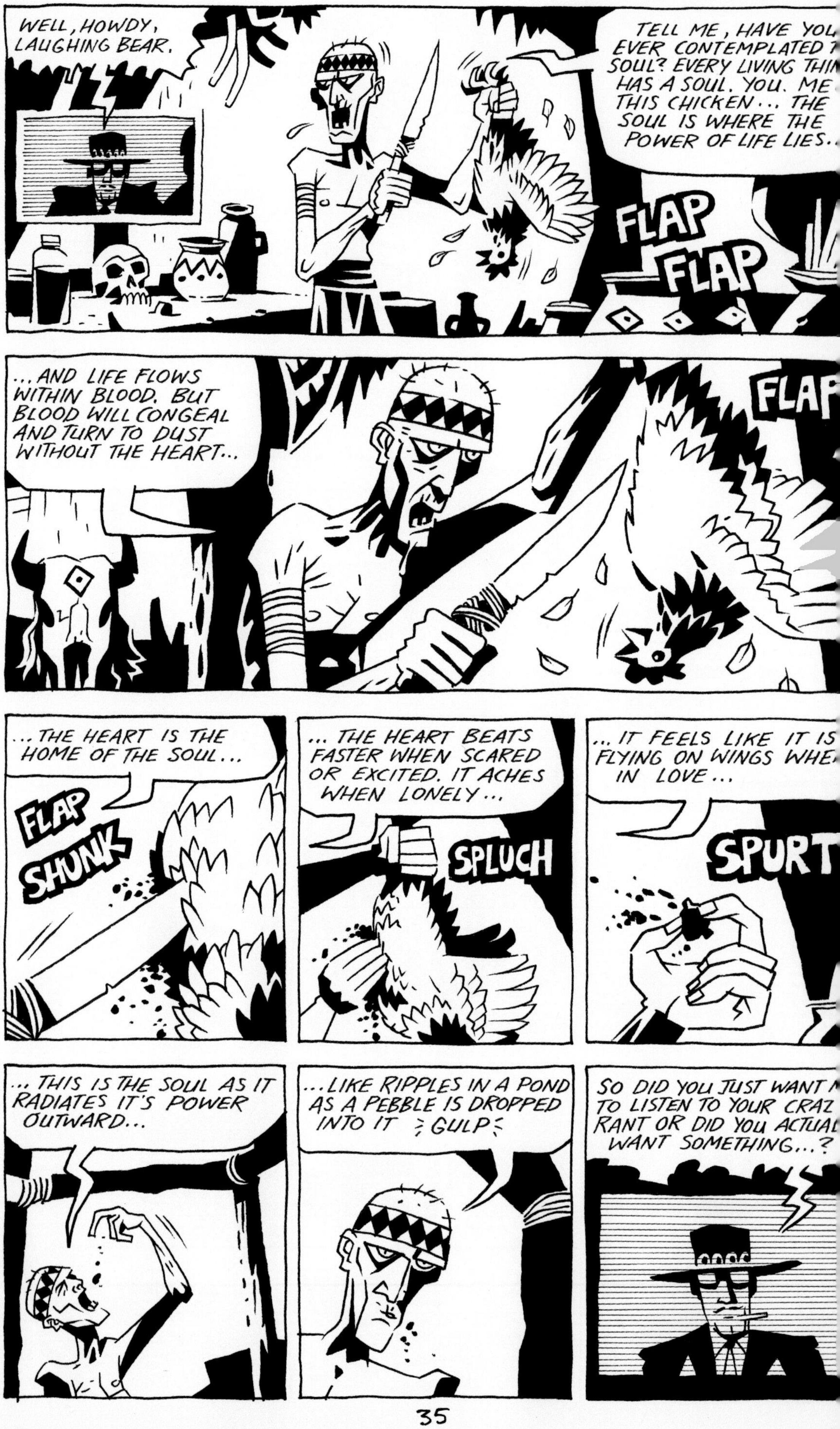
WELL, HOWDY, LAUGHING BEAR.
TELL ME, HAVE YOU EVER CONTEMPLATED THE SOUL? EVERY LIVING THING HAS A SOUL. YOU. ME. THIS CHICKEN... THE SOUL IS WHERE THE POWER OF LIFE LIES...
FLAP FLAP
...AND LIFE FLOWS WITHIN BLOOD. BUT BLOOD WILL CONGEAL AND TURN TO DUST WITHOUT THE HEART...
FLAP
...THE HEART IS THE HOME OF THE SOUL...
FLAP
SHUNK
...THE HEART BEATS FASTER WHEN SCARED OR EXCITED. IT ACHES WHEN LONELY...
SPLUCH
...IT FEELS LIKE IT IS FLYING ON WINGS WHEN IN LOVE...
SPURT
...THIS IS THE SOUL AS IT RADIATES IT'S POWER OUTWARD...
...LIKE RIPPLES IN A POND AS A PEBBLE IS DROPPED INTO IT ⸗GULP⸗
SO DID YOU JUST WANT ME TO LISTEN TO YOUR CRAZY RANT OR DID YOU ACTUALLY WANT SOMETHING...?

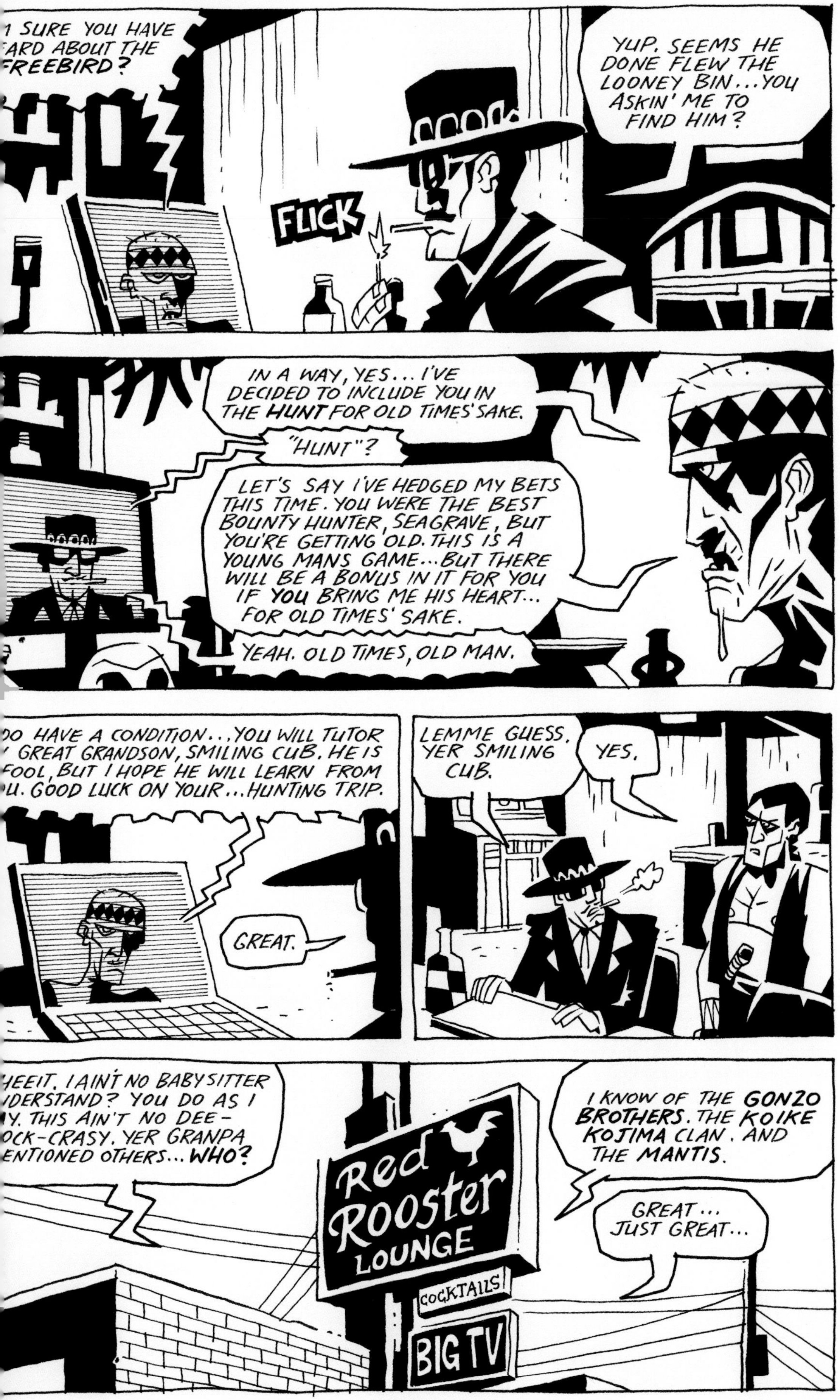
I SURE YOU HAVE
ARD ABOUT THE
FREEBIRD?
YUP. SEEMS HE DONE FLEW THE LOONEY BIN... YOU ASKIN' ME TO FIND HIM?
FLICK
IN A WAY, YES... I'VE DECIDED TO INCLUDE YOU IN THE HUNT FOR OLD TIMES' SAKE.
"HUNT"?
LET'S SAY I'VE HEDGED MY BETS THIS TIME. YOU WERE THE BEST BOUNTY HUNTER, SEAGRAVE, BUT YOU'RE GETTING OLD. THIS IS A YOUNG MANS GAME... BUT THERE WILL BE A BONUS IN IT FOR YOU IF YOU BRING ME HIS HEART... FOR OLD TIMES' SAKE.
YEAH. OLD TIMES, OLD MAN.
DO HAVE A CONDITION... YOU WILL TUTOR
GREAT GRANDSON, SMILING CUB. HE IS
FOOL, BUT I HOPE HE WILL LEARN FROM
U. GOOD LUCK ON YOUR... HUNTING TRIP.
GREAT.
LEMME GUESS. YER SMILING CUB.
YES.
HEEIT. I AIN'T NO BABYSITTER
IDERSTAND? YOU DO AS I
Y. THIS AIN'T NO DEE-
OCK-CRASY. YER GRANPA
ENTIONED OTHERS... WHO?
Red Rooster LOUNGE
COCKTAILS
BIG TV
I KNOW OF THE GONZO BROTHERS. THE KOIKE KOJIMA CLAN. AND THE MANTIS.
GREAT... JUST GREAT...

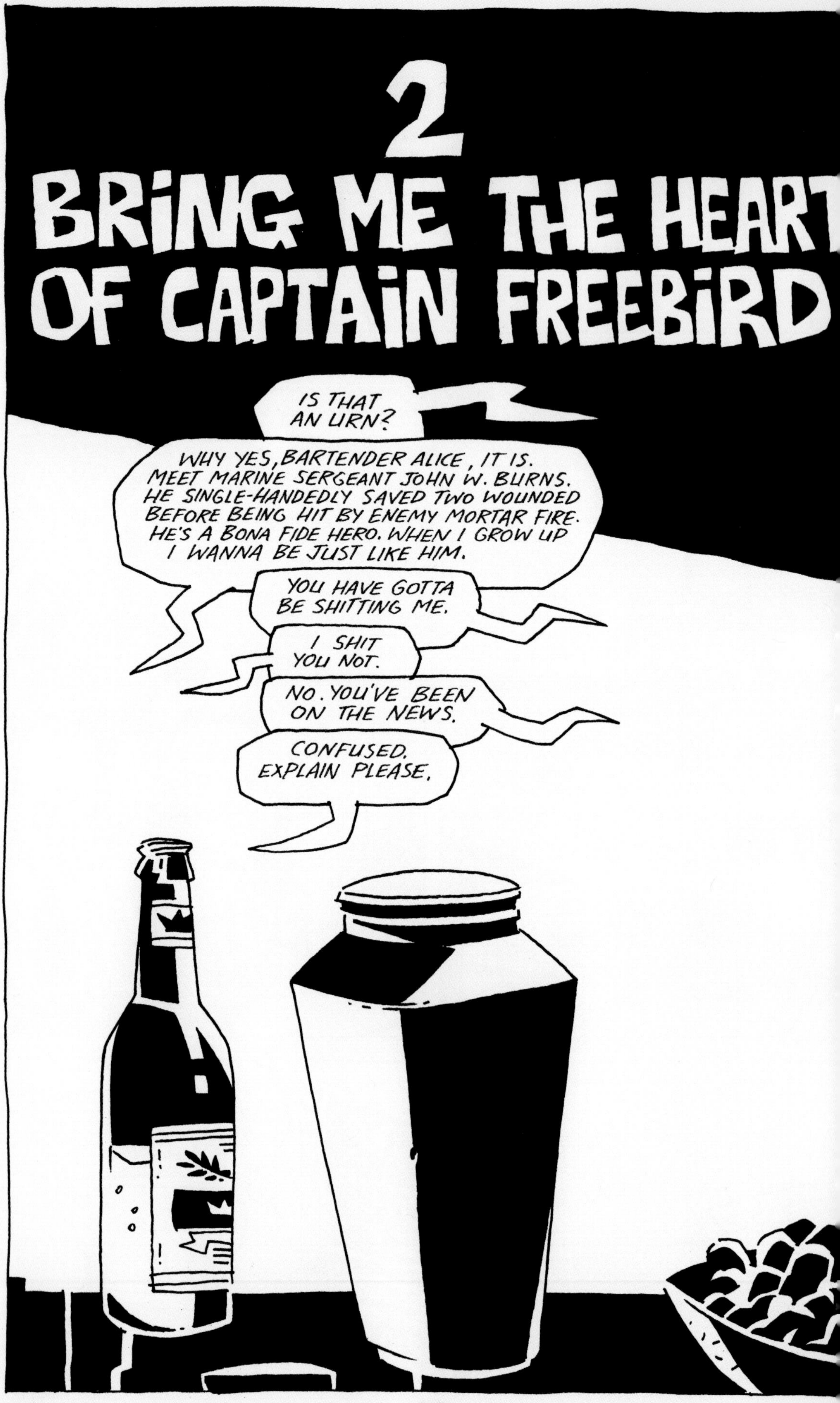

2
BRING ME THE HEART OF CAPTAIN FREEBIRD
IS THAT AN URN?
WHY YES, BARTENDER ALICE, IT IS. MEET MARINE SERGEANT JOHN W. BURNS. HE SINGLE-HANDEDLY SAVED TWO WOUNDED BEFORE BEING HIT BY ENEMY MORTAR FIRE. HE'S A BONA FIDE HERO. WHEN I GROW UP I WANNA BE JUST LIKE HIM.
YOU HAVE GOTTA BE SHITTING ME.
I SHIT YOU NOT.
NO. YOU'VE BEEN ON THE NEWS.
CONFUSED. EXPLAIN PLEASE.

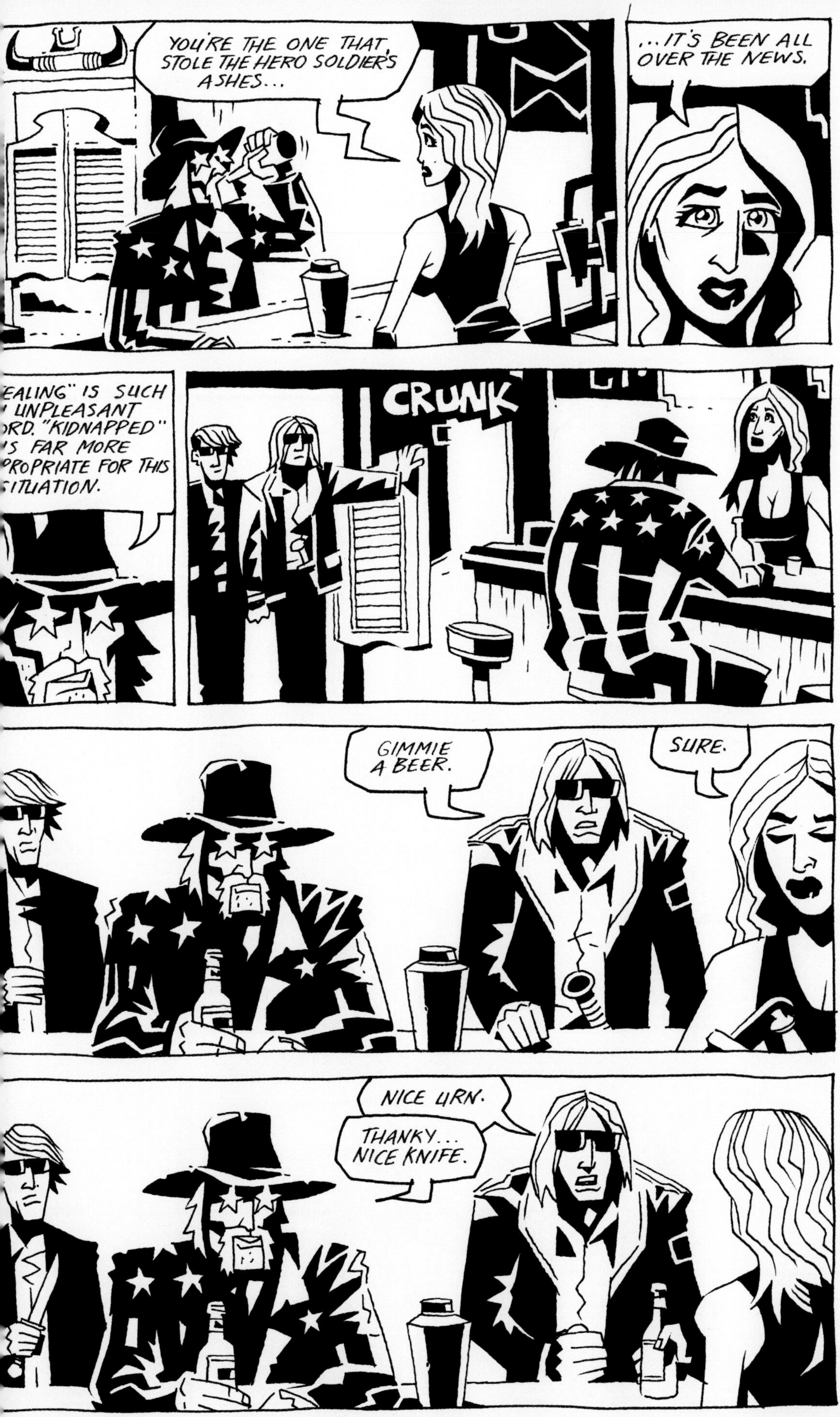
YOU'RE THE ONE THAT STOLE THE HERO SOLDIER'S ASHES...
...IT'S BEEN ALL OVER THE NEWS.
EALING" IS SUCH
UNPLEASANT
ORD. "KIDNAPPED"
'S FAR MORE
ROPRIATE FOR THIS
SITUATION.
CRUNK
GIMMIE A BEER.
SURE.
NICE URN.
THANKY... NICE KNIFE.

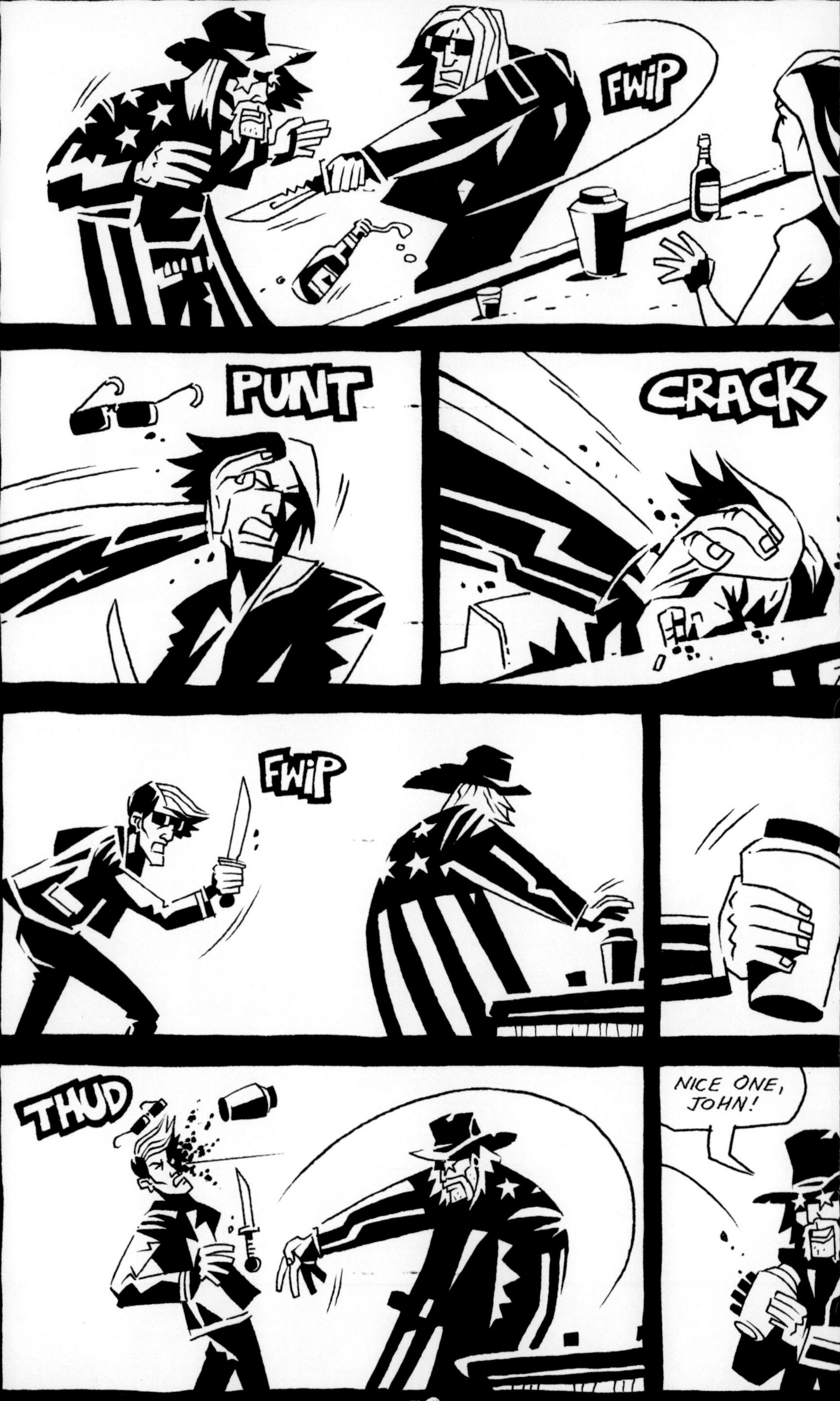
FWIP
PUNT
CRACK
FWIP
THUD
NICE ONE, JOHN!

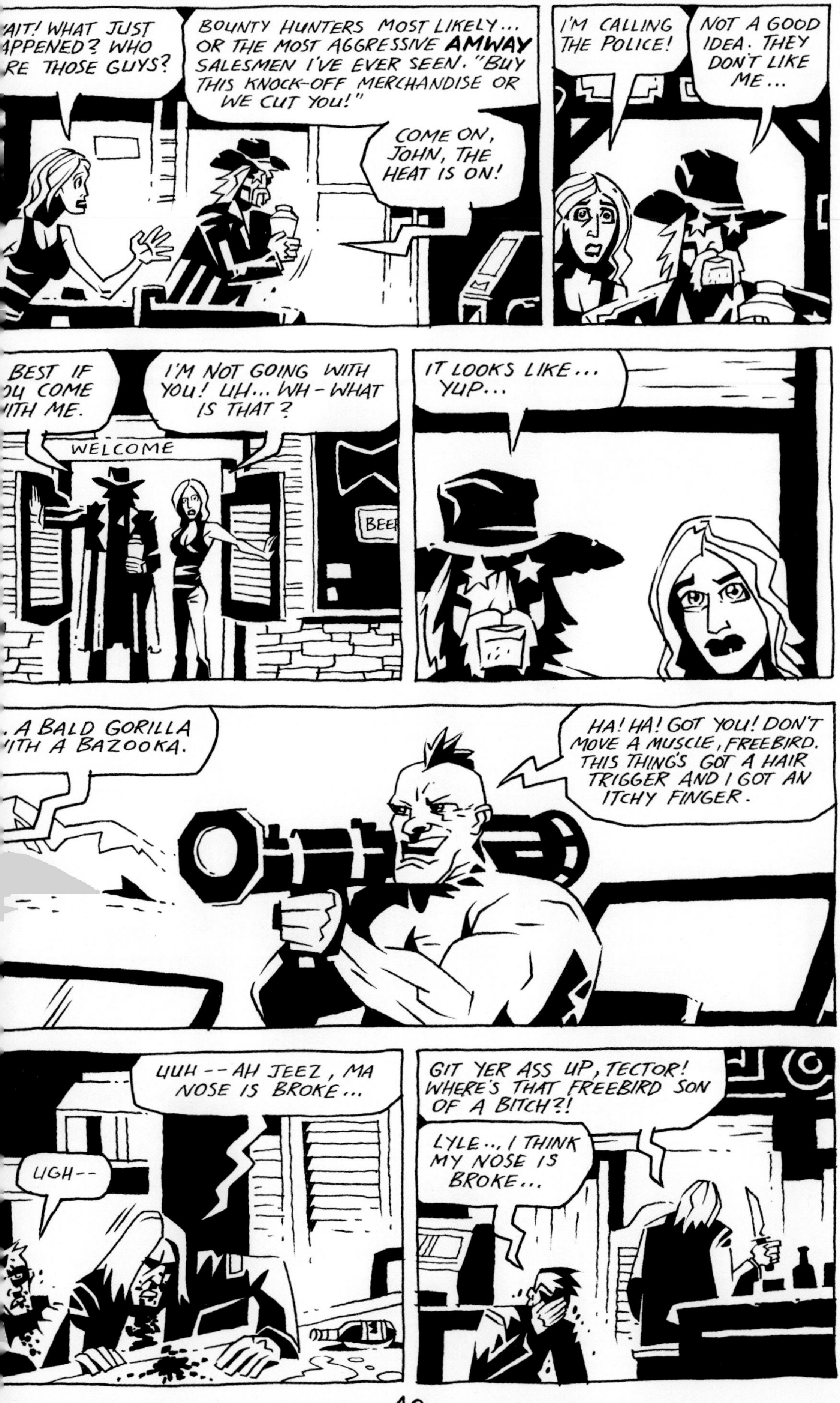
AIT! WHAT JUST APPENED? WHO RE THOSE GUYS?
BOUNTY HUNTERS MOST LIKELY... OR THE MOST AGGRESSIVE **AMWAY** SALESMEN I'VE EVER SEEN. "BUY THIS KNOCK-OFF MERCHANDISE OR WE CUT YOU!"
COME ON, JOHN, THE HEAT IS ON!
I'M CALLING THE POLICE!
NOT A GOOD IDEA. THEY DON'T LIKE ME...
BEST IF OU COME ITH ME.
I'M NOT GOING WITH YOU! UH... WH-WHAT IS THAT?
WELCOME
BEER
IT LOOKS LIKE... YUP...
. A BALD GORILLA ITH A BAZOOKA.
HA! HA! GOT YOU! DON'T MOVE A MUSCLE, FREEBIRD. THIS THING'S GOT A HAIR TRIGGER AND I GOT AN ITCHY FINGER.
UUH--AH JEEZ, MA NOSE IS BROKE...
UGH--
GIT YER ASS UP, TECTOR! WHERE'S THAT FREEBIRD SON OF A BITCH?!
LYLE.., I THINK MY NOSE IS BROKE...

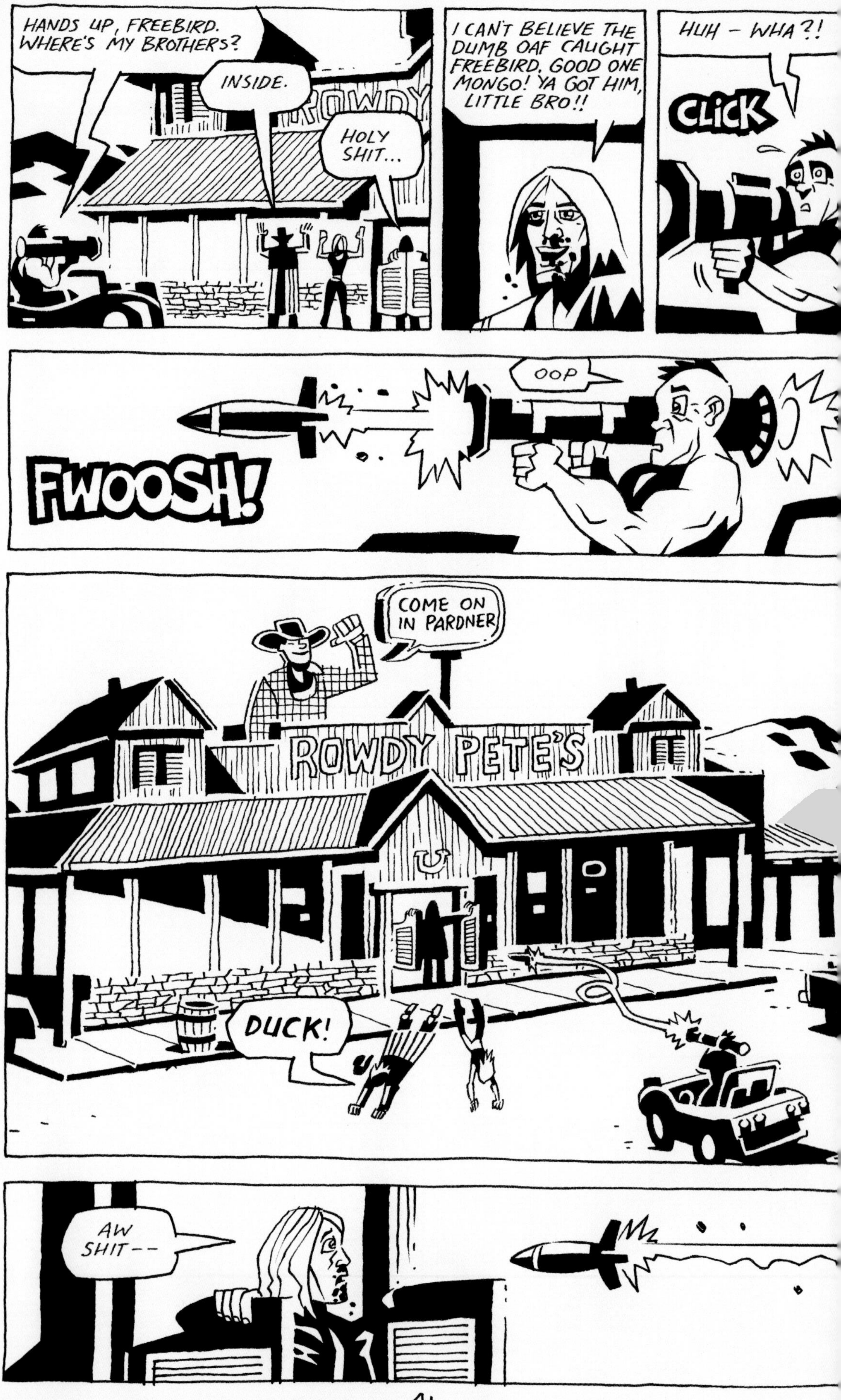
HANDS UP, FREEBIRD. WHERE'S MY BROTHERS?
INSIDE.
ROWDY
HOLY SHIT...
I CAN'T BELIEVE THE DUMB OAF CAUGHT FREEBIRD. GOOD ONE MONGO! YA GOT HIM, LITTLE BRO!!
HUH - WHA?!
CLICK
OOP
FWOOSH!
COME ON IN PARDNER
ROWDY PETE'S
DUCK!
AW SHIT--

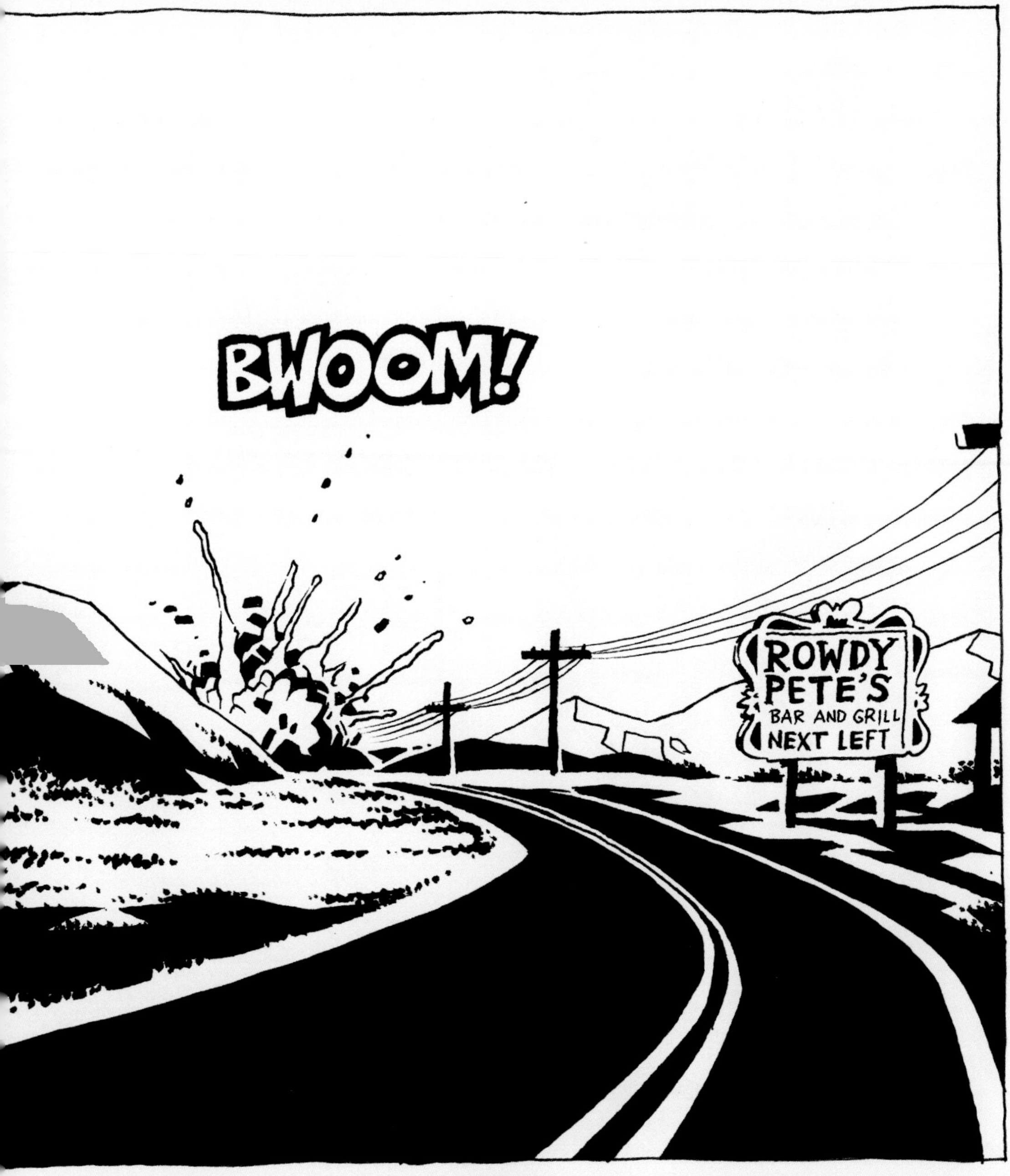
BWOOM!
ROWDY PETE'S BAR AND GRILL NEXT LEFT

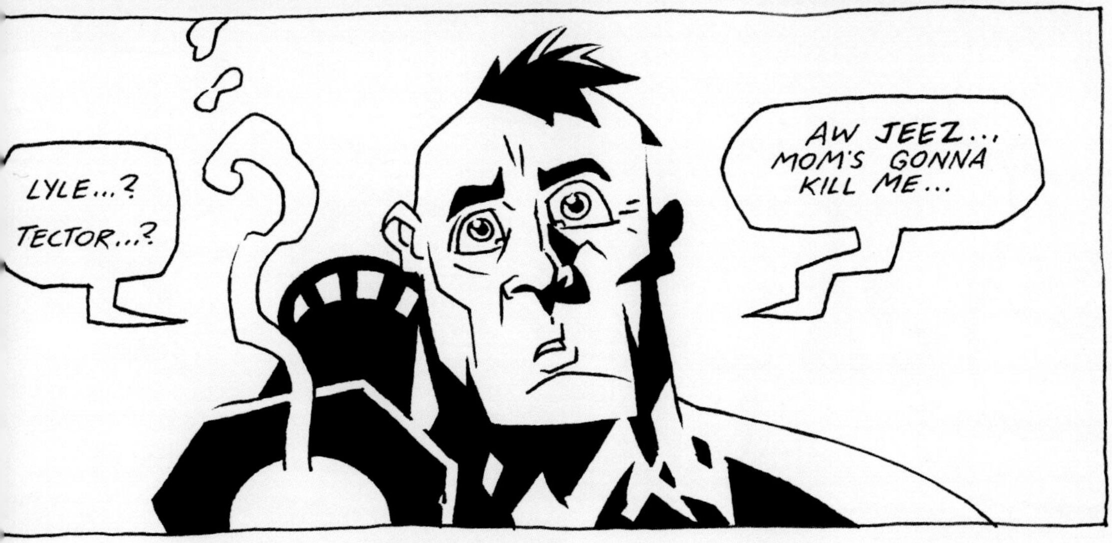
LYLE...? TECTOR...?
AW JEEZ... MOM'S GONNA KILL ME...

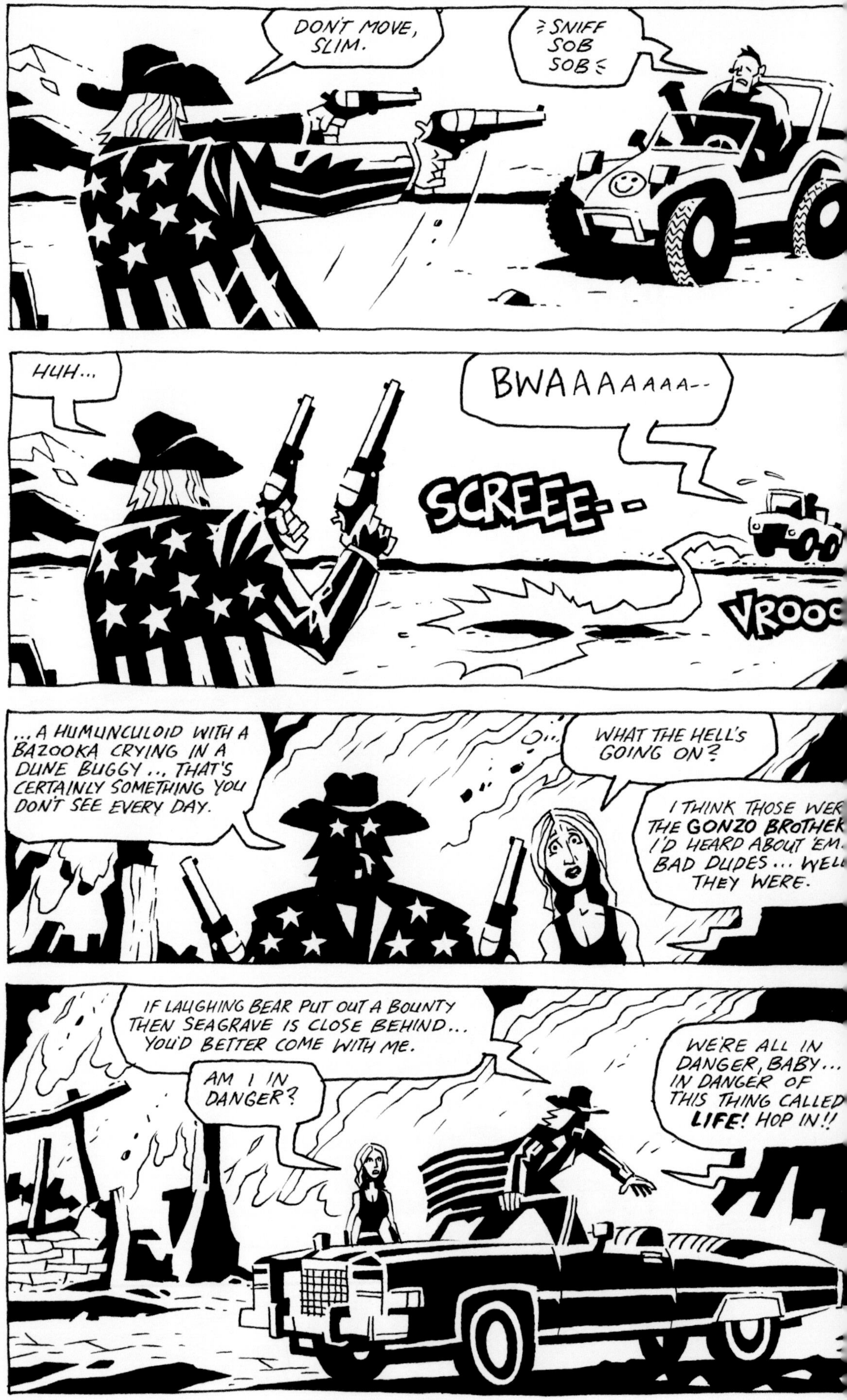
DON'T MOVE, SLIM.
≶ SNIFF SOB SOB ≶
HUH...
BWAAAAAAA--
SCREEE--
VROOO
...A HUMUNCULOID WITH A BAZOOKA CRYING IN A DUNE BUGGY..., THAT'S CERTAINLY SOMETHING YOU DON'T SEE EVERY DAY.
WHAT THE HELL'S GOING ON?
I THINK THOSE WER THE **GONZO BROTHEK** I'D HEARD ABOUT 'EM. BAD DUDES... WELL THEY WERE.
IF LAUGHING BEAR PUT OUT A BOUNTY THEN SEAGRAVE IS CLOSE BEHIND... YOU'D BETTER COME WITH ME.
AM I IN DANGER?
WE'RE ALL IN DANGER, BABY... IN DANGER OF THIS THING CALLED **LIFE**! HOP IN!!

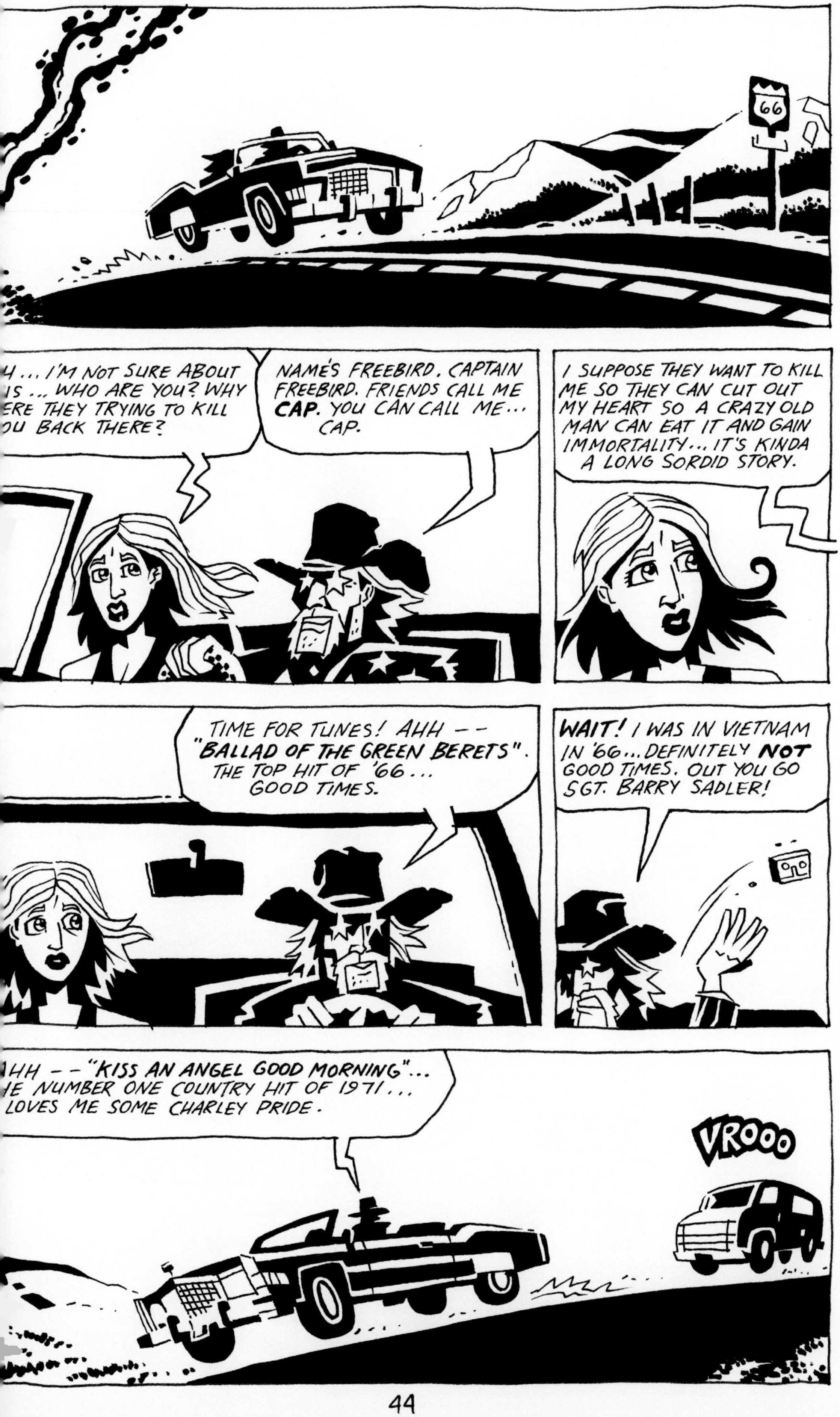
66
...I'M NOT SURE ABOUT ...IS... WHO ARE YOU? WHY ...ERE THEY TRYING TO KILL ...OU BACK THERE?
NAME'S FREEBIRD. CAPTAIN FREEBIRD. FRIENDS CALL ME **CAP**. YOU CAN CALL ME... CAP.
I SUPPOSE THEY WANT TO KILL ME SO THEY CAN CUT OUT MY HEART SO A CRAZY OLD MAN CAN EAT IT AND GAIN IMMORTALITY... IT'S KINDA A LONG SORDID STORY.
TIME FOR TUNES! AHH -- **"BALLAD OF THE GREEN BERETS"**. THE TOP HIT OF '66... GOOD TIMES.
WAIT! I WAS IN VIETNAM IN '66... DEFINITELY **NOT** GOOD TIMES. OUT YOU GO SGT. BARRY SADLER!
...HH -- **"KISS AN ANGEL GOOD MORNING"**... ...E NUMBER ONE COUNTRY HIT OF 1971... LOVES ME SOME CHARLEY PRIDE.
VROOO

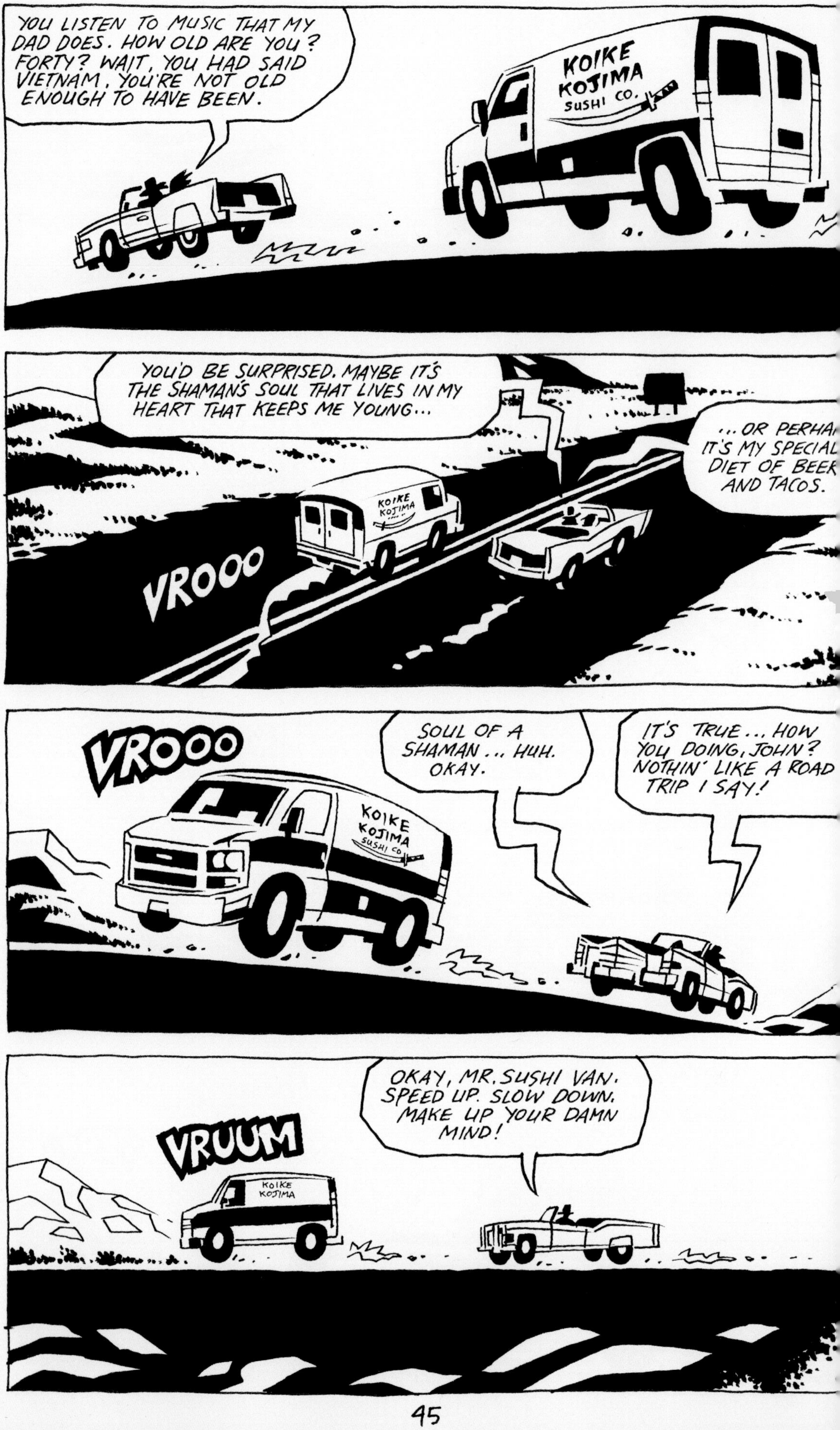
YOU LISTEN TO MUSIC THAT MY DAD DOES. HOW OLD ARE YOU? FORTY? WAIT, YOU HAD SAID VIETNAM, YOU'RE NOT OLD ENOUGH TO HAVE BEEN.
KOIKE KOJIMA SUSHI CO.
YOU'D BE SURPRISED. MAYBE IT'S THE SHAMAN'S SOUL THAT LIVES IN MY HEART THAT KEEPS ME YOUNG...
...OR PERHA IT'S MY SPECIAL DIET OF BEER AND TACOS.
KOIKE KOJIMA
VROOO
VROOO
KOIKE KOJIMA SUSHI CO.
SOUL OF A SHAMAN... HUH. OKAY.
IT'S TRUE... HOW YOU DOING, JOHN? NOTHIN' LIKE A ROAD TRIP I SAY!
OKAY, MR. SUSHI VAN. SPEED UP. SLOW DOWN. MAKE UP YOUR DAMN MIND!
VRUUM
KOIKE KOJIMA

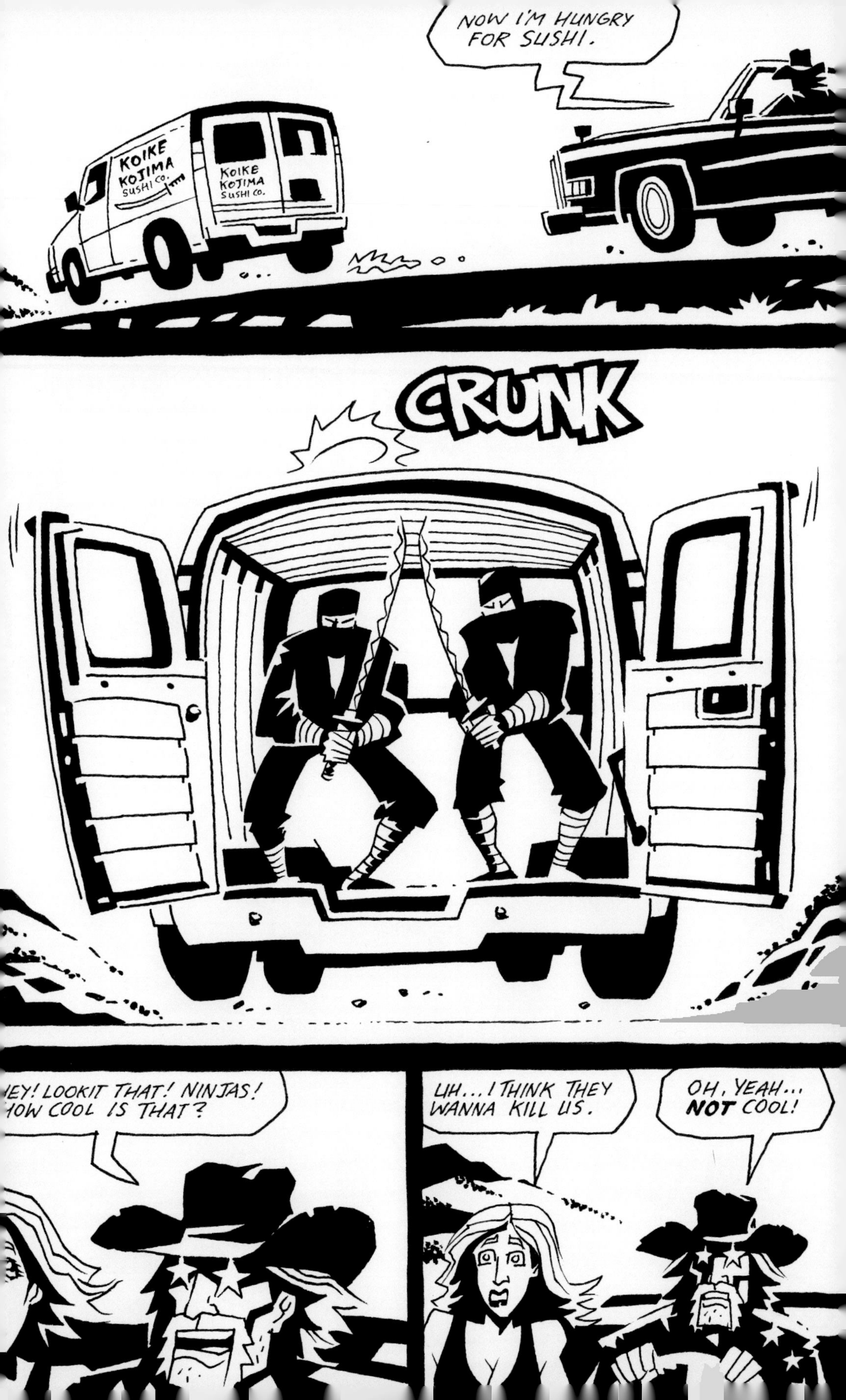
NOW I'M HUNGRY FOR SUSHI.
KOIKE KOJIMA SUSHI CO.
KOIKE KOJIMA SUSHI CO.
CRUNK
EY! LOOKIT THAT! NINJAS! OW COOL IS THAT?
UH... I THINK THEY WANNA KILL US.
OH, YEAH... **NOT** COOL!

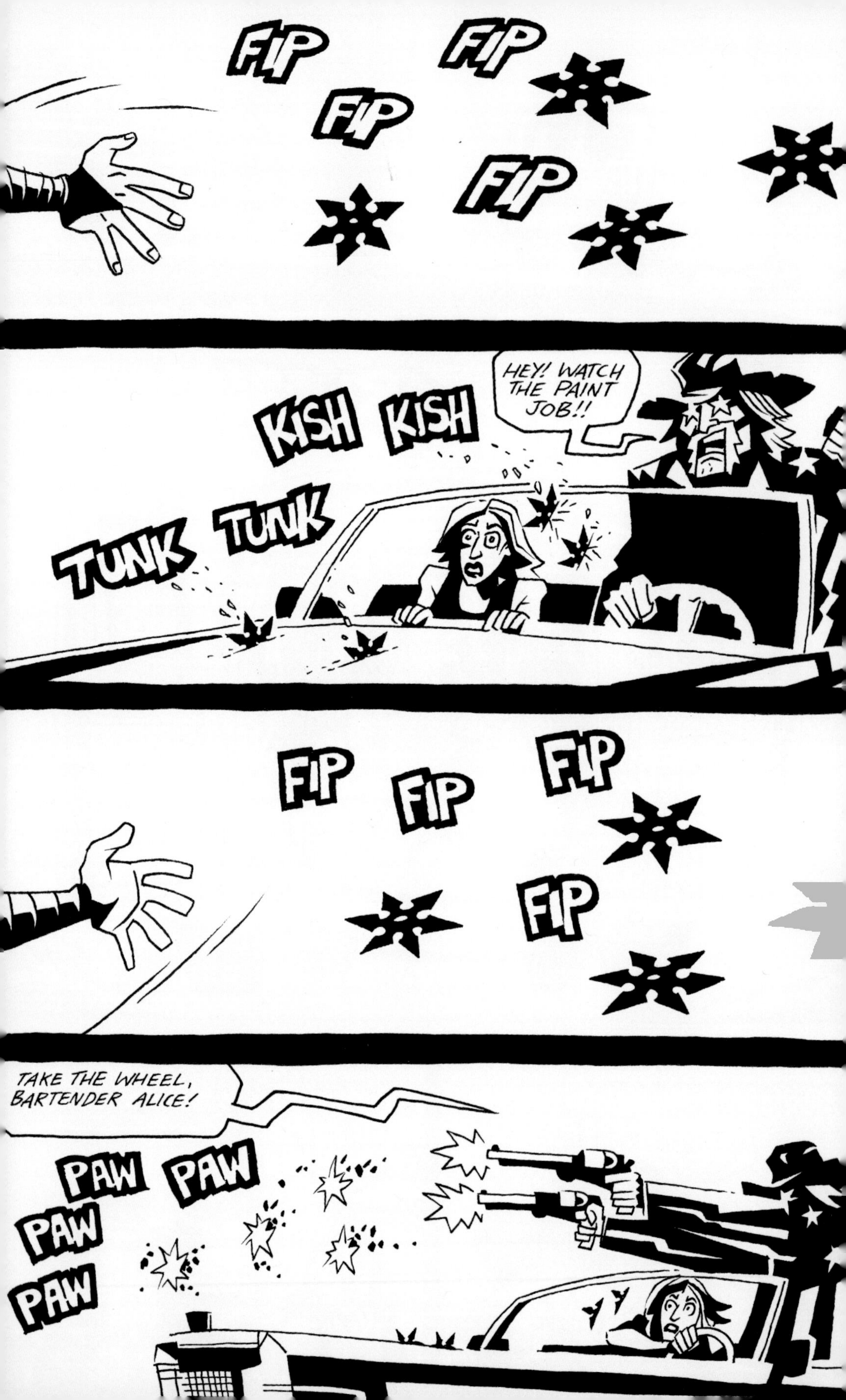
FIP FIP
FIP
FIP
KISH KISH
HEY! WATCH THE PAINT JOB!!
TUNK TUNK
FIP FIP FIP
FIP
TAKE THE WHEEL, BARTENDER ALICE!
PAW PAW
PAW
PAW

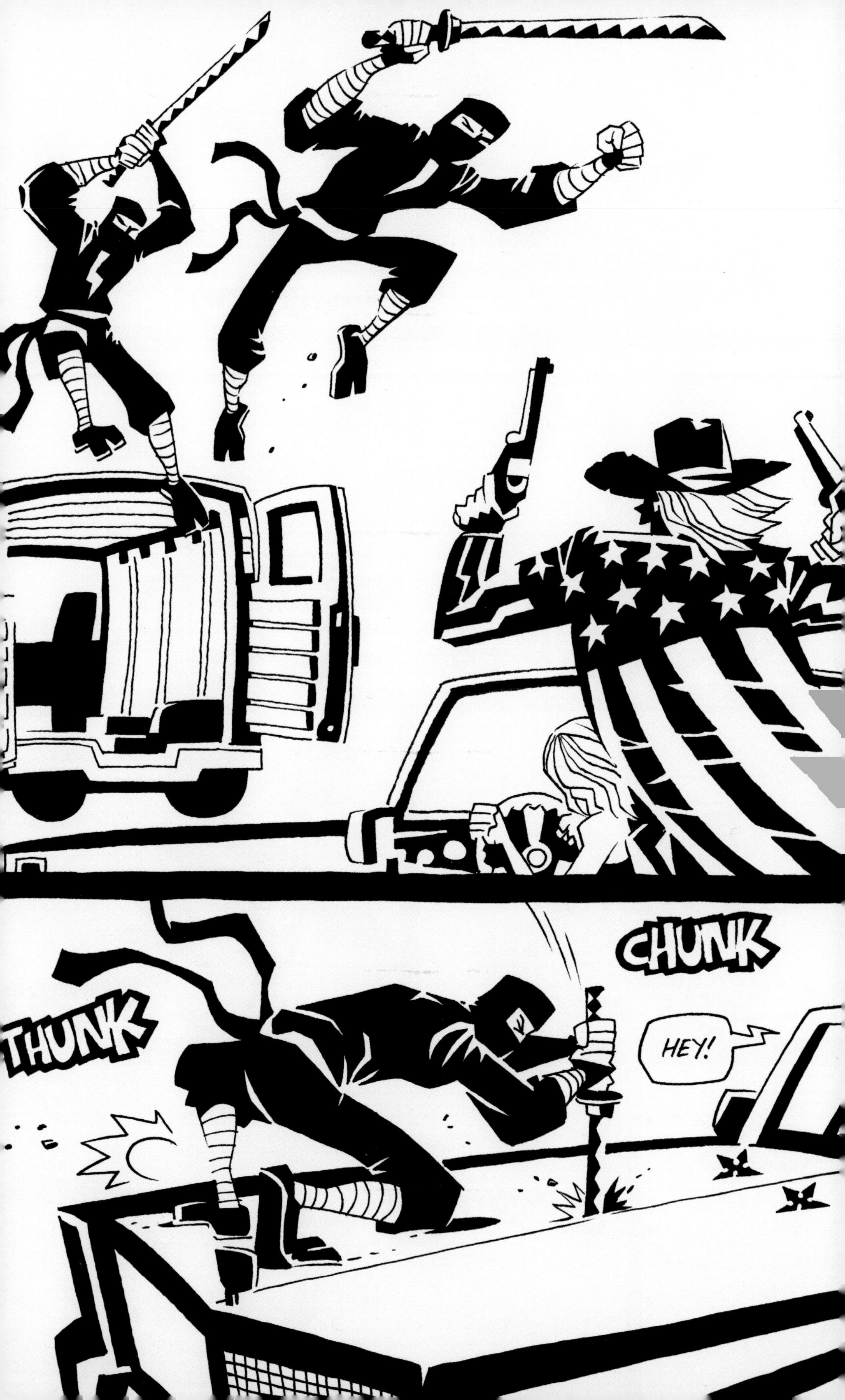
THUNK
CHUNK
HEY!

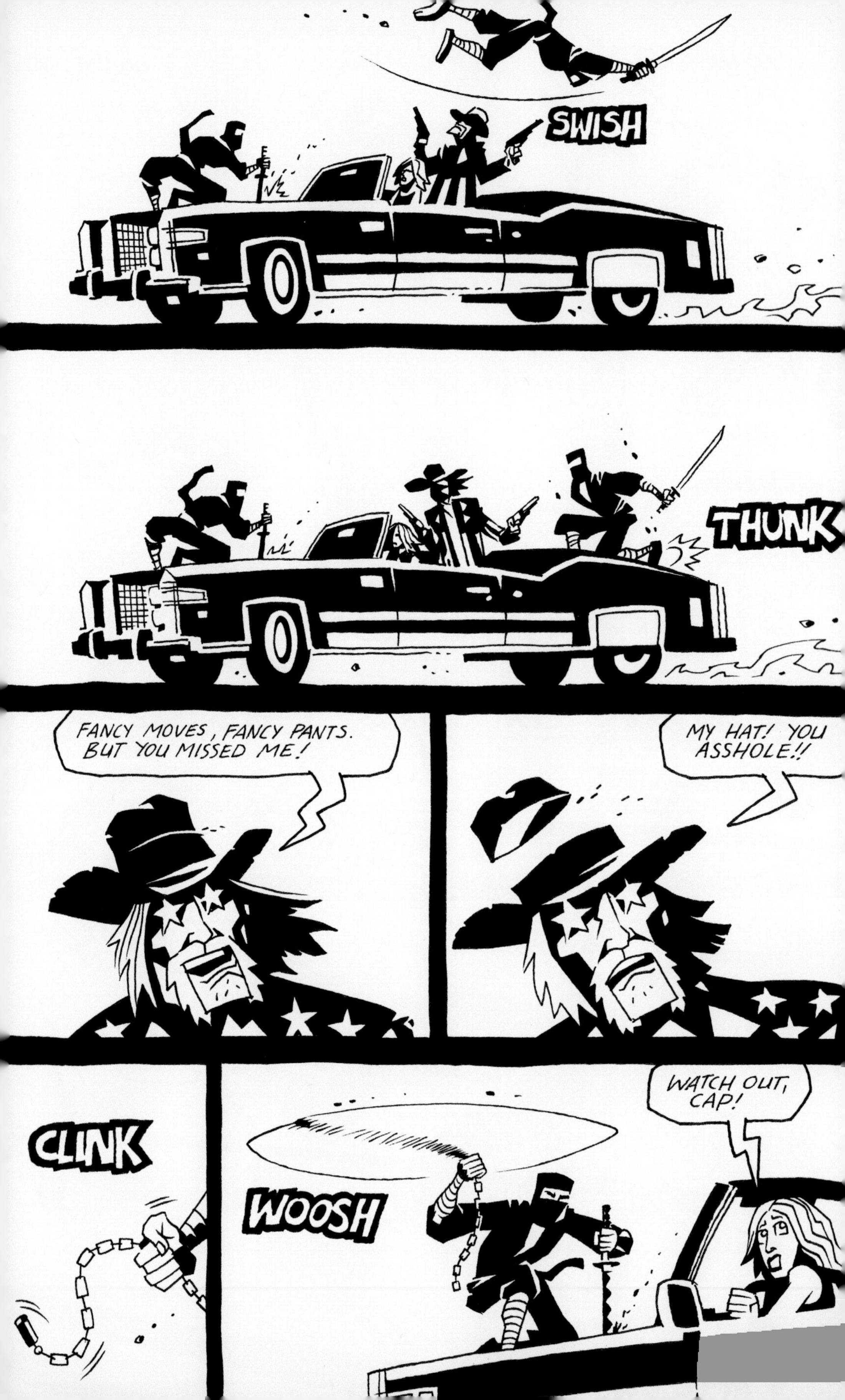
SWISH
THUNK
FANCY MOVES, FANCY PANTS. BUT YOU MISSED ME!
MY HAT! YOU ASSHOLE!!
CLINK
WOOSH
WATCH OUT, CAP!

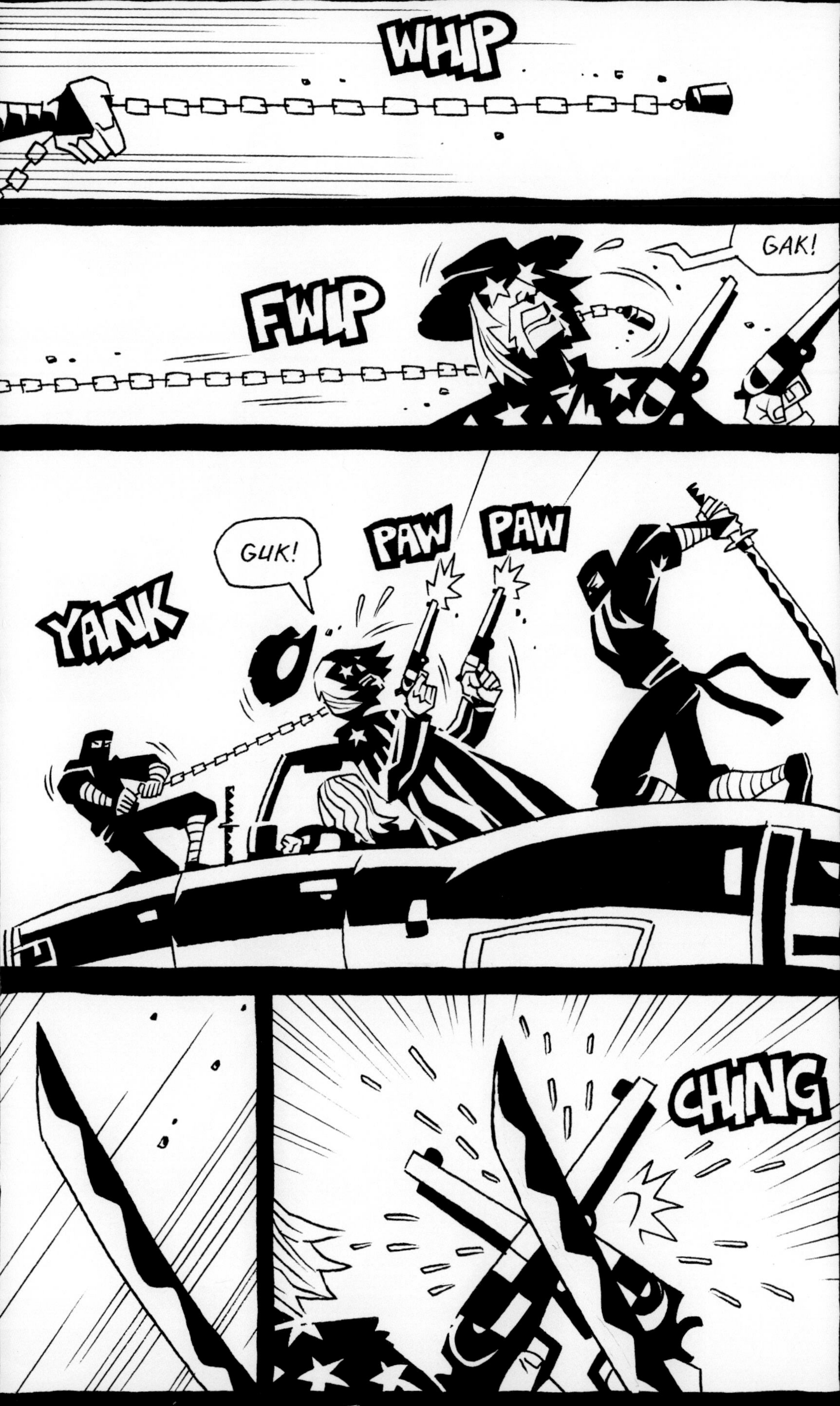
WHIP
FWIP
GAK!
YANK
GUK!
PAW
PAW
CHING

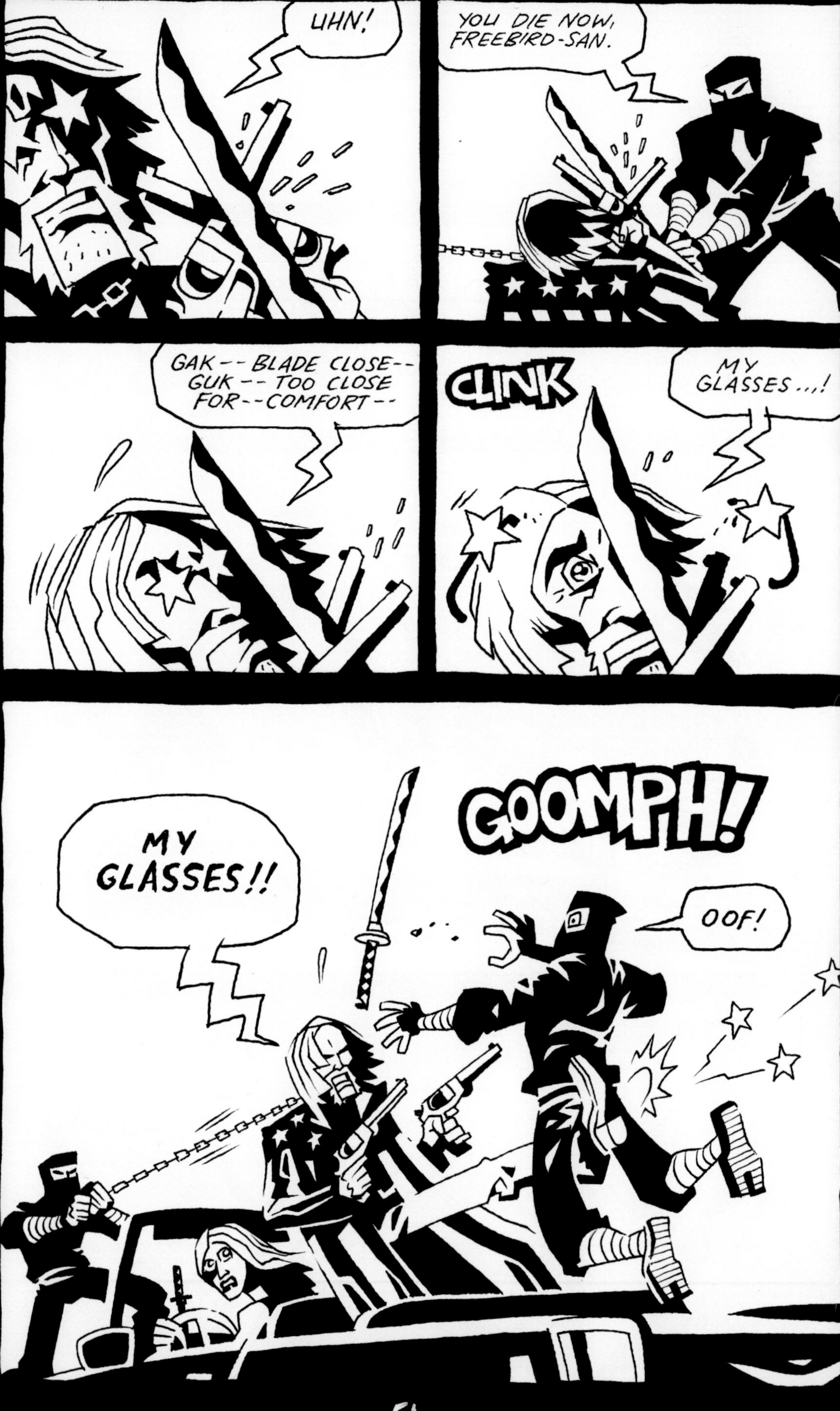
UHN!
YOU DIE NOW, FREEBIRD-SAN.
GAK-- BLADE CLOSE-- GUK -- TOO CLOSE FOR--COMFORT--
CLINK
MY GLASSES...!
MY GLASSES!!
GOOMPH!
OOF!

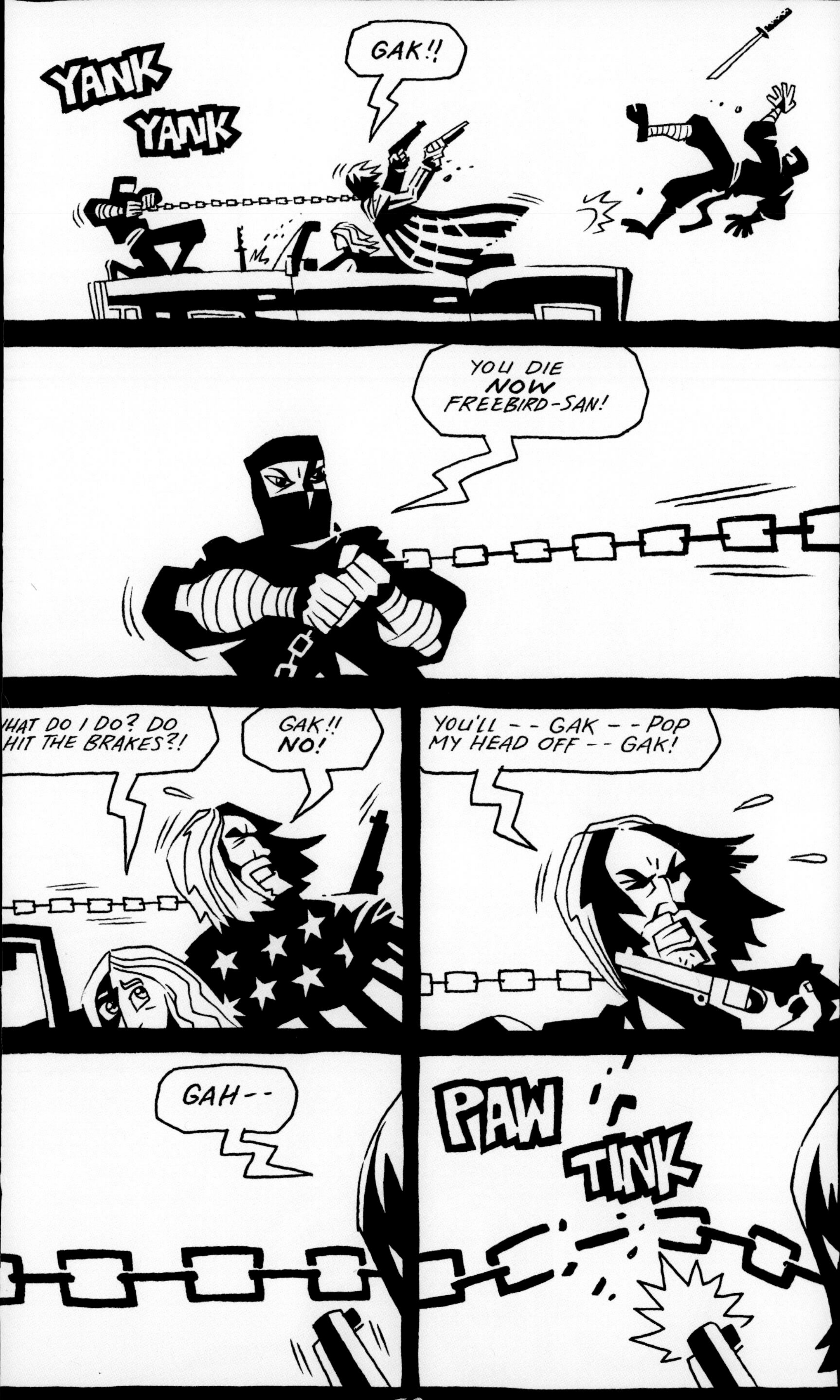
YANK
YANK
GAK!!
YOU DIE NOW FREEBIRD-SAN!
WHAT DO I DO? DO HIT THE BRAKES?!
GAK!! NO!
YOU'LL -- GAK -- POP MY HEAD OFF -- GAK!
GAH--
PAW
TINK

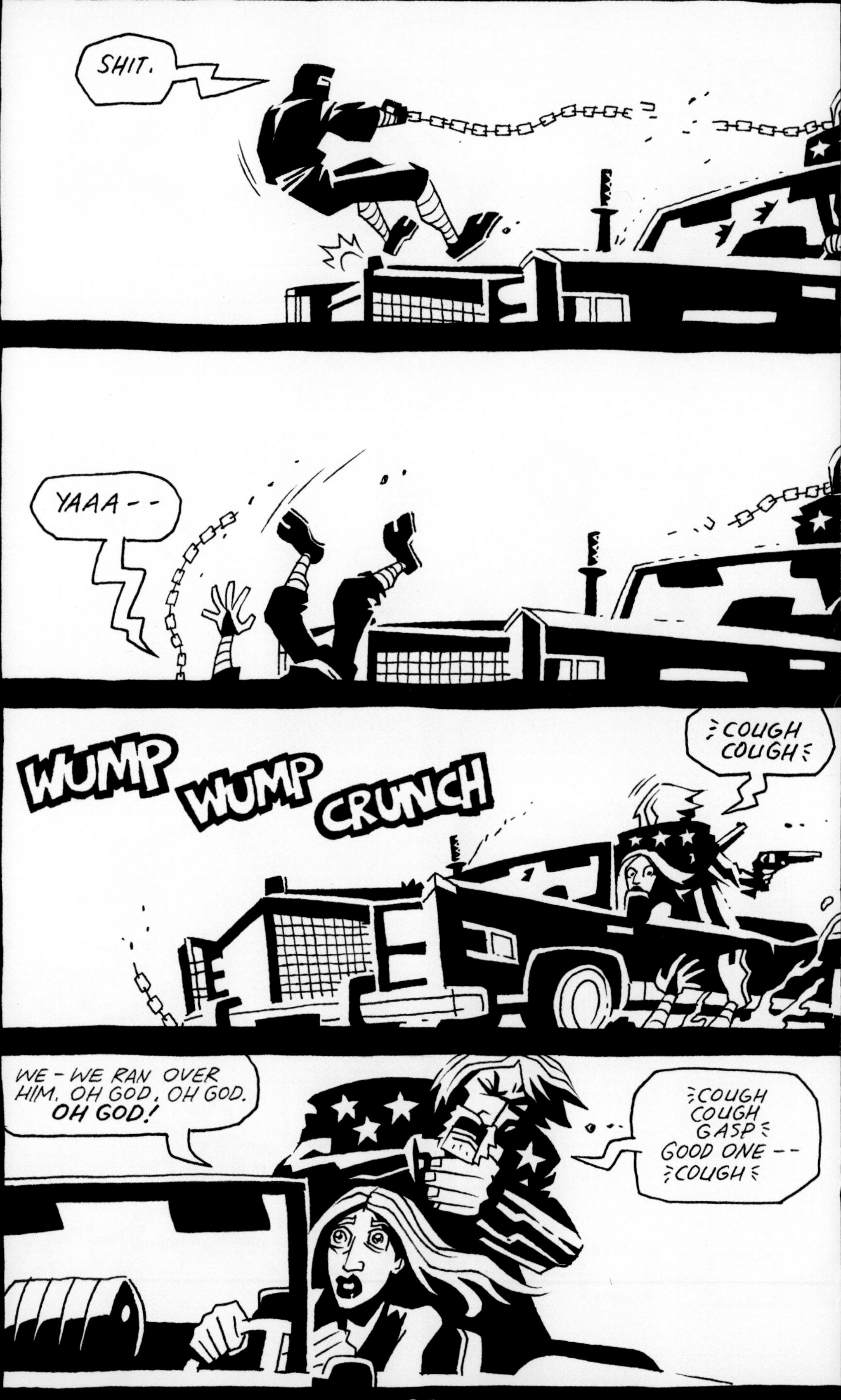
SHIT.
YAAA--
WUMP WUMP CRUNCH
COUGH COUGH
WE-WE RAN OVER HIM. OH GOD. OH GOD. OH GOD!
COUGH COUGH GASP GOOD ONE-- COUGH

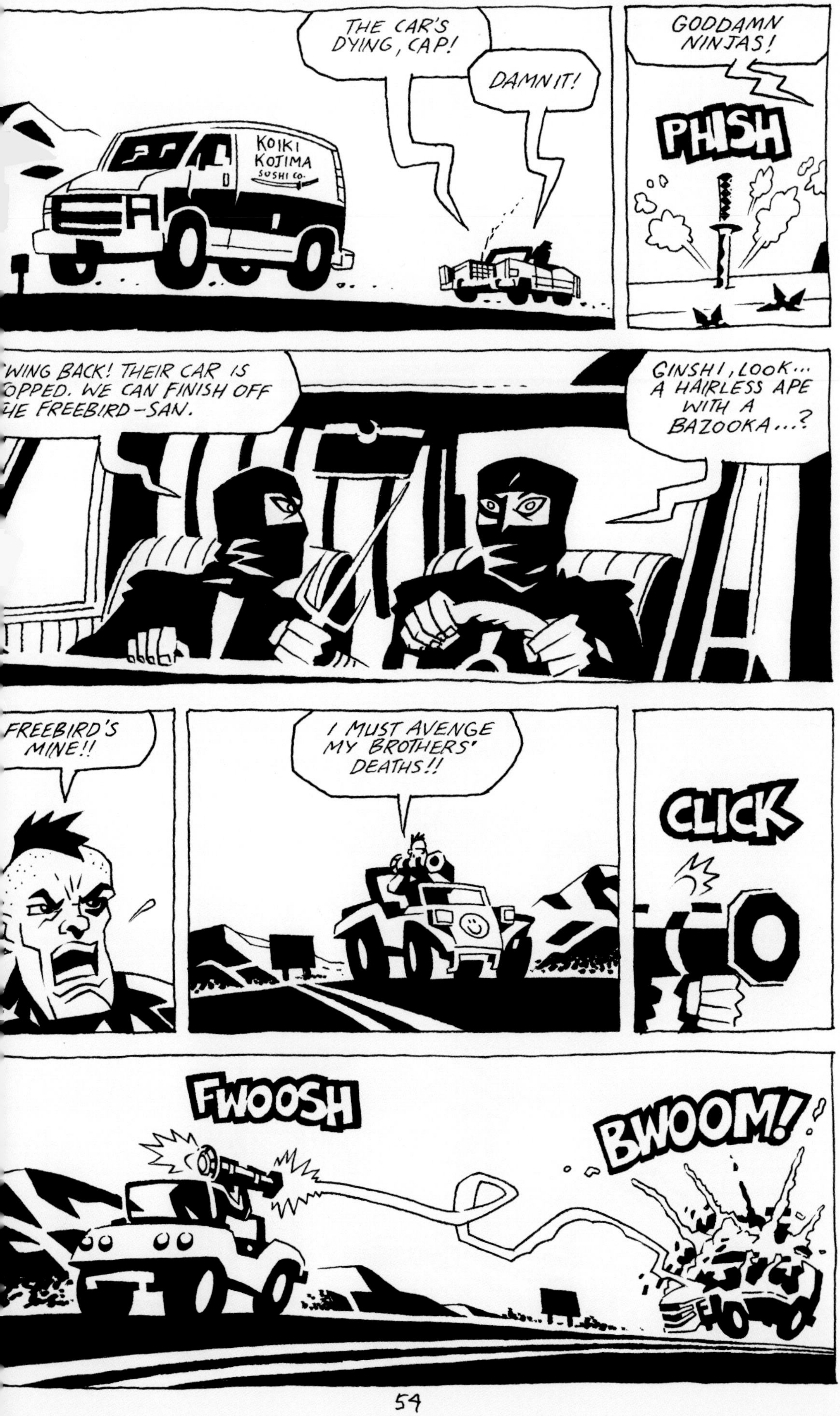
THE CAR'S DYING, CAP!
DAMNIT!
KOIKI KOJIMA SUSHI CO.
GODDAMN NINJAS!
PHISH
'WING BACK! THEIR CAR IS OPPED. WE CAN FINISH OFF HE FREEBIRD-SAN.
GINSHI, LOOK... A HAIRLESS APE WITH A BAZOOKA...?
FREEBIRD'S MINE!!
I MUST AVENGE MY BROTHERS' DEATHS!!
CLICK
FWOOSH
BWOOM!

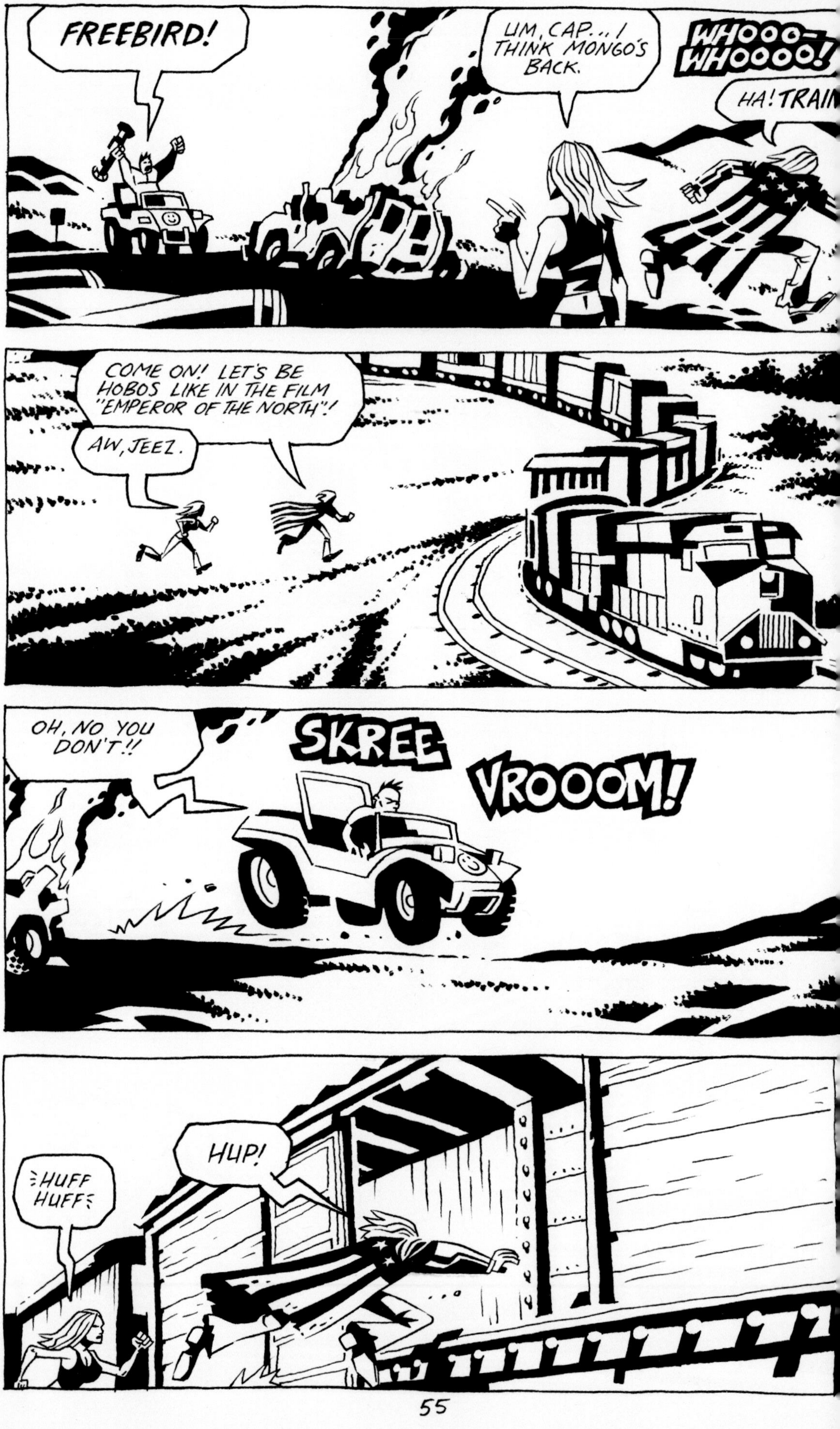

FREEBIRD!
UM, CAP... I THINK MONGO'S BACK.
WHOOO-WHOOOO!
HA! TRAIN
COME ON! LET'S BE HOBOS LIKE IN THE FILM "EMPEROR OF THE NORTH"!
AW, JEEZ.
OH, NO YOU DON'T!!
SKREE
VROOOM!
HUP!
HUFF HUFF

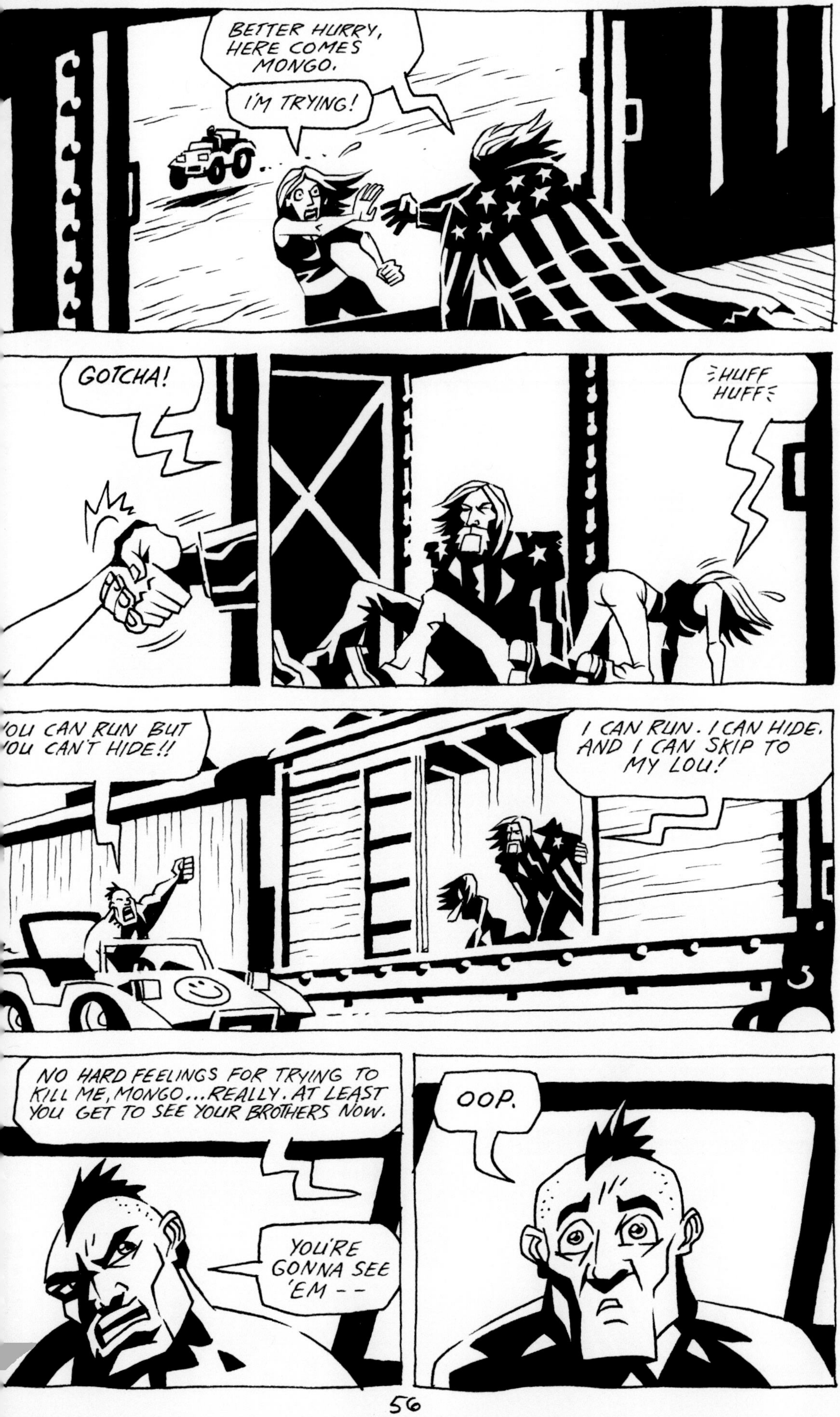
BETTER HURRY, HERE COMES MONGO.
I'M TRYING!
GOTCHA!
HUFF HUFF
YOU CAN RUN BUT YOU CAN'T HIDE!!
I CAN RUN. I CAN HIDE. AND I CAN SKIP TO MY LOU!
NO HARD FEELINGS FOR TRYING TO KILL ME, MONGO...REALLY. AT LEAST YOU GET TO SEE YOUR BROTHERS NOW.
YOU'RE GONNA SEE 'EM --
OOP.

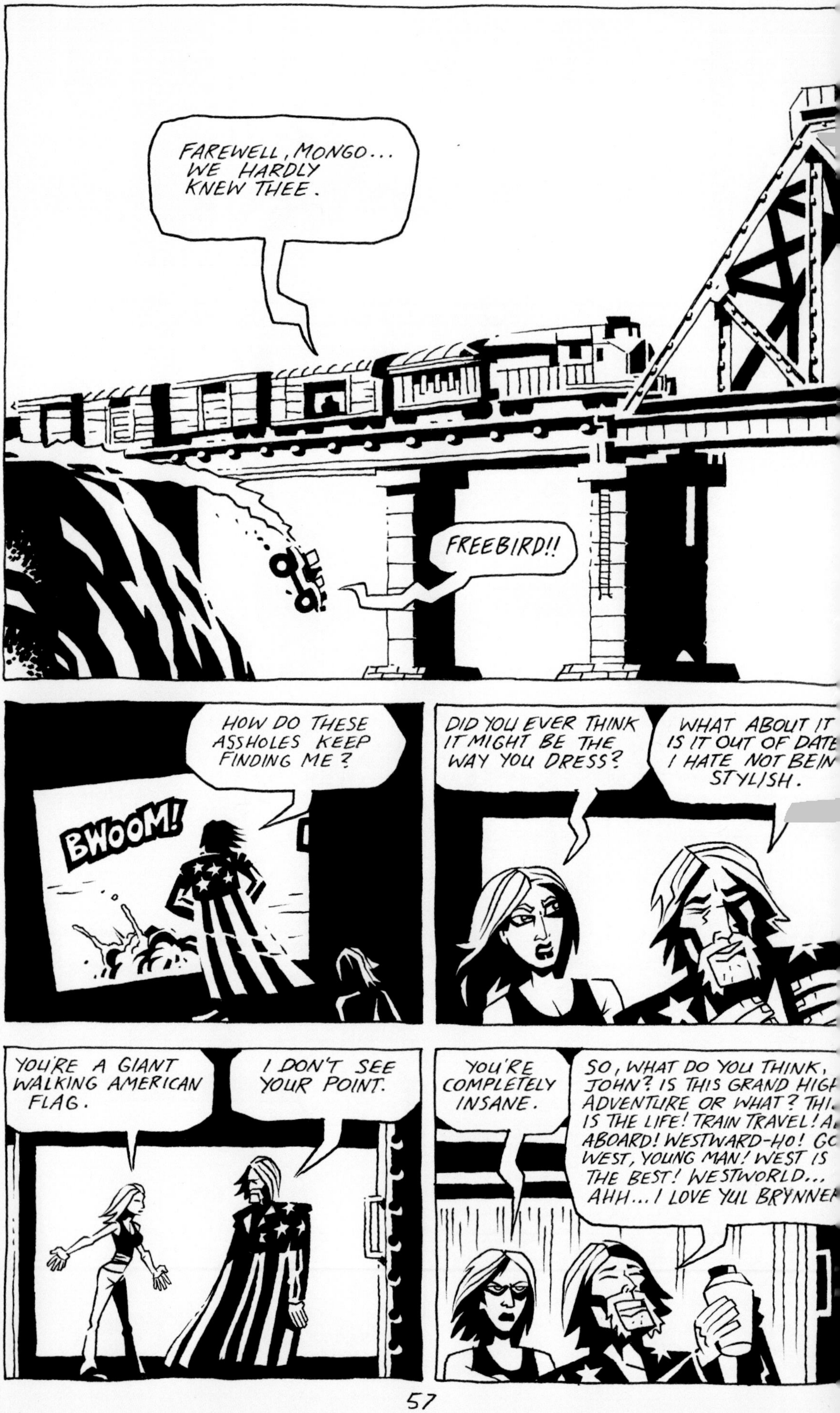
FAREWELL, MONGO... WE HARDLY KNEW THEE.
FREEBIRD!!
HOW DO THESE ASSHOLES KEEP FINDING ME?
BWOOM!
DID YOU EVER THINK IT MIGHT BE THE WAY YOU DRESS?
WHAT ABOUT IT? IS IT OUT OF DATE? I HATE NOT BEIN STYLISH.
YOU'RE A GIANT WALKING AMERICAN FLAG.
I DON'T SEE YOUR POINT.
YOU'RE COMPLETELY INSANE.
SO, WHAT DO YOU THINK, JOHN? IS THIS GRAND HIGH ADVENTURE OR WHAT? THI IS THE LIFE! TRAIN TRAVEL! A ABOARD! WESTWARD-HO! GO WEST, YOUNG MAN! WEST IS THE BEST! WESTWORLD... AHH... I LOVE YUL BRYNNER

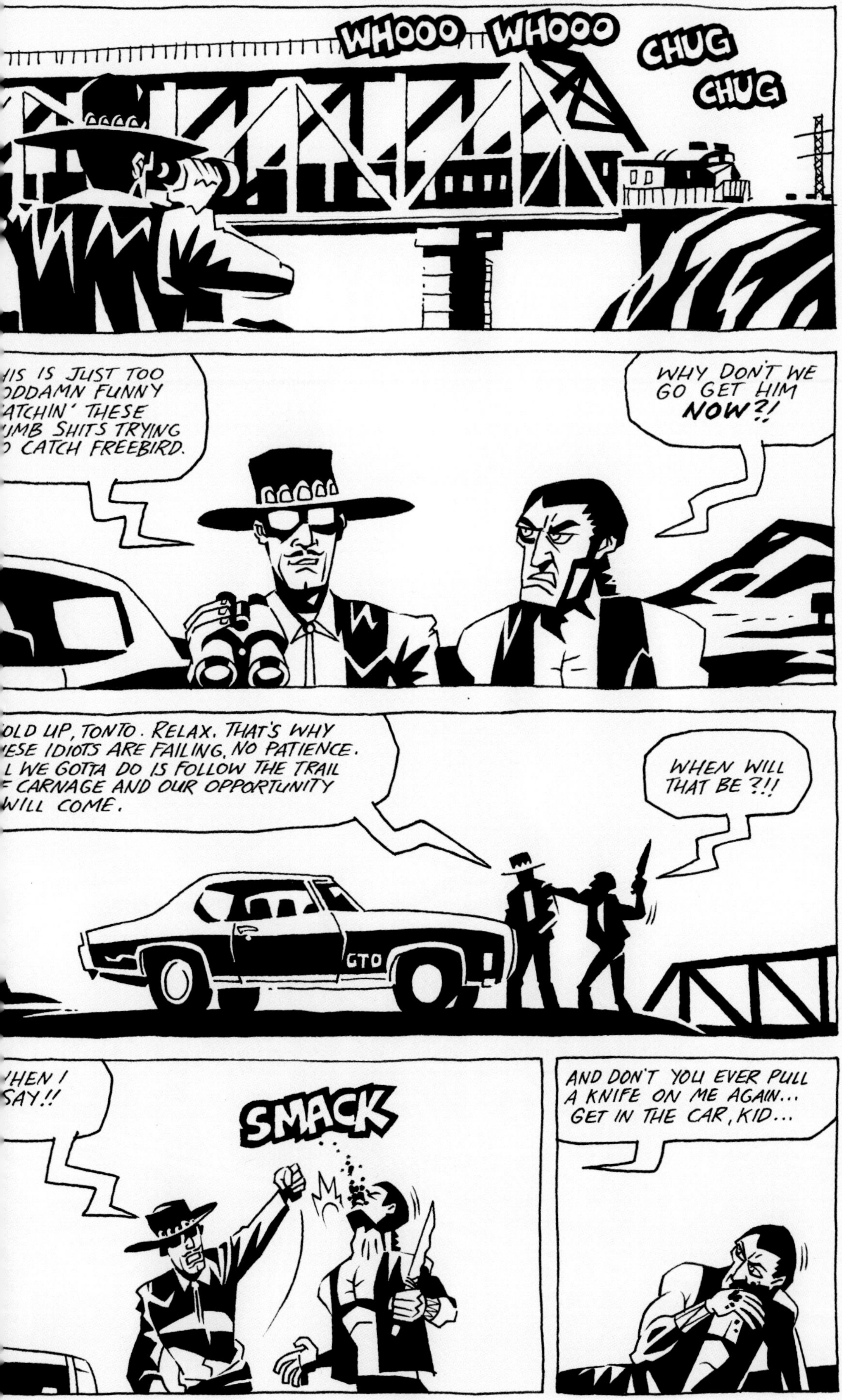

WHOOO WHOOO
CHUG CHUG
HIS IS JUST TOO ODDAMN FUNNY ATCHIN' THESE UMB SHITS TRYING O CATCH FREEBIRD.
WHY DON'T WE GO GET HIM NOW?!
OLD UP, TONTO. RELAX. THAT'S WHY HESE IDIOTS ARE FAILING. NO PATIENCE. L WE GOTTA DO IS FOLLOW THE TRAIL F CARNAGE AND OUR OPPORTUNITY WILL COME.
WHEN WILL THAT BE?!!
GTO
HEN I SAY!!
SMACK
AND DON'T YOU EVER PULL A KNIFE ON ME AGAIN... GET IN THE CAR, KID...

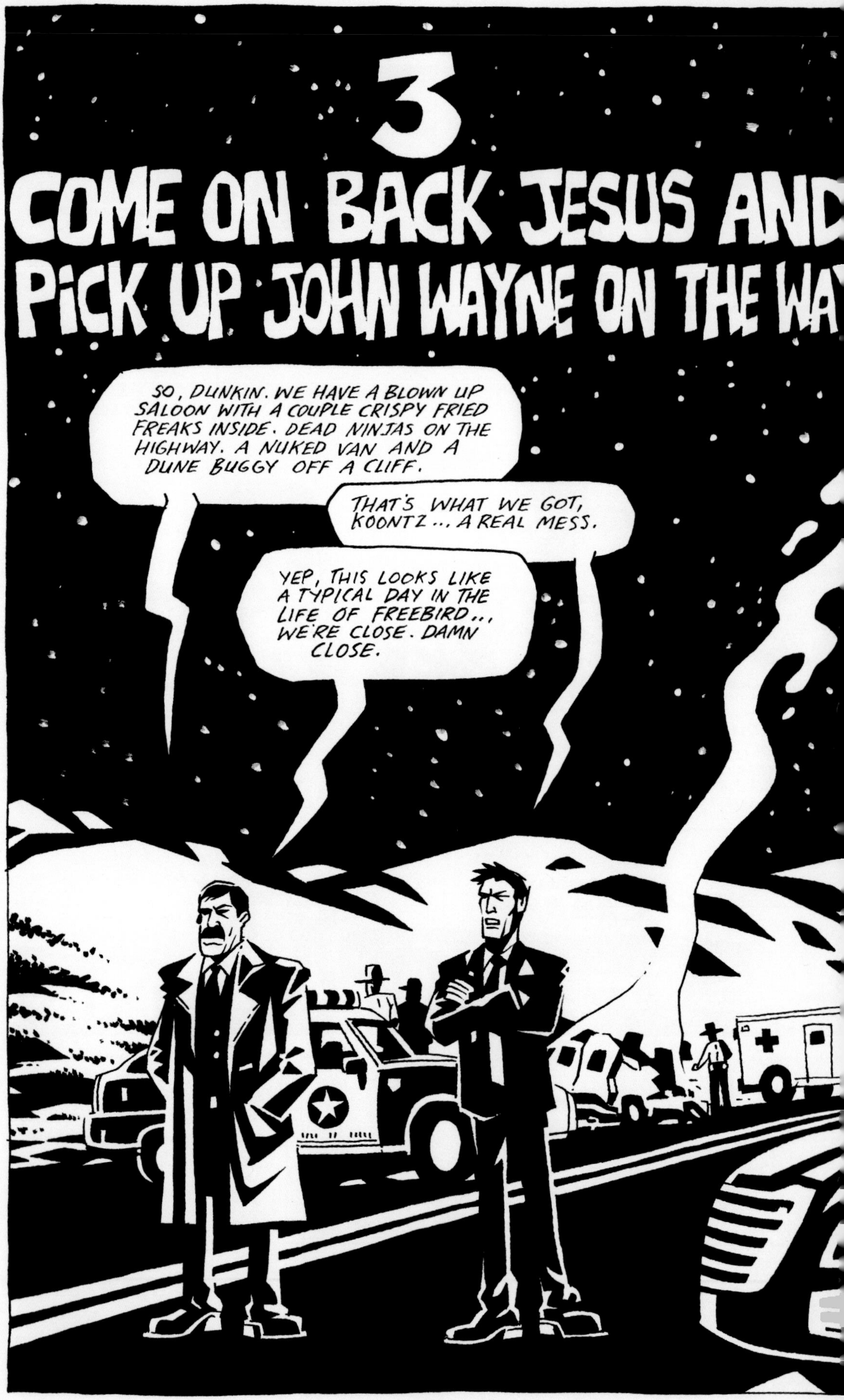
3
COME ON BACK JESUS AND PICK UP JOHN WAYNE ON THE WAY
SO, DUNKIN. WE HAVE A BLOWN UP SALOON WITH A COUPLE CRISPY FRIED FREAKS INSIDE. DEAD NINJAS ON THE HIGHWAY. A NUKED VAN AND A DUNE BUGGY OFF A CLIFF.
THAT'S WHAT WE GOT, KOONTZ... A REAL MESS.
YEP, THIS LOOKS LIKE A TYPICAL DAY IN THE LIFE OF FREEBIRD... WE'RE CLOSE. DAMN CLOSE.

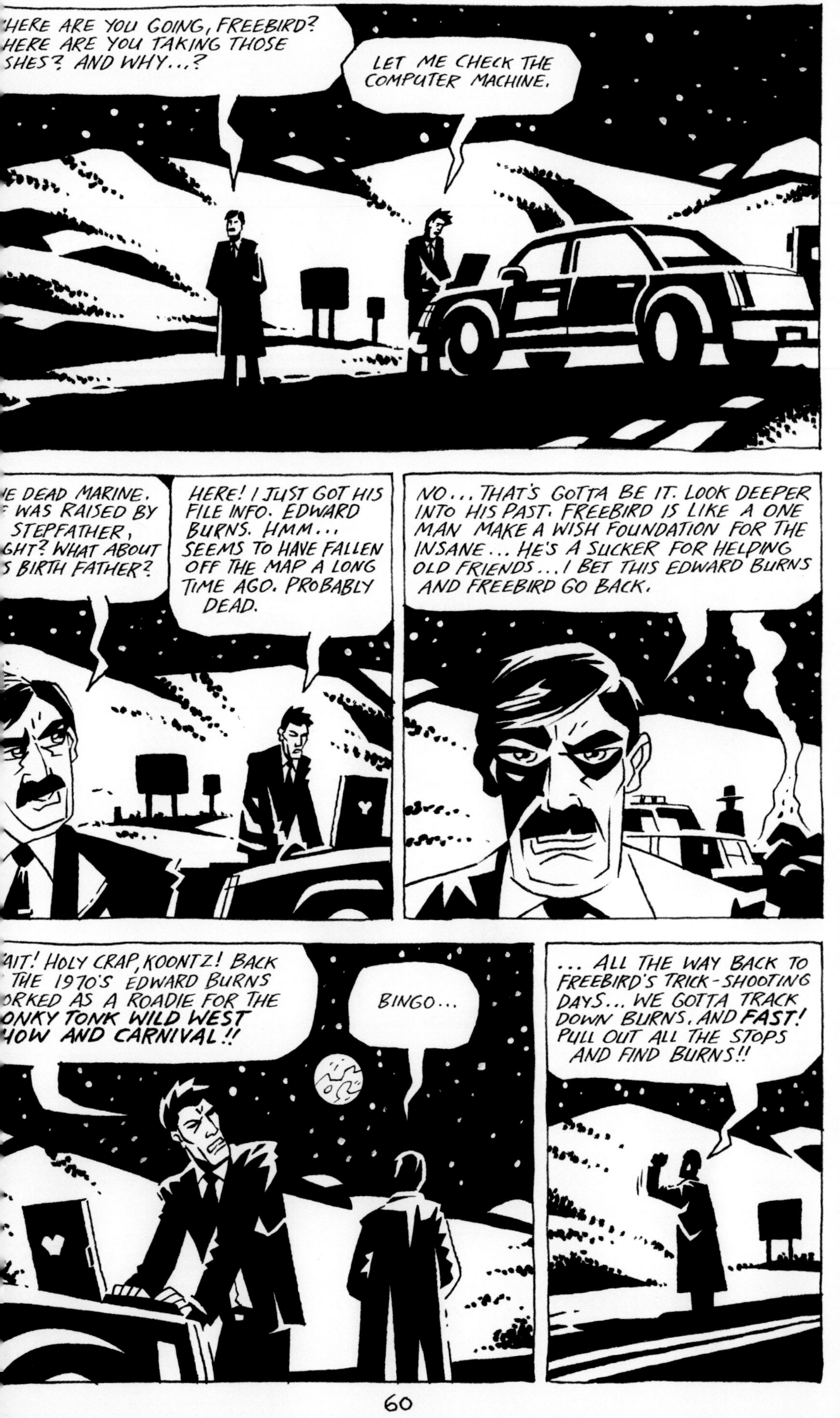
HERE ARE YOU GOING, FREEBIRD? HERE ARE YOU TAKING THOSE SHES? AND WHY...?
LET ME CHECK THE COMPUTER MACHINE.
E DEAD MARINE. WAS RAISED BY STEPFATHER, GHT? WHAT ABOUT BIRTH FATHER?
HERE! I JUST GOT HIS FILE INFO. EDWARD BURNS. HMM... SEEMS TO HAVE FALLEN OFF THE MAP A LONG TIME AGO. PROBABLY DEAD.
NO... THAT'S GOTTA BE IT. LOOK DEEPER INTO HIS PAST. FREEBIRD IS LIKE A ONE MAN MAKE A WISH FOUNDATION FOR THE INSANE... HE'S A SUCKER FOR HELPING OLD FRIENDS... I BET THIS EDWARD BURNS AND FREEBIRD GO BACK.
AIT! HOLY CRAP, KOONTZ! BACK THE 1970'S EDWARD BURNS ORKED AS A ROADIE FOR THE ONKY TONK WILD WEST HOW AND CARNIVAL!!
BINGO...
... ALL THE WAY BACK TO FREEBIRD'S TRICK-SHOOTING DAYS... WE GOTTA TRACK DOWN BURNS, AND FAST! PULL OUT ALL THE STOPS AND FIND BURNS!!

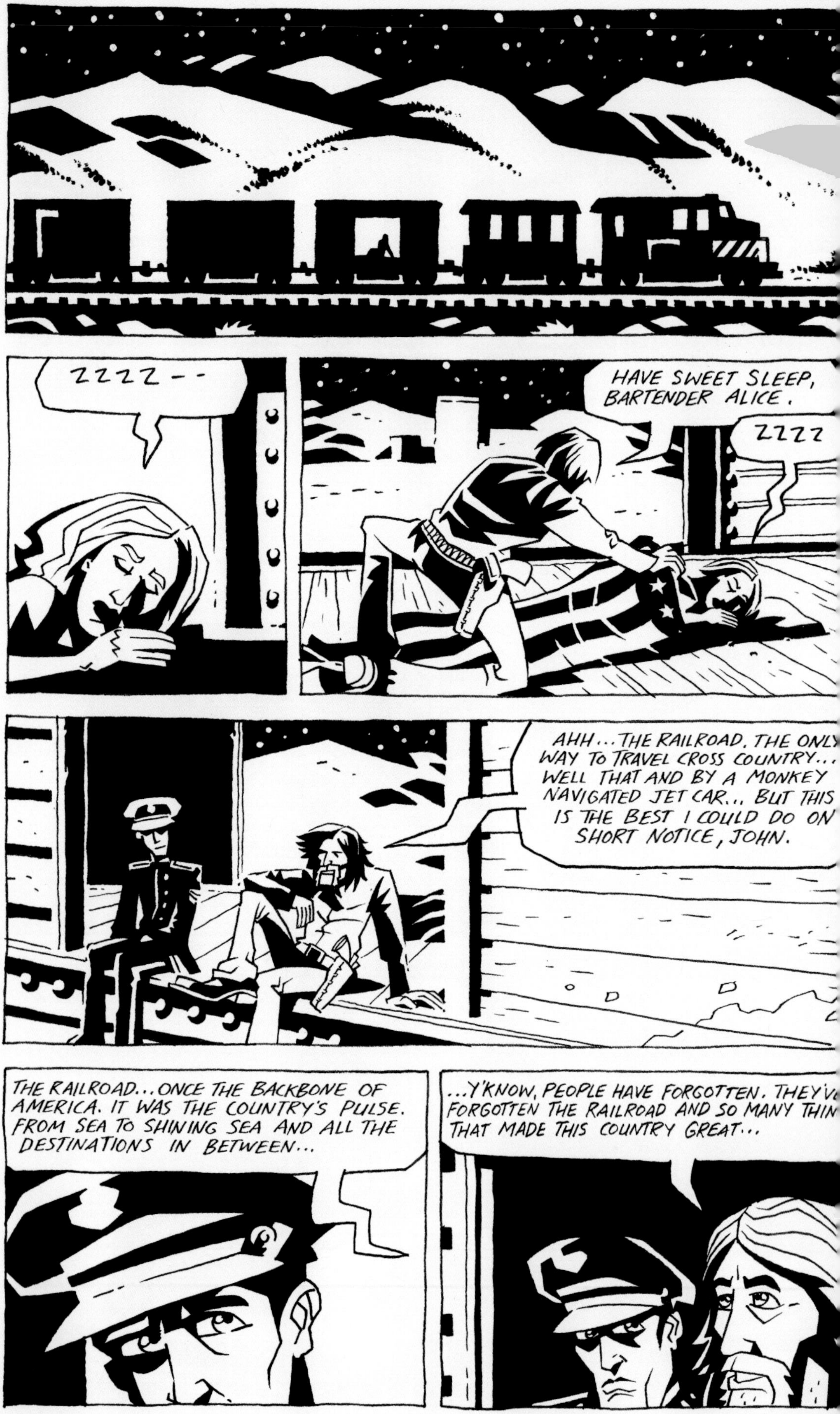
ZZZZ--
HAVE SWEET SLEEP, BARTENDER ALICE.
ZZZZ
AHH...THE RAILROAD. THE ONLY WAY TO TRAVEL CROSS COUNTRY... WELL THAT AND BY A MONKEY NAVIGATED JET CAR... BUT THIS IS THE BEST I COULD DO ON SHORT NOTICE, JOHN.
THE RAILROAD...ONCE THE BACKBONE OF AMERICA. IT WAS THE COUNTRY'S PULSE. FROM SEA TO SHINING SEA AND ALL THE DESTINATIONS IN BETWEEN...
...Y'KNOW, PEOPLE HAVE FORGOTTEN. THEY'VE FORGOTTEN THE RAILROAD AND SO MANY THIN THAT MADE THIS COUNTRY GREAT...

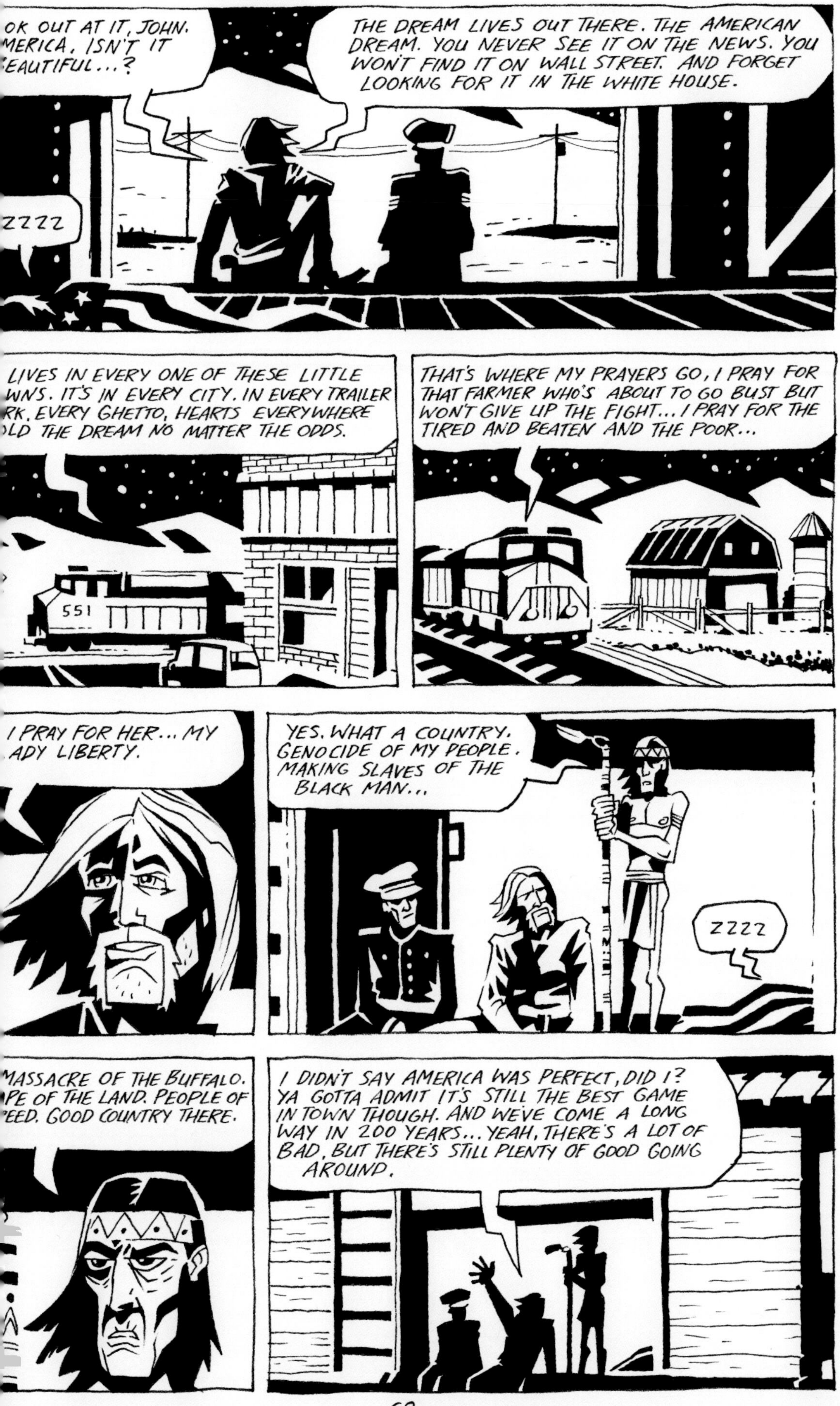
OK OUT AT IT, JOHN. MERICA. ISN'T IT EAUTIFUL...?
THE DREAM LIVES OUT THERE. THE AMERICAN DREAM. YOU NEVER SEE IT ON THE NEWS. YOU WON'T FIND IT ON WALL STREET. AND FORGET LOOKING FOR IT IN THE WHITE HOUSE.
ZZZZ
LIVES IN EVERY ONE OF THESE LITTLE WNS. IT'S IN EVERY CITY. IN EVERY TRAILER RK. EVERY GHETTO. HEARTS EVERYWHERE LD THE DREAM NO MATTER THE ODDS.
551
THAT'S WHERE MY PRAYERS GO. I PRAY FOR THAT FARMER WHO'S ABOUT TO GO BUST BUT WON'T GIVE UP THE FIGHT... I PRAY FOR THE TIRED AND BEATEN AND THE POOR...
I PRAY FOR HER... MY ADY LIBERTY.
YES. WHAT A COUNTRY. GENOCIDE OF MY PEOPLE. MAKING SLAVES OF THE BLACK MAN...
ZZZZ
MASSACRE OF THE BUFFALO. PE OF THE LAND. PEOPLE OF EED. GOOD COUNTRY THERE.
I DIDN'T SAY AMERICA WAS PERFECT, DID I? YA GOTTA ADMIT IT'S STILL THE BEST GAME IN TOWN THOUGH. AND WE'VE COME A LONG WAY IN 200 YEARS... YEAH, THERE'S A LOT OF BAD, BUT THERE'S STILL PLENTY OF GOOD GOING AROUND.

IF I MAY INTERJECT...

...FORGIVENESS IS THE TRAIT OF THE TRULY ENLIGHTENED SOUL.

THE WAY I SEE IT, SCREW 'EM IF THEY CAN'T TAKE A JOKE.

PARDON US. MY ASSOCIATE AND I JUST HOPPED ON THE FRIEGHT AND WE DO APPRECIATE A GOOD CONVERSATION. I'M J.C. AND THIS IS DUKE.

I'M FREEBIRD. THIS MOJO RISING AND JOHN. NICE TO MEET YOU.

LIKEWISE.

SIT. SIT! SO WHAT BRINGS YOU TO RIDE THE RAILS?

LOOKING FOR KINDRID SPIRITS SUCH AS YOURSELF WHO ARE KEEPING THE FLAME.

DAMN STRAIGHT.

ZZZZ --

OKAY, WHO'S UP FOR SOME POKER?

UH--WHA?

DEAL 'EM UP, PILGRIM.

I GOTTA BE DREAMIN ZZZZ...

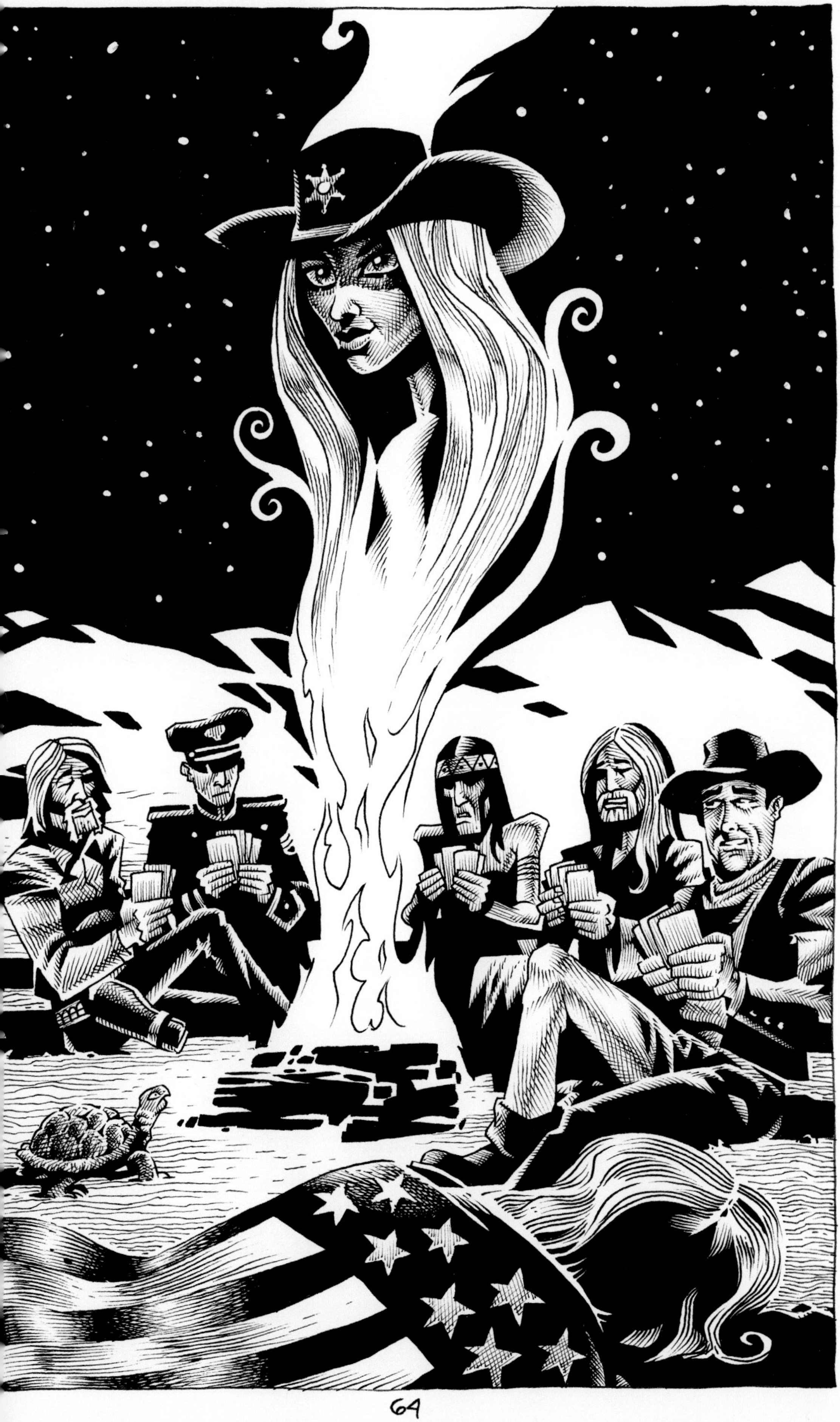

4
A BAD CASE OF GONE

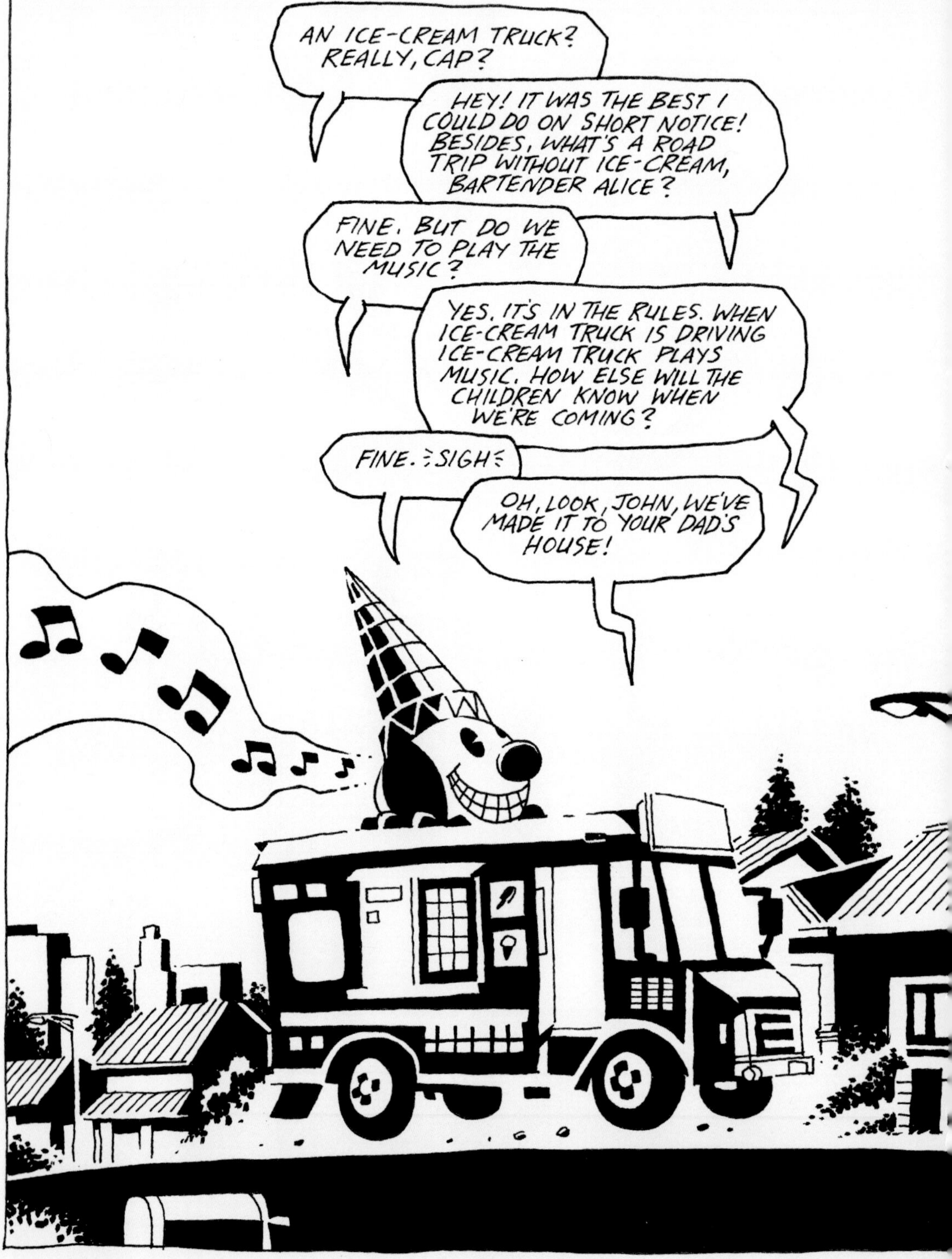

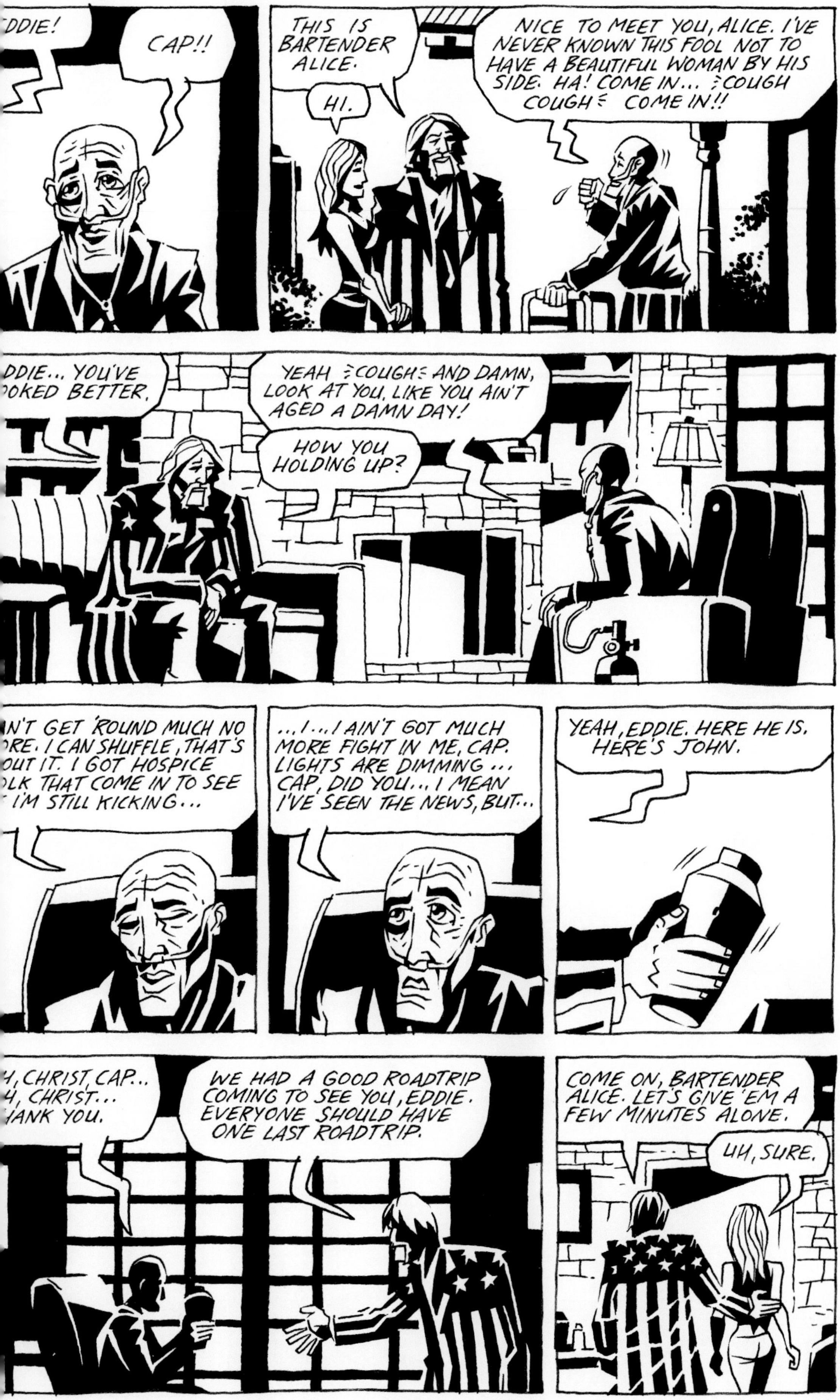
DDIE!
CAP!!
THIS IS BARTENDER ALICE.
HI.
NICE TO MEET YOU, ALICE. I'VE NEVER KNOWN THIS FOOL NOT TO HAVE A BEAUTIFUL WOMAN BY HIS SIDE. HA! COME IN... COUGH COUGH COME IN!!
DDIE... YOU'VE OOKED BETTER.
YEAH COUGH AND DAMN, LOOK AT YOU, LIKE YOU AIN'T AGED A DAMN DAY!
HOW YOU HOLDING UP?
N'T GET 'ROUND MUCH NO ORE. I CAN SHUFFLE, THAT'S OUT IT. I GOT HOSPICE OLK THAT COME IN TO SEE I'M STILL KICKING...
...I...I AIN'T GOT MUCH MORE FIGHT IN ME, CAP. LIGHTS ARE DIMMING... CAP, DID YOU... I MEAN I'VE SEEN THE NEWS, BUT...
YEAH, EDDIE. HERE HE IS. HERE'S JOHN.
H, CHRIST, CAP... H, CHRIST... HANK YOU.
WE HAD A GOOD ROADTRIP COMING TO SEE YOU, EDDIE. EVERYONE SHOULD HAVE ONE LAST ROADTRIP.
COME ON, BARTENDER ALICE. LET'S GIVE 'EM A FEW MINUTES ALONE.
UH, SURE.

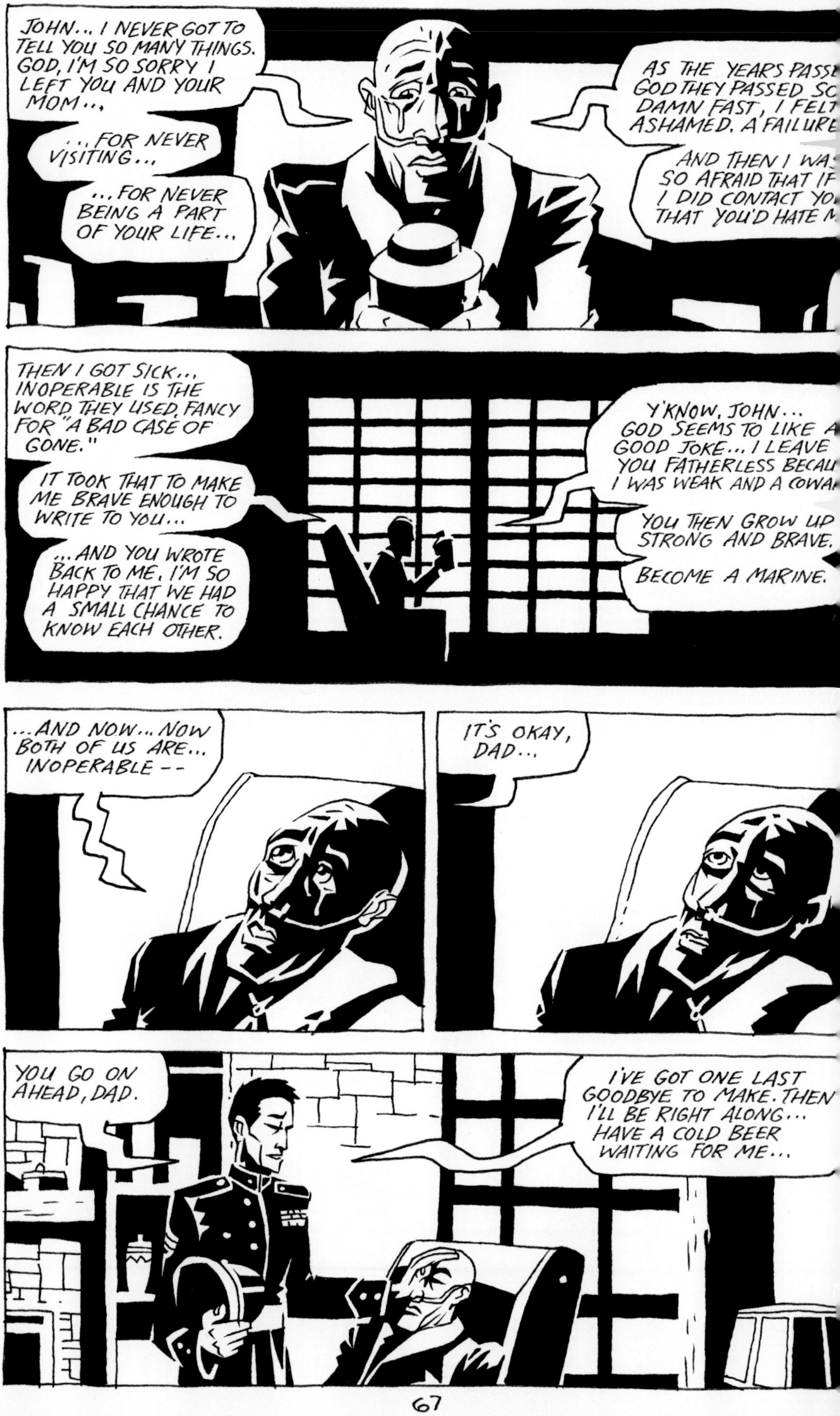
JOHN... I NEVER GOT TO TELL YOU SO MANY THINGS. GOD, I'M SO SORRY I LEFT YOU AND YOUR MOM...,
...FOR NEVER VISITING...,
...FOR NEVER BEING A PART OF YOUR LIFE...
AS THE YEARS PASS GOD THEY PASSED SO DAMN FAST, I FELT ASHAMED. A FAILURE
AND THEN I WAS SO AFRAID THAT IF I DID CONTACT YO THAT YOU'D HATE
THEN I GOT SICK..., INOPERABLE IS THE WORD THEY USED, FANCY FOR "A BAD CASE OF GONE."
IT TOOK THAT TO MAKE ME BRAVE ENOUGH TO WRITE TO YOU...
...AND YOU WROTE BACK TO ME. I'M SO HAPPY THAT WE HAD A SMALL CHANCE TO KNOW EACH OTHER.
Y'KNOW, JOHN... GOD SEEMS TO LIKE A GOOD JOKE... I LEAVE YOU FATHERLESS BECAU I WAS WEAK AND A COWA
YOU THEN GROW UP STRONG AND BRAVE.
BECOME A MARINE.
...AND NOW... NOW BOTH OF US ARE... INOPERABLE --
IT'S OKAY, DAD...
YOU GO ON AHEAD, DAD.
I'VE GOT ONE LAST GOODBYE TO MAKE. THEN I'LL BE RIGHT ALONG... HAVE A COLD BEER WAITING FOR ME...

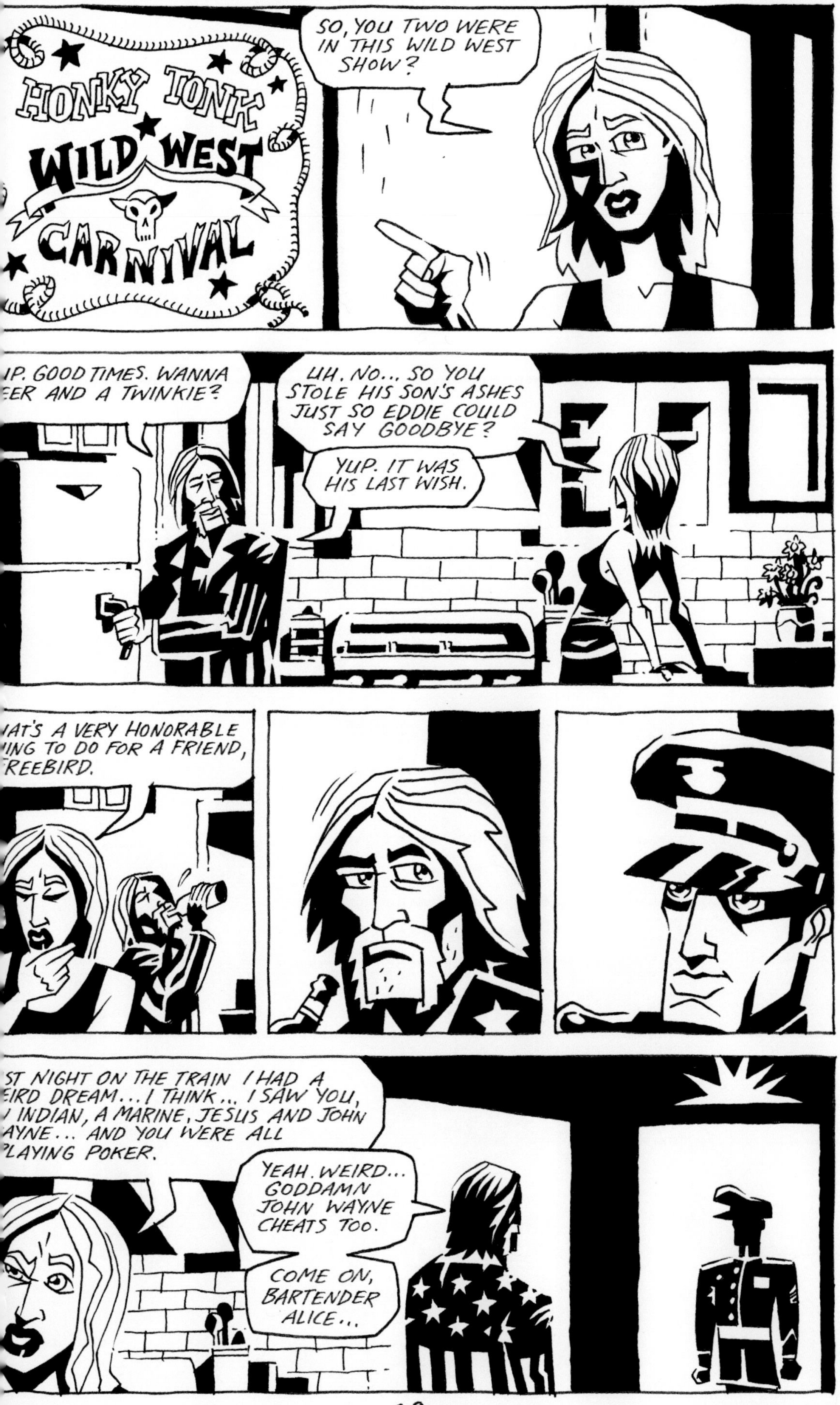
HONKY TONK WILD WEST CARNIVAL
SO, YOU TWO WERE IN THIS WILD WEST SHOW?
IP. GOOD TIMES. WANNA EER AND A TWINKIE?
UH. NO... SO YOU STOLE HIS SON'S ASHES JUST SO EDDIE COULD SAY GOODBYE?
YUP. IT WAS HIS LAST WISH.
IAT'S A VERY HONORABLE IING TO DO FOR A FRIEND, FREEBIRD.
ST NIGHT ON THE TRAIN I HAD A EIRD DREAM... I THINK... I SAW YOU, INDIAN, A MARINE, JESUS AND JOHN AYNE... AND YOU WERE ALL PLAYING POKER.
YEAH. WEIRD... GODDAMN JOHN WAYNE CHEATS TOO.
COME ON, BARTENDER ALICE...

IS HE...?

YUP, GODSPEED, OLD BUDDY... GODSPEED.

SO YOU'RE FINISHED WITH YOUR MISSION...? UH, I MEAN YOUR FAVOR?

YUP, JUST GOTTA MAKE SURE JOHN GETS BACK HOME TO SAY GOODBYE TO HIS MOTHER.

GOOD, I'VE ALWAYS HONORED COMPLETION OF A TASK, I'LL MAKE SURE JOHN MAKES IT HOME TO HIS MOTHER.

UH, OKAY, I GUESS...BUT WE'D BETTER SKEE-DADDLE. MY SPIDER-SENSES... TINGLING...

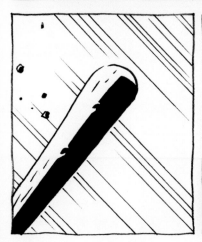

THUD!

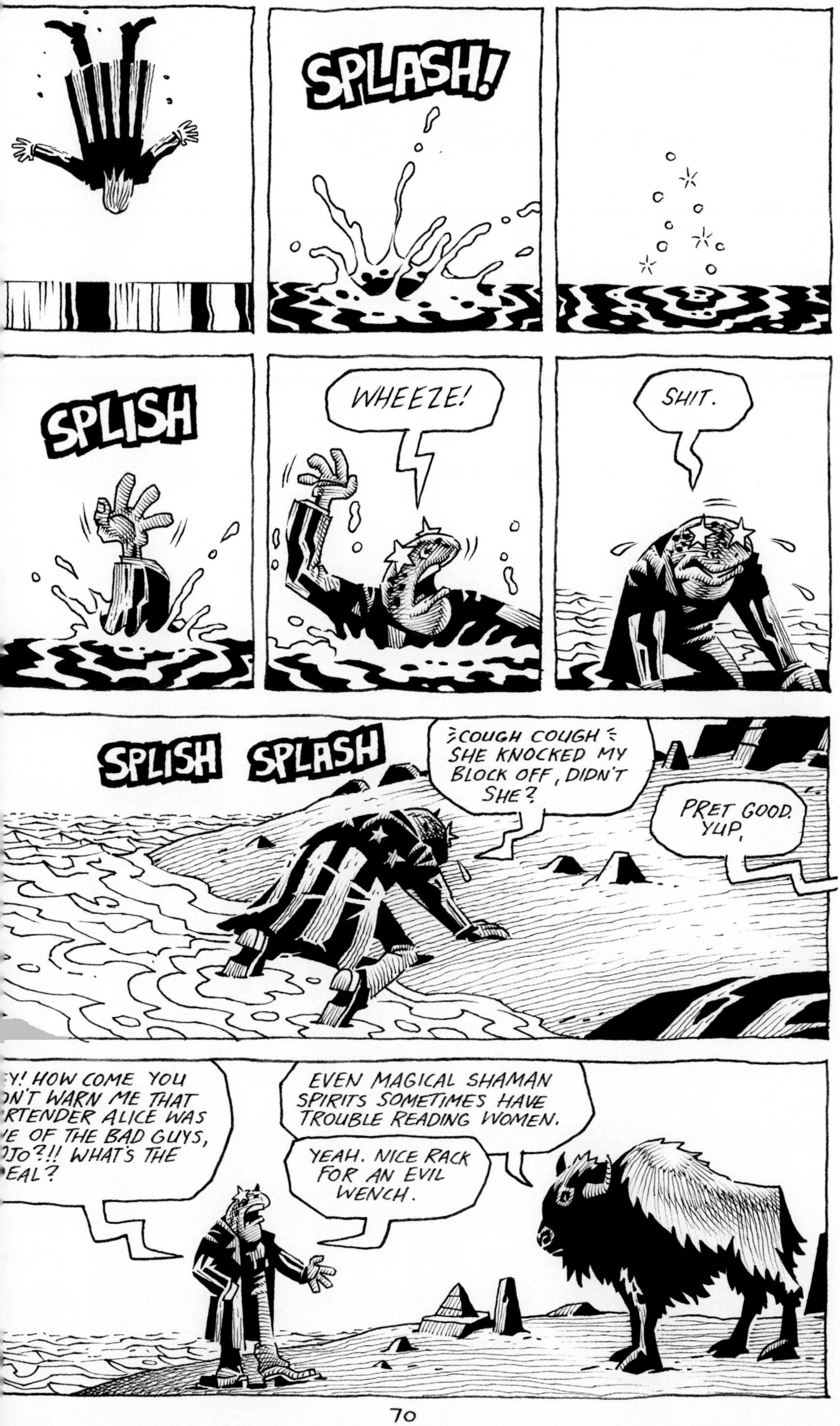

SPLASH!
SPLISH
WHEEZE!
SHIT.
SPLISH SPLASH
COUGH COUGH SHE KNOCKED MY BLOCK OFF, DIDN'T SHE?
PRET GOOD. YUP.
Y! HOW COME YOU N'T WARN ME THAT RTENDER ALICE WAS E OF THE BAD GUYS, JO?!! WHAT'S THE EAL?
YEAH. NICE RACK FOR AN EVIL WENCH.
EVEN MAGICAL SHAMAN SPIRITS SOMETIMES HAVE TROUBLE READING WOMEN.

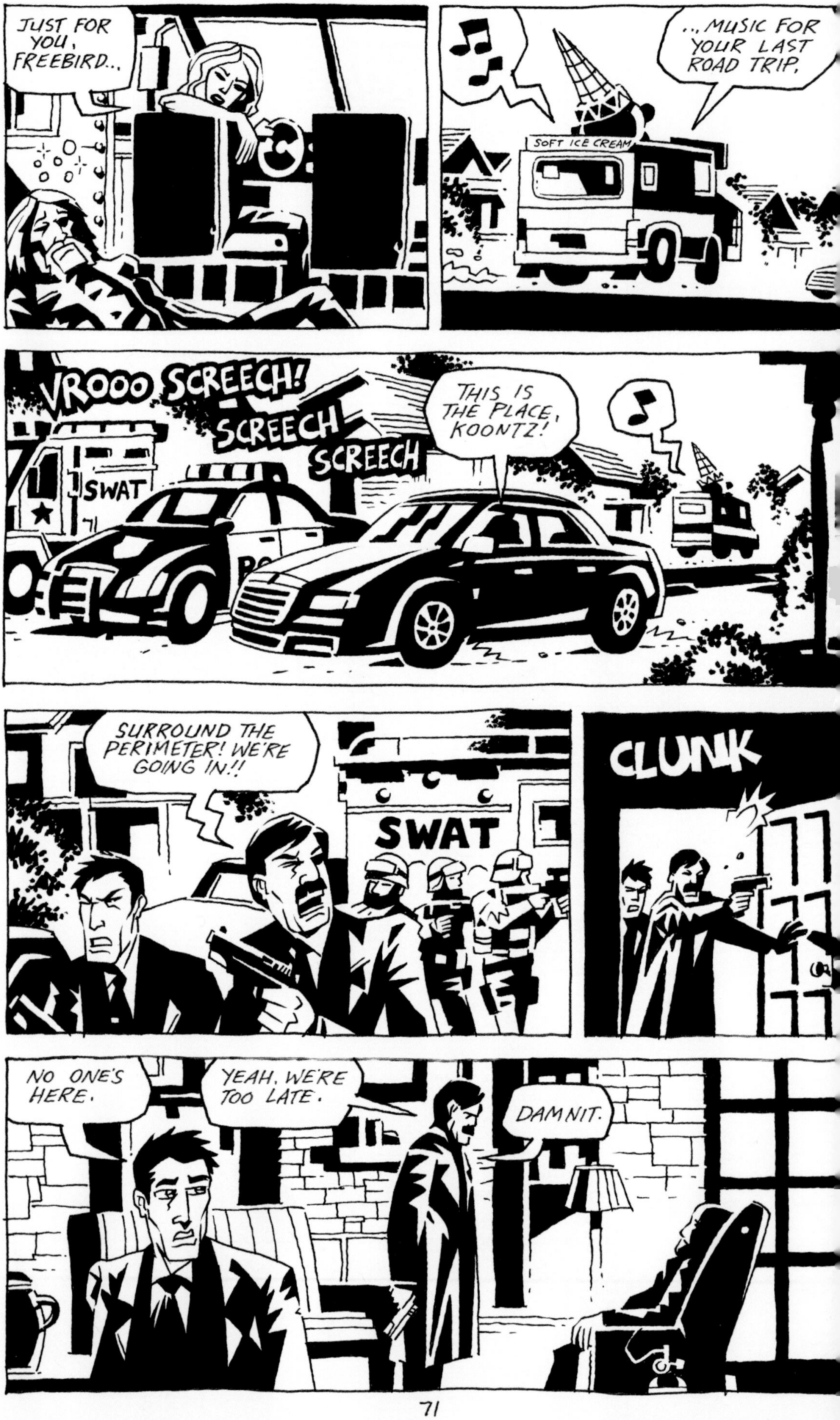
JUST FOR YOU, FREEBIRD...
..., MUSIC FOR YOUR LAST ROAD TRIP,
SOFT ICE CREAM
VROOO SCREECH!
SCREECH
SCREECH
SWAT
THIS IS THE PLACE, KOONTZ!
SURROUND THE PERIMETER! WE'RE GOING IN!!
SWAT
CLUNK
NO ONE'S HERE.
YEAH. WE'RE TOO LATE.
DAMNIT.

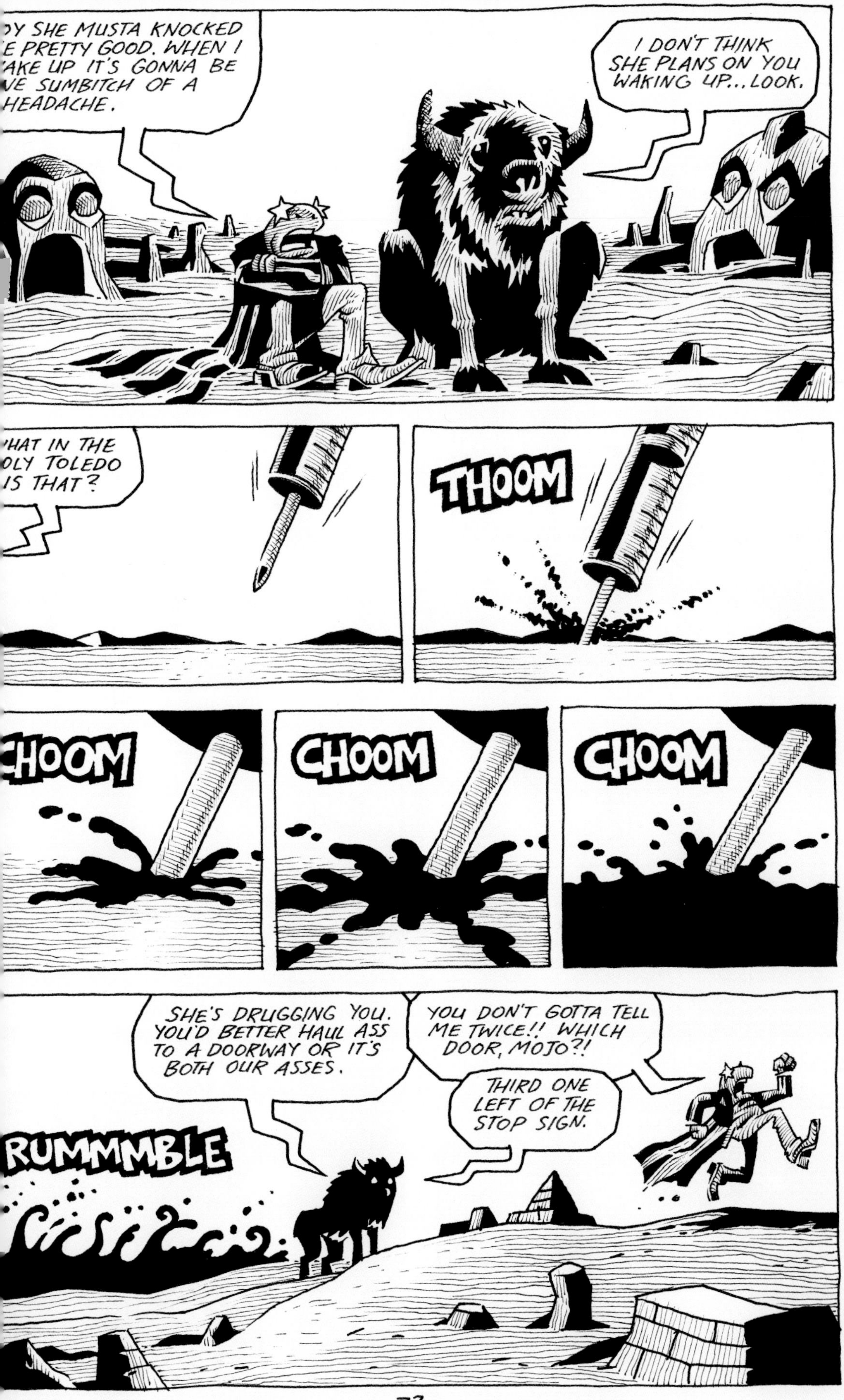

OY SHE MUSTA KNOCKED E PRETTY GOOD. WHEN I AKE UP IT'S GONNA BE NE SUMBITCH OF A HEADACHE.
I DON'T THINK SHE PLANS ON YOU WAKING UP... LOOK.
HAT IN THE OLY TOLEDO IS THAT?
THOOM
CHOOM
CHOOM
CHOOM
SHE'S DRUGGING YOU. YOU'D BETTER HAUL ASS TO A DOORWAY OR IT'S BOTH OUR ASSES.
YOU DON'T GOTTA TELL ME TWICE!! WHICH DOOR, MOJO?!
THIRD ONE LEFT OF THE STOP SIGN.
RUMMMBLE

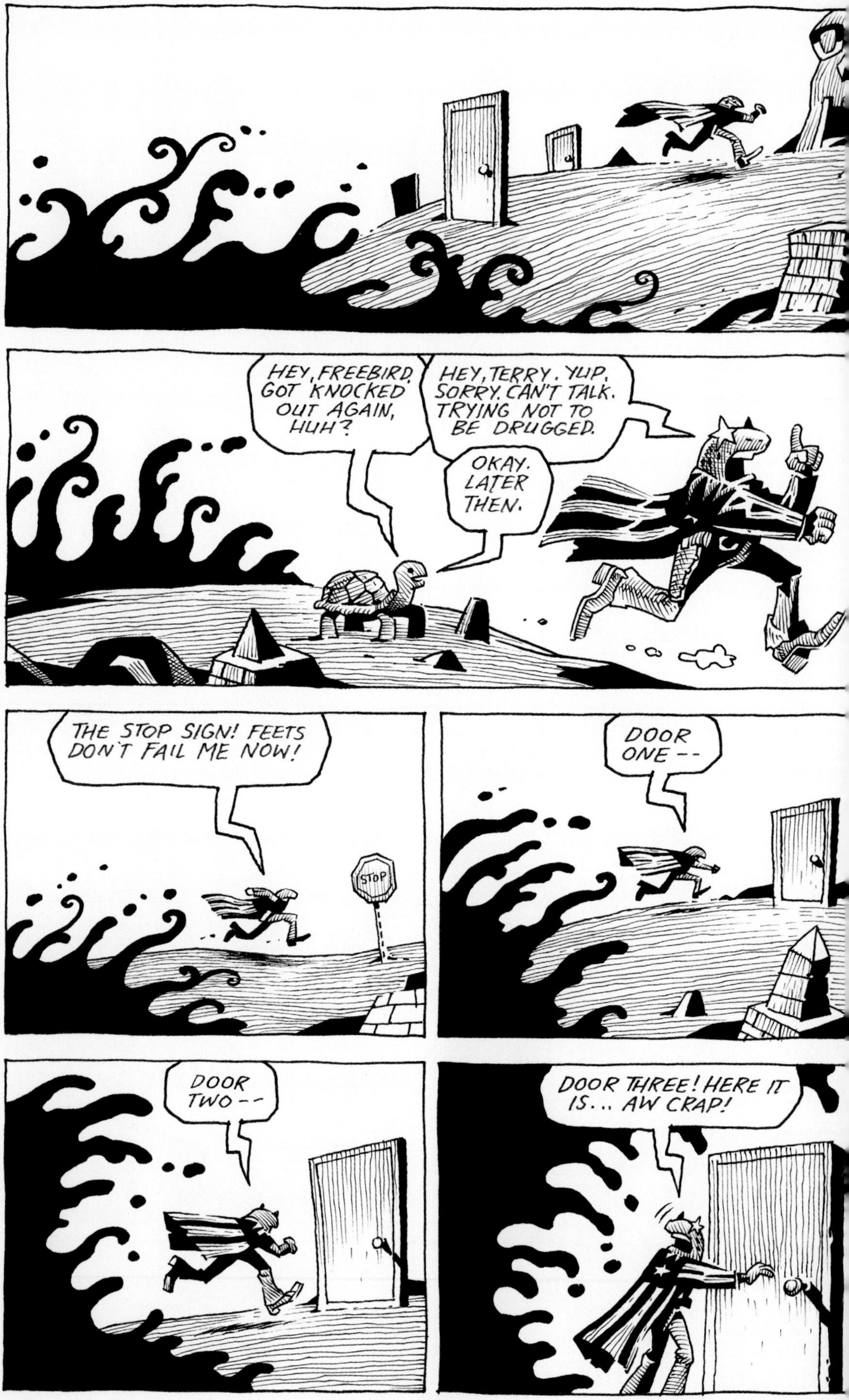
HEY, FREEBIRD. GOT KNOCKED OUT AGAIN, HUH?
HEY, TERRY. YUP. SORRY. CAN'T TALK. TRYING NOT TO BE DRUGGED.
OKAY. LATER THEN.
THE STOP SIGN! FEETS DON'T FAIL ME NOW!
STOP
DOOR ONE --
DOOR TWO --
DOOR THREE! HERE IT IS... AW CRAP!

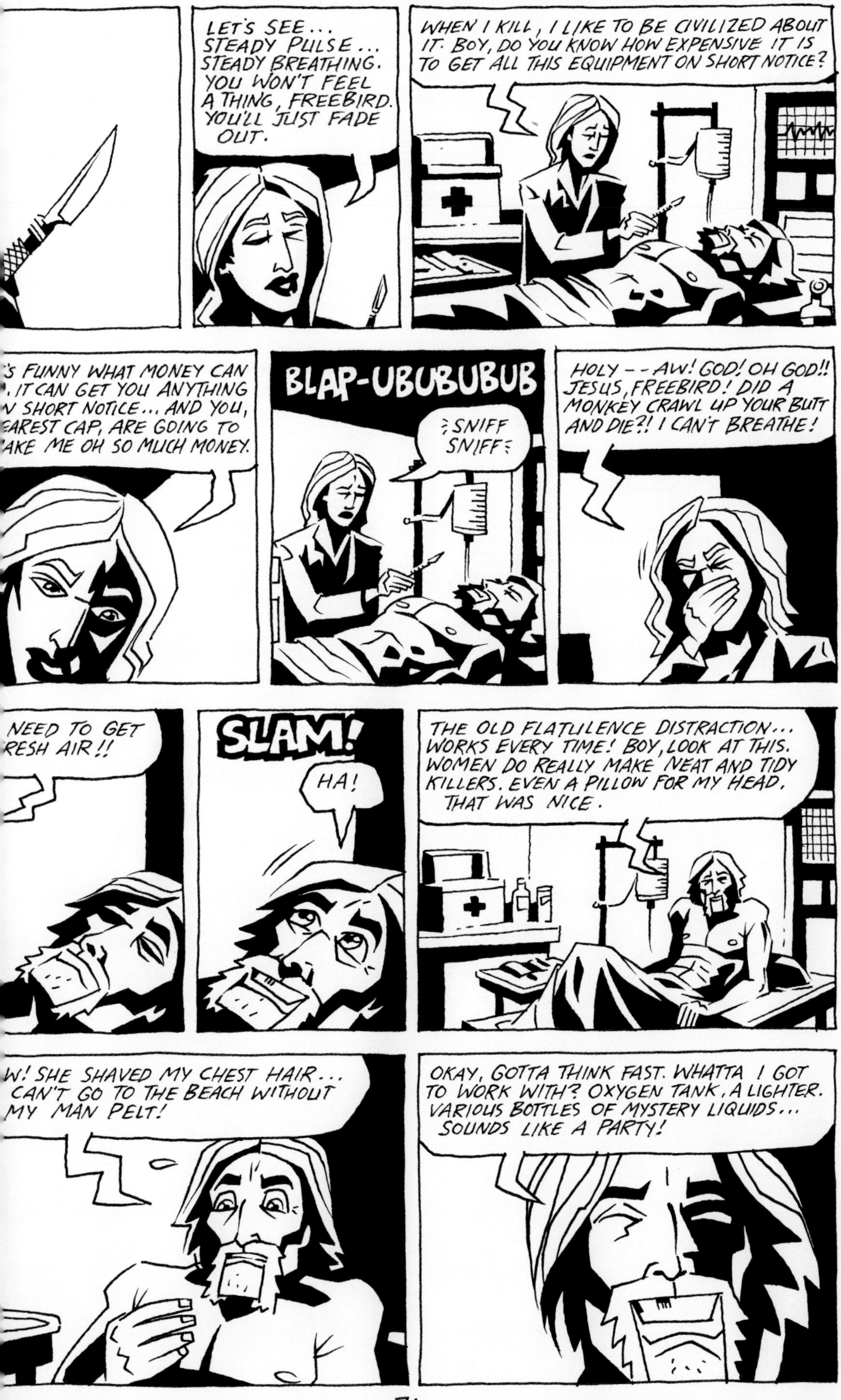

LET'S SEE... STEADY PULSE... STEADY BREATHING. YOU WON'T FEEL A THING, FREEBIRD. YOU'LL JUST FADE OUT.
WHEN I KILL, I LIKE TO BE CIVILIZED ABOUT IT. BOY, DO YOU KNOW HOW EXPENSIVE IT IS TO GET ALL THIS EQUIPMENT ON SHORT NOTICE?
'S FUNNY WHAT MONEY CAN . IT CAN GET YOU ANYTHING N SHORT NOTICE... AND YOU, EAREST CAP, ARE GOING TO AKE ME OH SO MUCH MONEY.
BLAP-UBUBUBUB
SNIFF SNIFF
HOLY --AW! GOD! OH GOD!! JESUS, FREEBIRD! DID A MONKEY CRAWL UP YOUR BUTT AND DIE?! I CAN'T BREATHE!
NEED TO GET RESH AIR!!
SLAM!
HA!
THE OLD FLATULENCE DISTRACTION... WORKS EVERY TIME! BOY, LOOK AT THIS. WOMEN DO REALLY MAKE NEAT AND TIDY KILLERS. EVEN A PILLOW FOR MY HEAD. THAT WAS NICE.
W! SHE SHAVED MY CHEST HAIR... CAN'T GO TO THE BEACH WITHOUT MY MAN PELT!
OKAY, GOTTA THINK FAST. WHATTA I GOT TO WORK WITH? OXYGEN TANK, A LIGHTER. VARIOUS BOTTLES OF MYSTERY LIQUIDS... SOUNDS LIKE A PARTY!

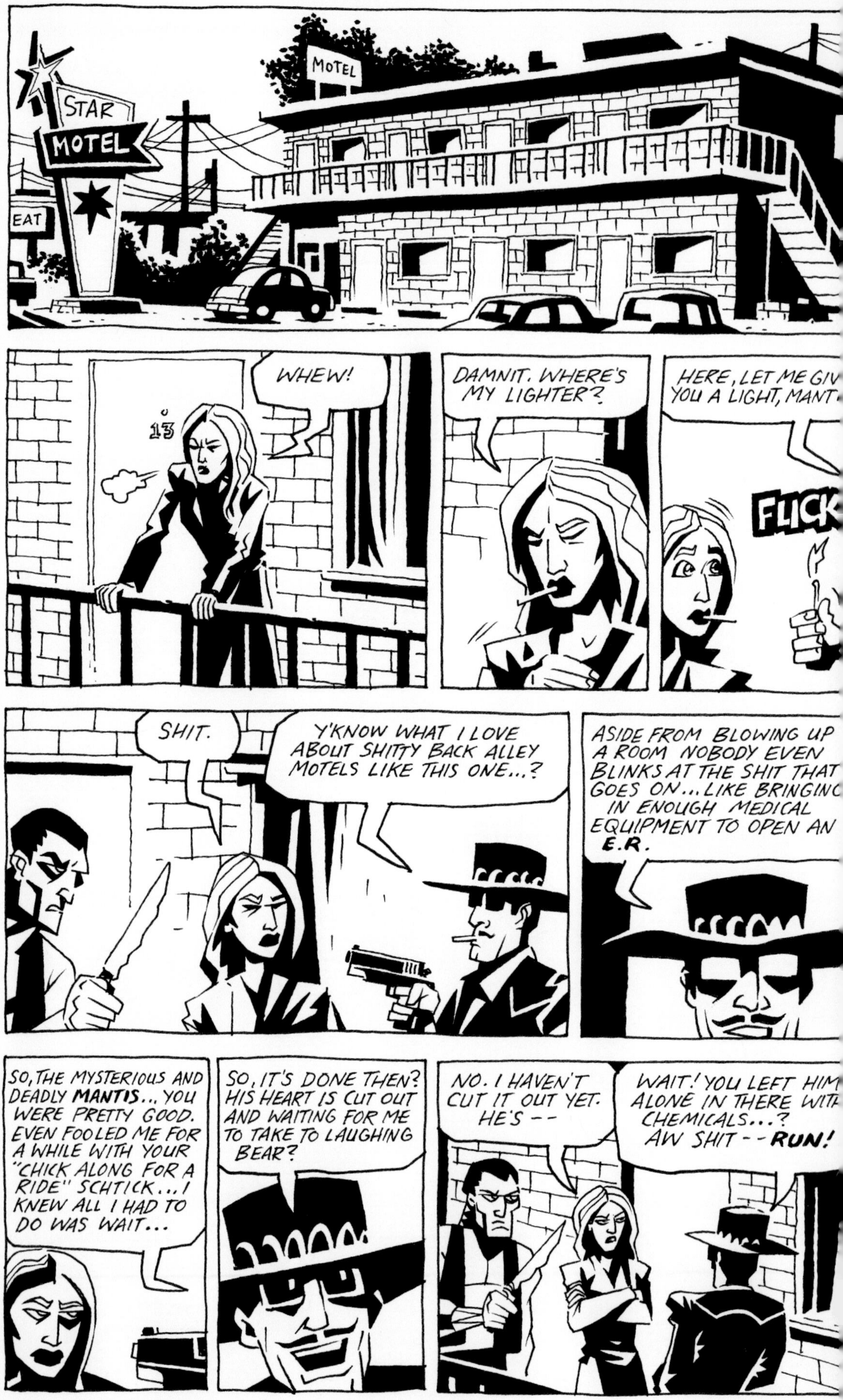
MOTEL
STAR
MOTEL
EAT
WHEW!
13
DAMNIT. WHERE'S MY LIGHTER?
HERE, LET ME GIV YOU A LIGHT, MANT
FLICK
SHIT.
Y'KNOW WHAT I LOVE ABOUT SHITTY BACK ALLEY MOTELS LIKE THIS ONE...?
ASIDE FROM BLOWING UP A ROOM NOBODY EVEN BLINKS AT THE SHIT THAT GOES ON... LIKE BRINGING IN ENOUGH MEDICAL EQUIPMENT TO OPEN AN **E.R.**
SO, THE MYSTERIOUS AND DEADLY **MANTIS**... YOU WERE PRETTY GOOD. EVEN FOOLED ME FOR A WHILE WITH YOUR "CHICK ALONG FOR A RIDE" SCHTICK... I KNEW ALL I HAD TO DO WAS WAIT...
SO, IT'S DONE THEN? HIS HEART IS CUT OUT AND WAITING FOR ME TO TAKE TO LAUGHING BEAR?
NO. I HAVEN'T CUT IT OUT YET. HE'S --
WAIT! YOU LEFT HIM ALONE IN THERE WIT CHEMICALS...? AW SHIT -- **RUN!**

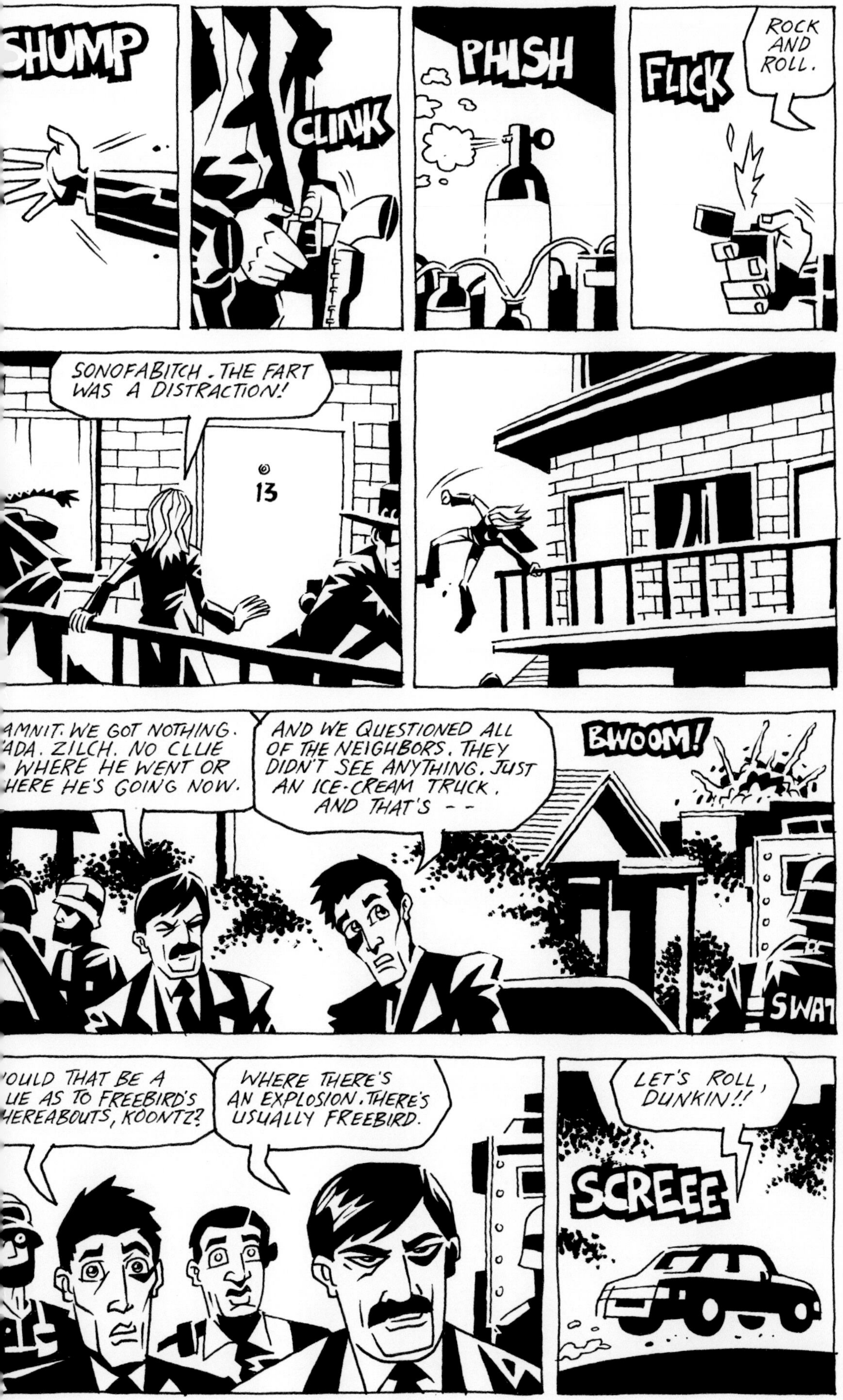
SHUMP
CLINK
PHISH
FLICK
ROCK AND ROLL.
SONOFABITCH. THE FART WAS A DISTRACTION!
13
AMNIT. WE GOT NOTHING. ADA. ZILCH. NO CLUE WHERE HE WENT OR HERE HE'S GOING NOW.
AND WE QUESTIONED ALL OF THE NEIGHBORS. THEY DIDN'T SEE ANYTHING. JUST AN ICE-CREAM TRUCK. AND THAT'S --
BWOOM!
SWAT
OULD THAT BE A UE AS TO FREEBIRD'S HEREABOUTS, KOONTZ?
WHERE THERE'S AN EXPLOSION. THERE'S USUALLY FREEBIRD.
LET'S ROLL, DUNKIN!!
SCREEE

WOO! THAT BATHROOM WINDOW WAS FURTHER UP THAN I THOUGHT. OUCH. HOW YOU HOLDIN' OUT, JOHN?

SWEET! MY ICE-CREAM TRUCK! WHAT I WOULDN'T DO FOR A KLONDIKE BAR.

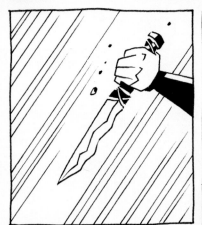

GAH!

SHUNK

THUD

FIP

THUP

FUP

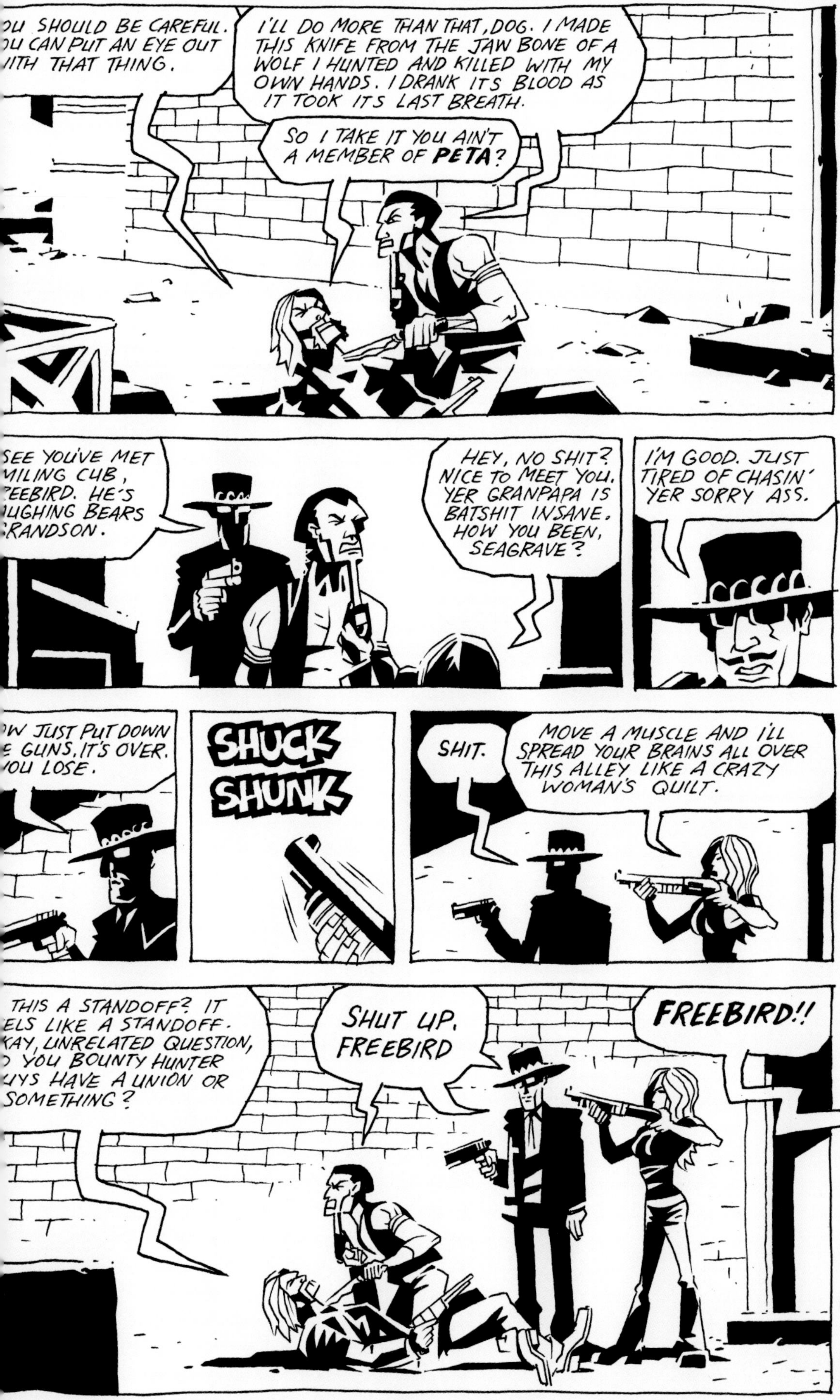
OU SHOULD BE CAREFUL. OU CAN PUT AN EYE OUT ITH THAT THING.
I'LL DO MORE THAN THAT, DOG. I MADE THIS KNIFE FROM THE JAW BONE OF A WOLF I HUNTED AND KILLED WITH MY OWN HANDS. I DRANK ITS BLOOD AS IT TOOK ITS LAST BREATH.
SO I TAKE IT YOU AIN'T A MEMBER OF PETA?
SEE YOU'VE MET MILING CUB, EEBIRD. HE'S UGHING BEARS RANDSON.
HEY, NO SHIT? NICE TO MEET YOU. YER GRANPAPA IS BATSHIT INSANE. HOW YOU BEEN, SEAGRAVE?
I'M GOOD. JUST TIRED OF CHASIN' YER SORRY ASS.
W JUST PUT DOWN E GUNS. IT'S OVER. OU LOSE.
SHUCK
SHUNK
SHIT.
MOVE A MUSCLE AND I'LL SPREAD YOUR BRAINS ALL OVER THIS ALLEY LIKE A CRAZY WOMAN'S QUILT.
THIS A STANDOFF? IT ELS LIKE A STANDOFF. KAY, UNRELATED QUESTION, YOU BOUNTY HUNTER UYS HAVE A UNION OR SOMETHING?
SHUT UP. FREEBIRD
FREEBIRD!!

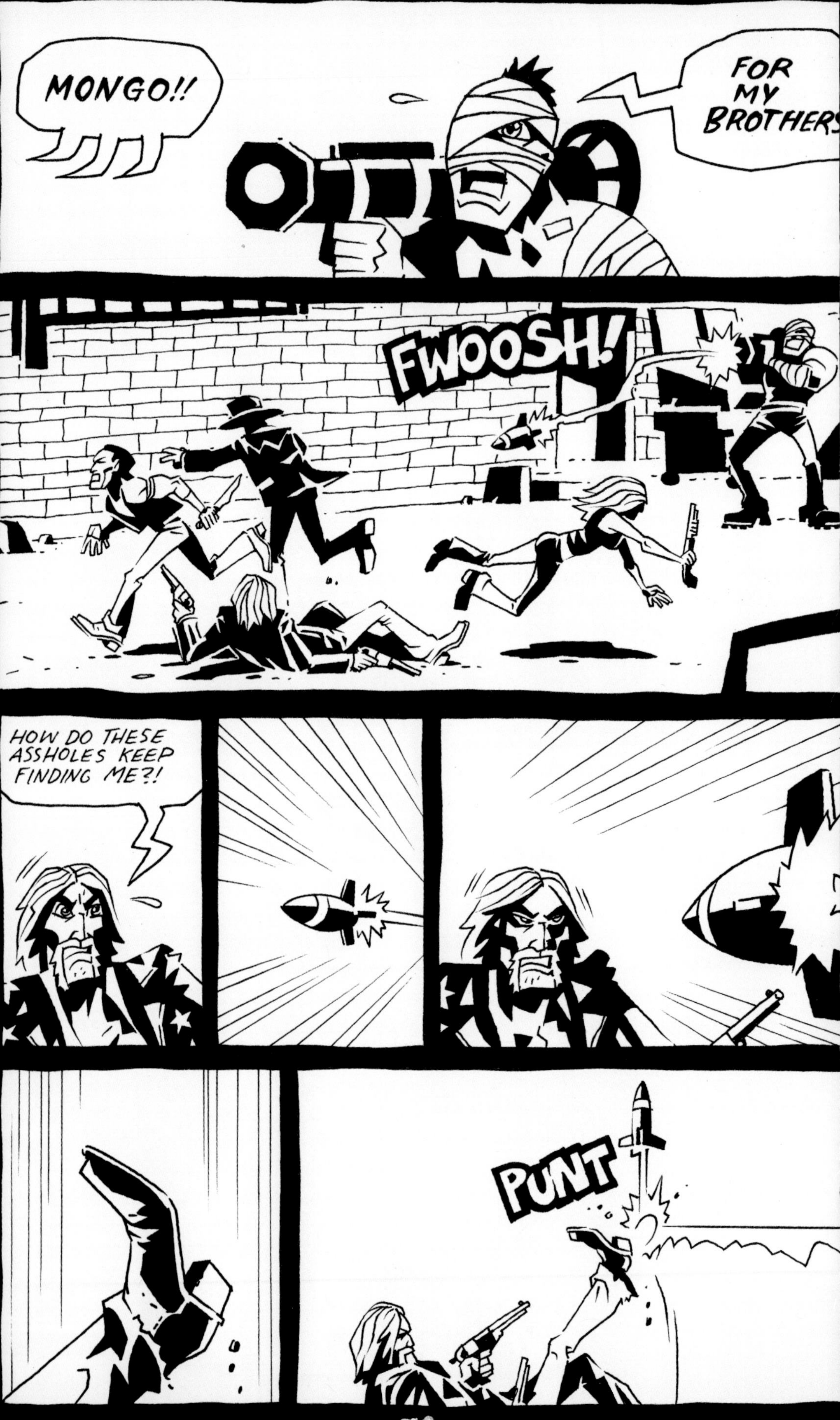
MONGO!!
FOR MY BROTHERS
FWOOSH!
HOW DO THESE ASSHOLES KEEP FINDING ME?!
PUNT

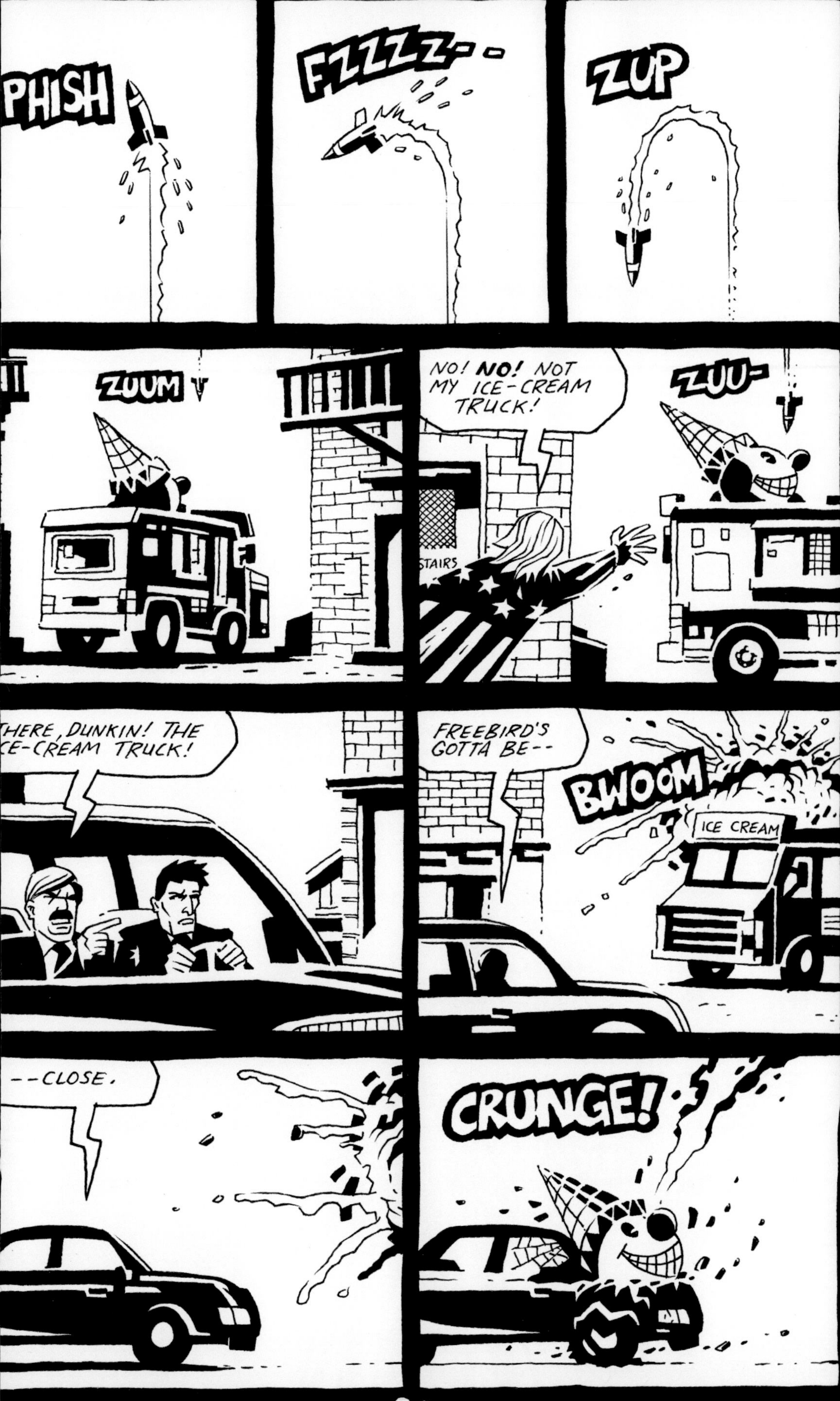
PHISH
FZZZZ-
ZUP
ZUUM
NO! **NO!** NOT MY ICE-CREAM TRUCK!
ZUU-
STAIRS
THERE, DUNKIN! THE ICE-CREAM TRUCK!
FREEBIRD'S GOTTA BE--
BWOOM
ICE CREAM
--CLOSE.
CRUNGE!

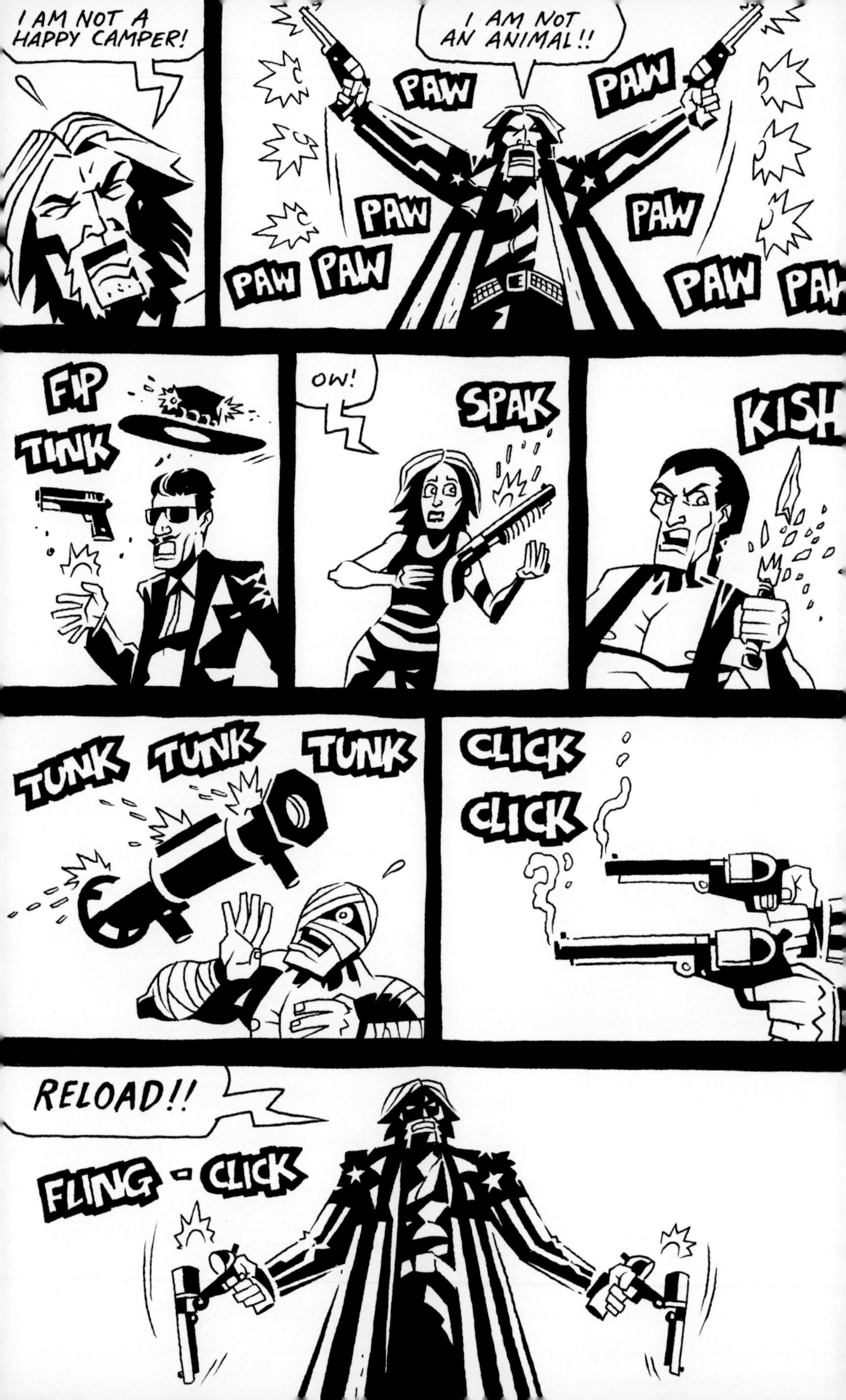
I AM NOT A HAPPY CAMPER!
I AM NOT AN ANIMAL!!
PAW
PAW
PAW
PAW
PAW
PAW
PAW
PAW
FIP
TINK
OW!
SPAK
KISH
TUNK
TUNK
TUNK
CLICK
CLICK
RELOAD!!
FLING - CLICK

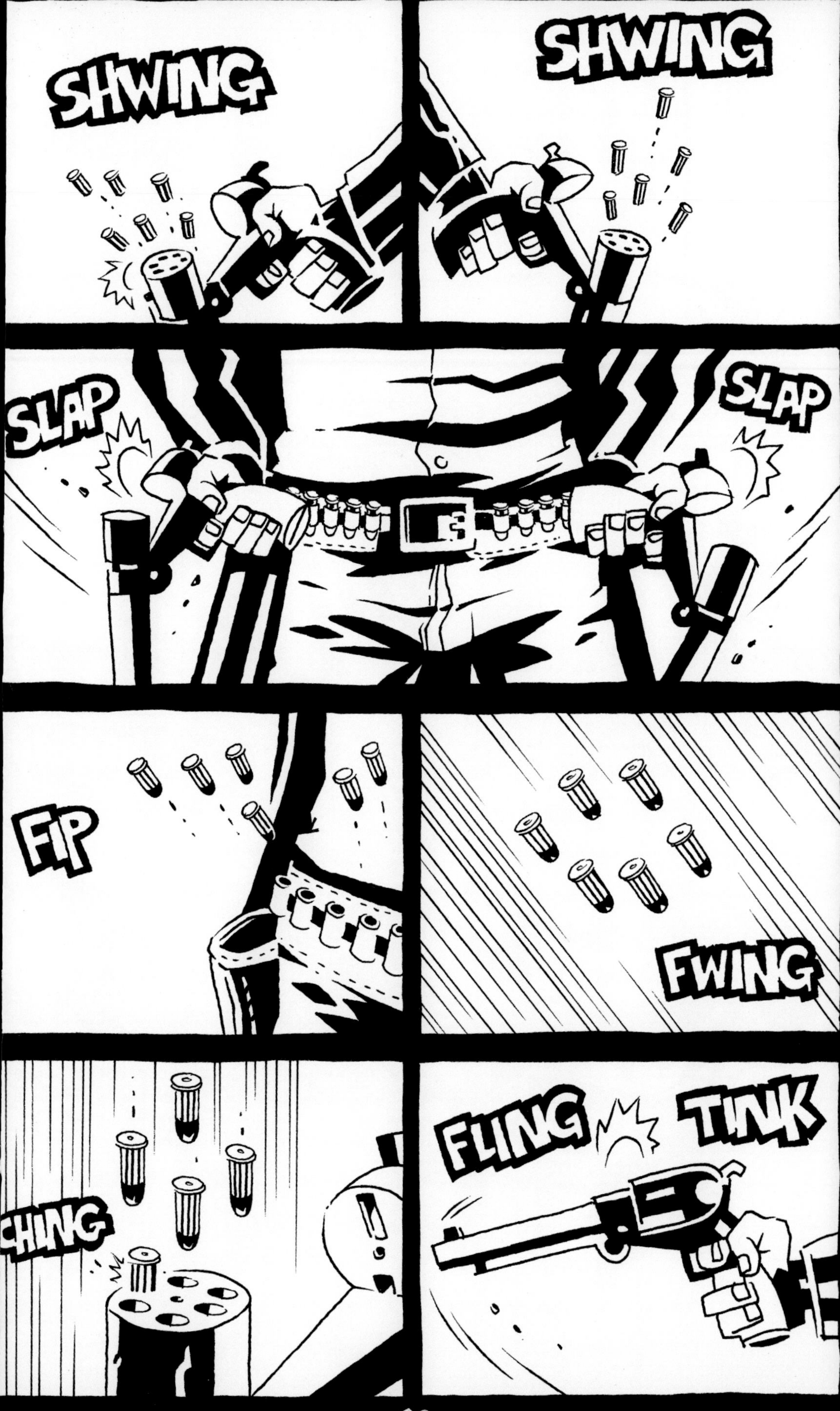
SHWING
SHWING
SLAP
SLAP
FIP
FWING
CHING
FLING
TINK

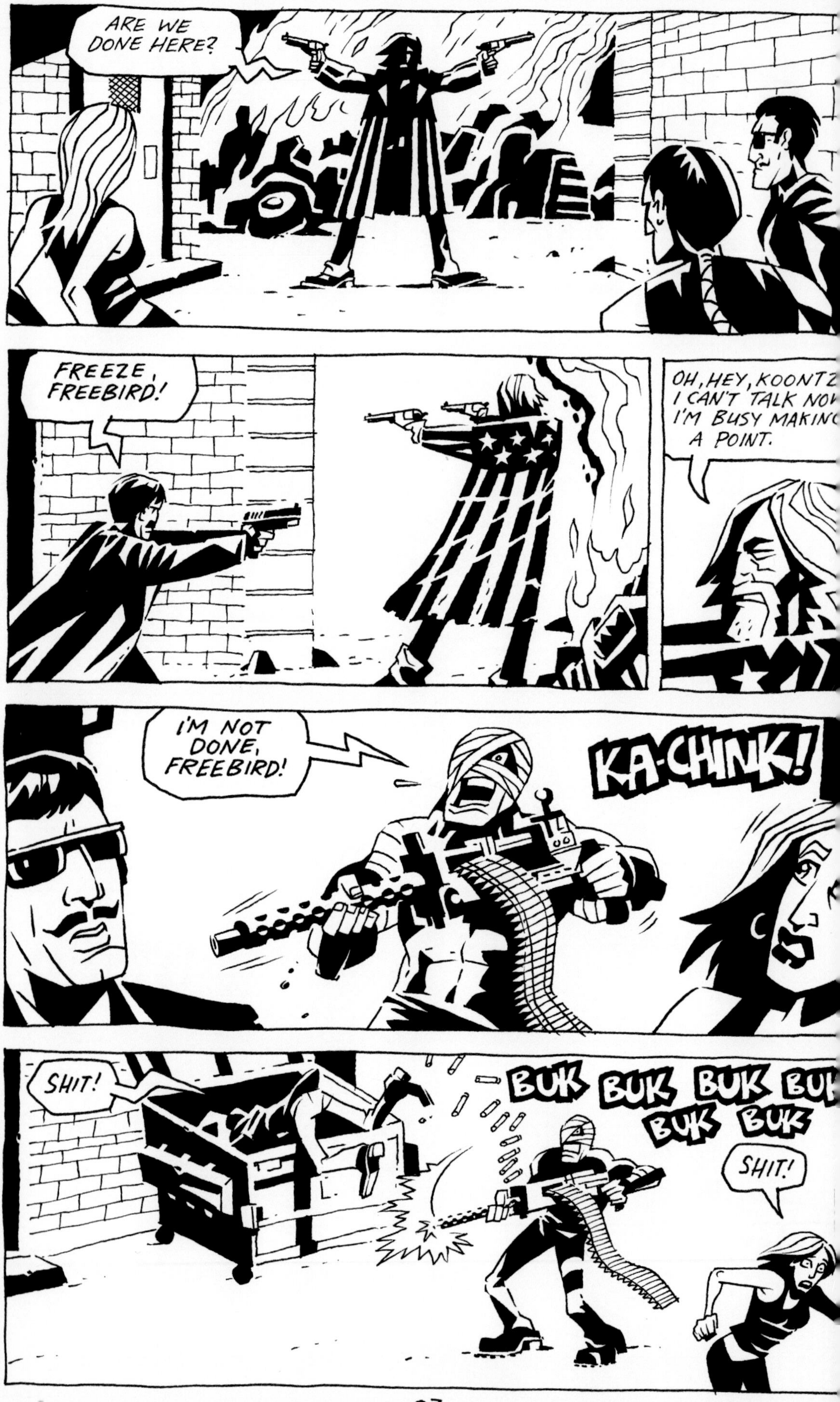
ARE WE DONE HERE?
FREEZE, FREEBIRD!
OH, HEY, KOONTZ. I CAN'T TALK NOW. I'M BUSY MAKING A POINT.
I'M NOT DONE, FREEBIRD!
KA-CHINK!
SHIT!
BUK BUK BUK BUK BUK BUK
SHIT!

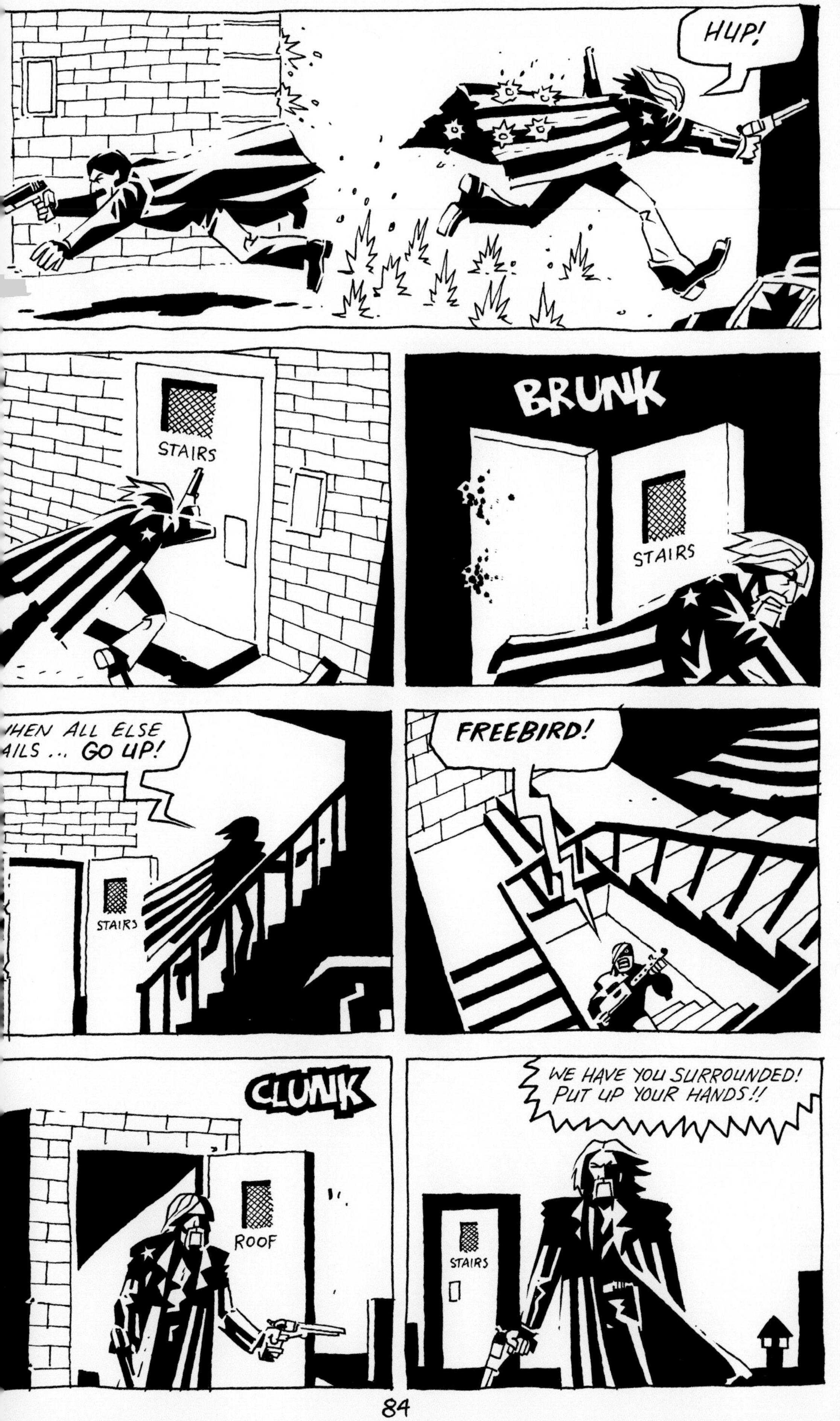
HUP!
STAIRS
BRUNK
STAIRS
HEN ALL ELSE
AILS ... GO UP!
STAIRS
FREEBIRD!
CLUNK
ROOF
WE HAVE YOU SURROUNDED! PUT UP YOUR HANDS!!
STAIRS

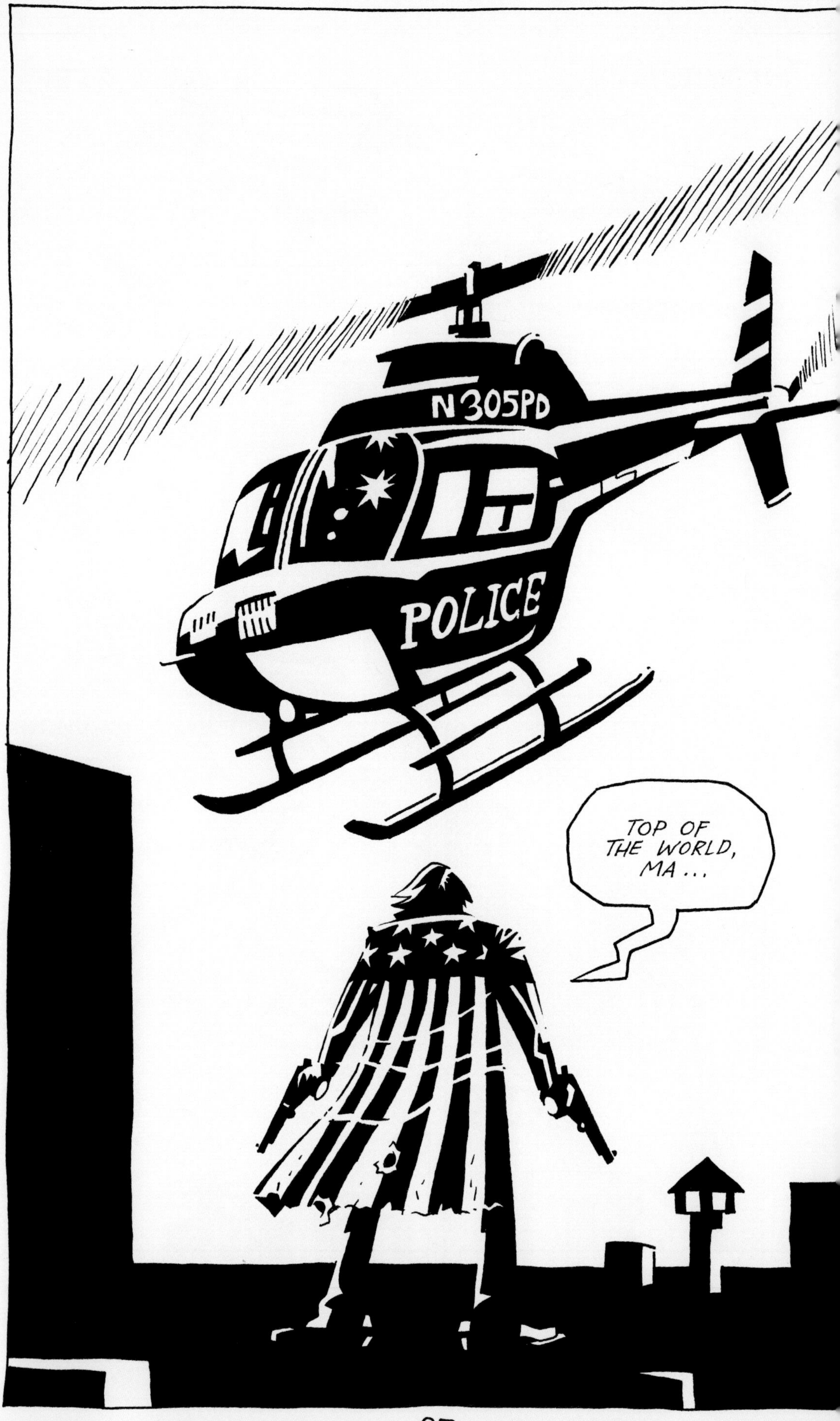
N305PD
POLICE
TOP OF THE WORLD, MA...

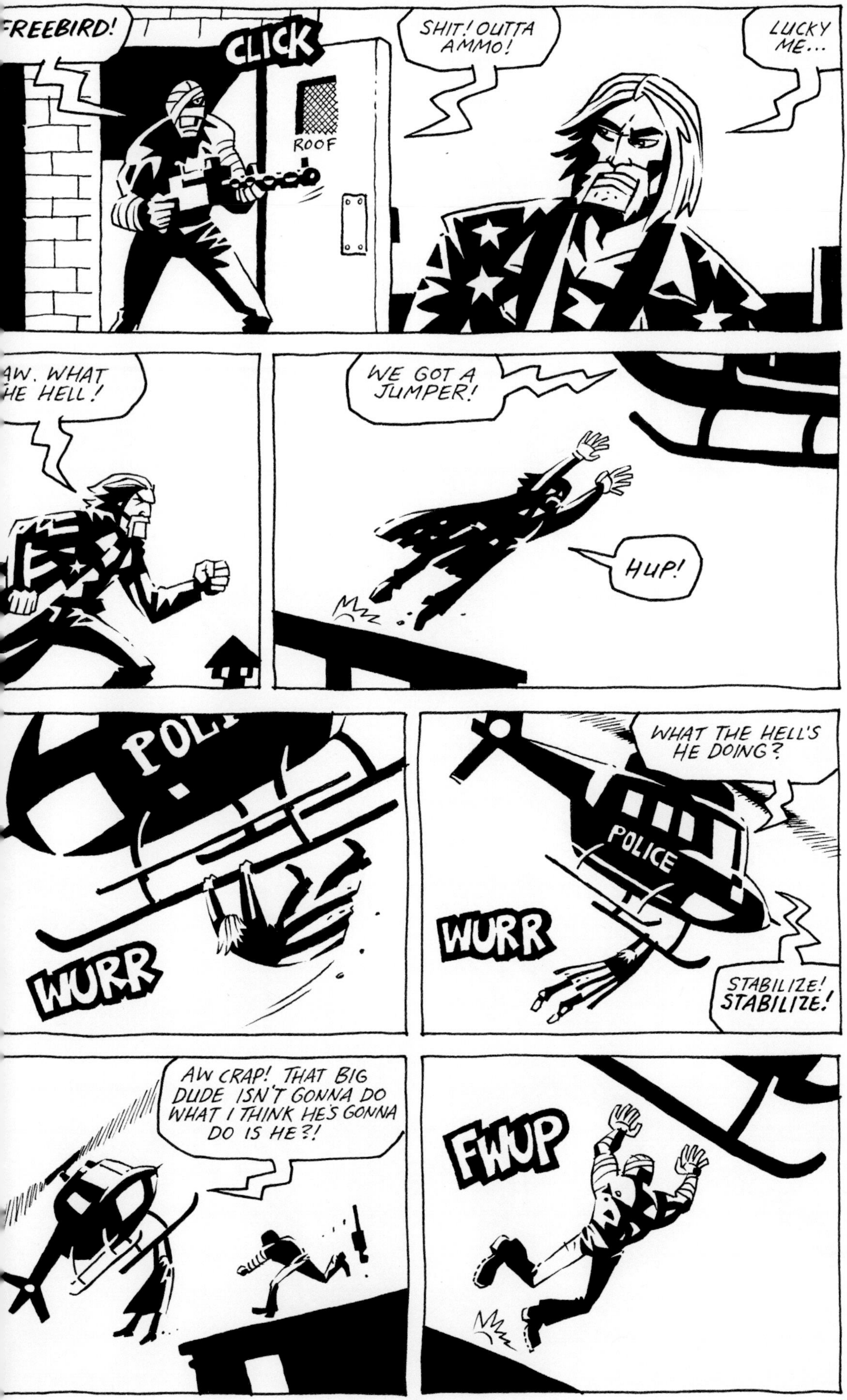
FREEBIRD!
CLICK
ROOF
SHIT! OUTTA AMMO!
LUCKY ME...
AW. WHAT THE HELL!
WE GOT A JUMPER!
HUP!
POL
WURR
WHAT THE HELL'S HE DOING?
POLICE
WURR
STABILIZE! STABILIZE!
AW CRAP! THAT BIG DUDE ISN'T GONNA DO WHAT I THINK HE'S GONNA DO IS HE?!
FWUP

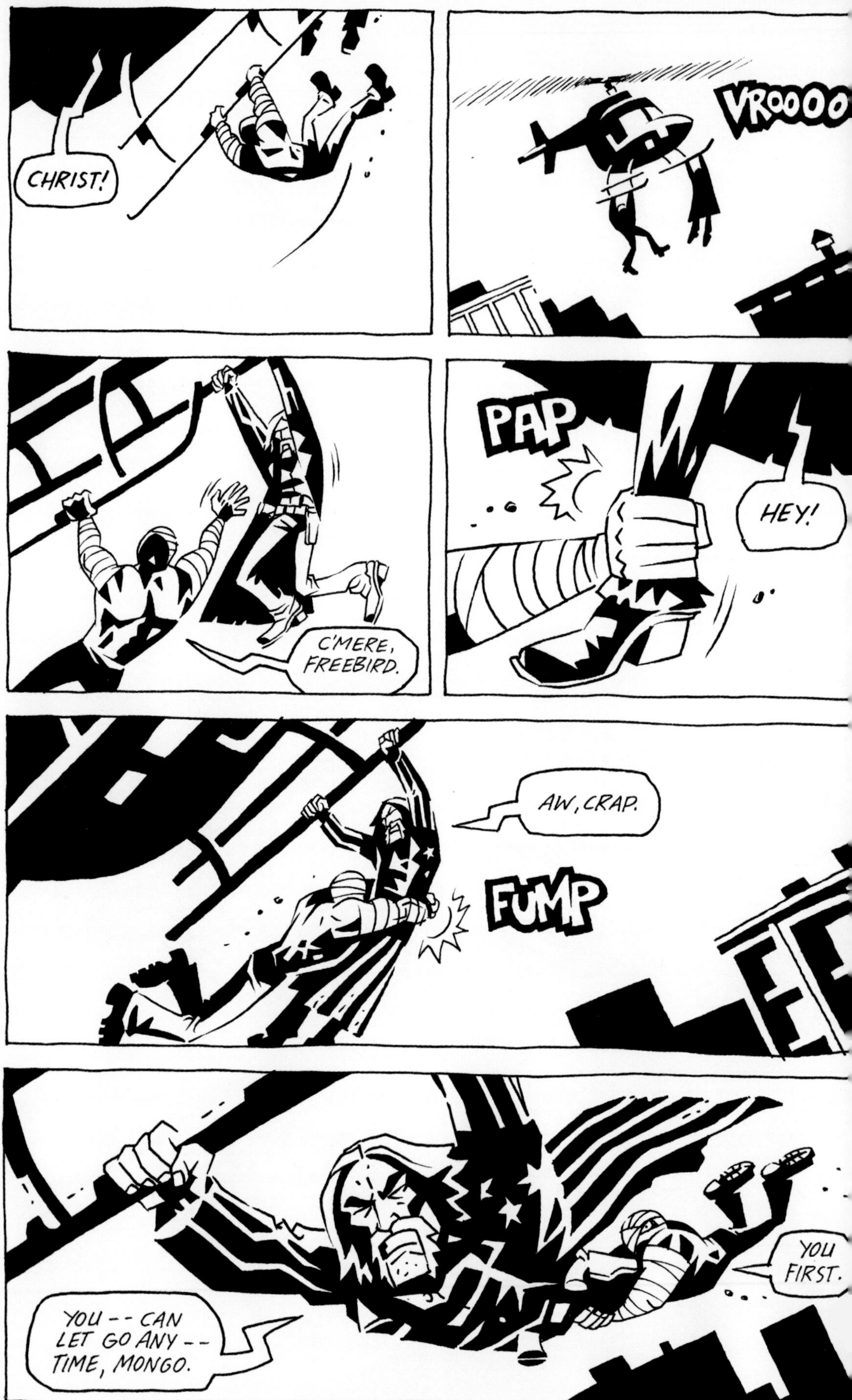
CHRIST!
VROOOO
C'MERE, FREEBIRD.
PAP
HEY!
AW, CRAP.
FUMP
YOU -- CAN LET GO ANY -- TIME, MONGO.
YOU FIRST.

STABILIZE! STABILIZE! STABILIZE!!

I'M TRYING!!

POLICE

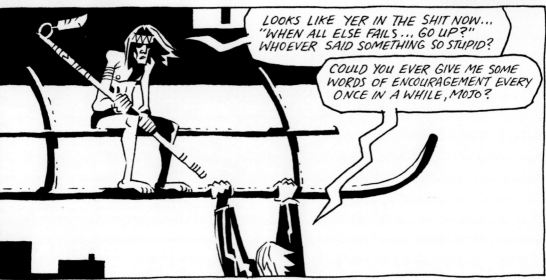

LOOKS LIKE YER IN THE SHIT NOW... "WHEN ALL ELSE FAILS... GO UP?" WHOEVER SAID SOMETHING SO STUPID?

COULD YOU EVER GIVE ME SOME WORDS OF ENCOURAGEMENT EVERY ONCE IN A WHILE, MOJO?

THIS DON'T LOOK GOOD FOR US.

UNG!

CAN'T HOLD... ON...

FIP

88

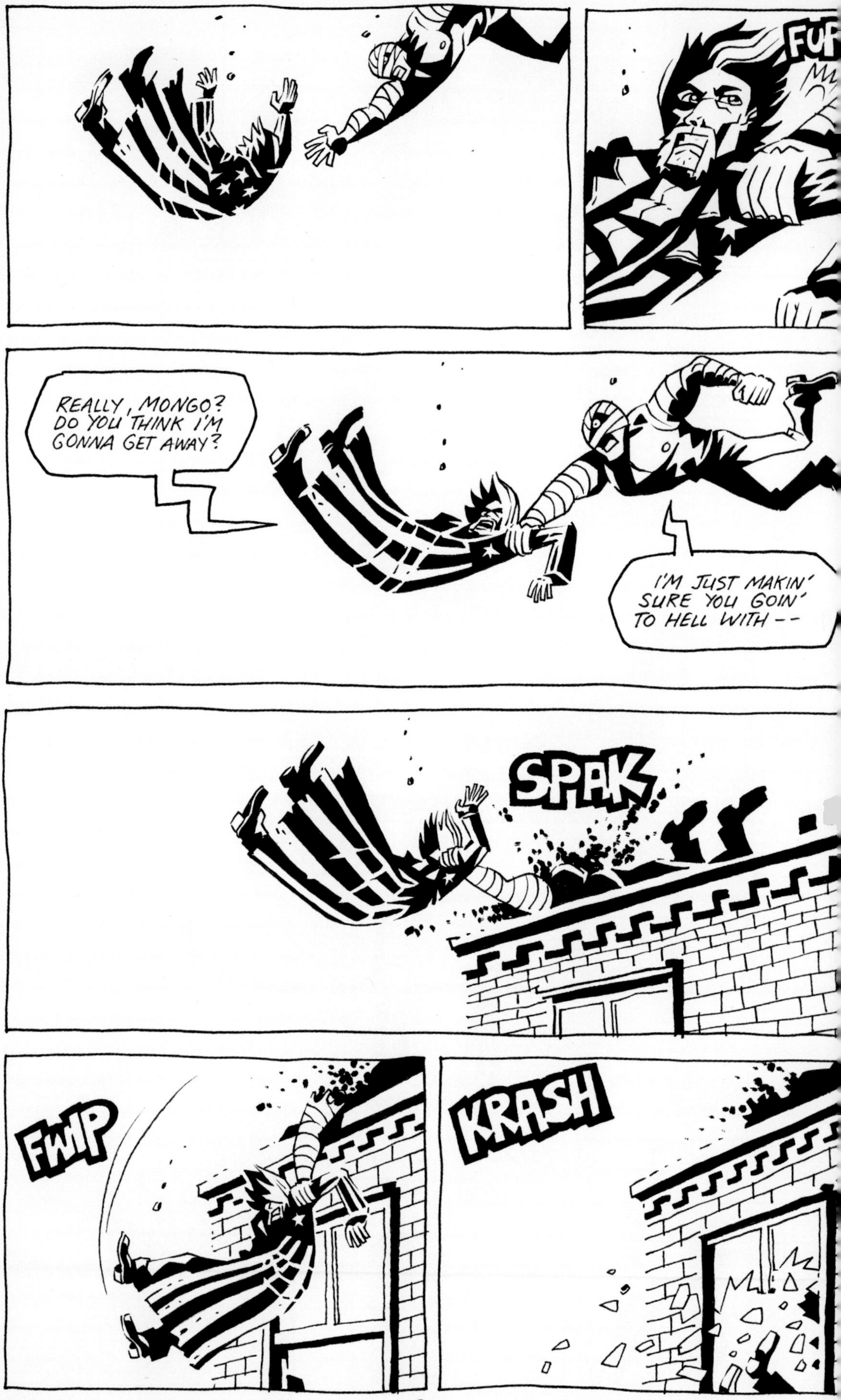
FUF
REALLY, MONGO? DO YOU THINK I'M GONNA GET AWAY?
I'M JUST MAKIN' SURE YOU GOIN' TO HELL WITH --
SPAK
FWIP
KRASH

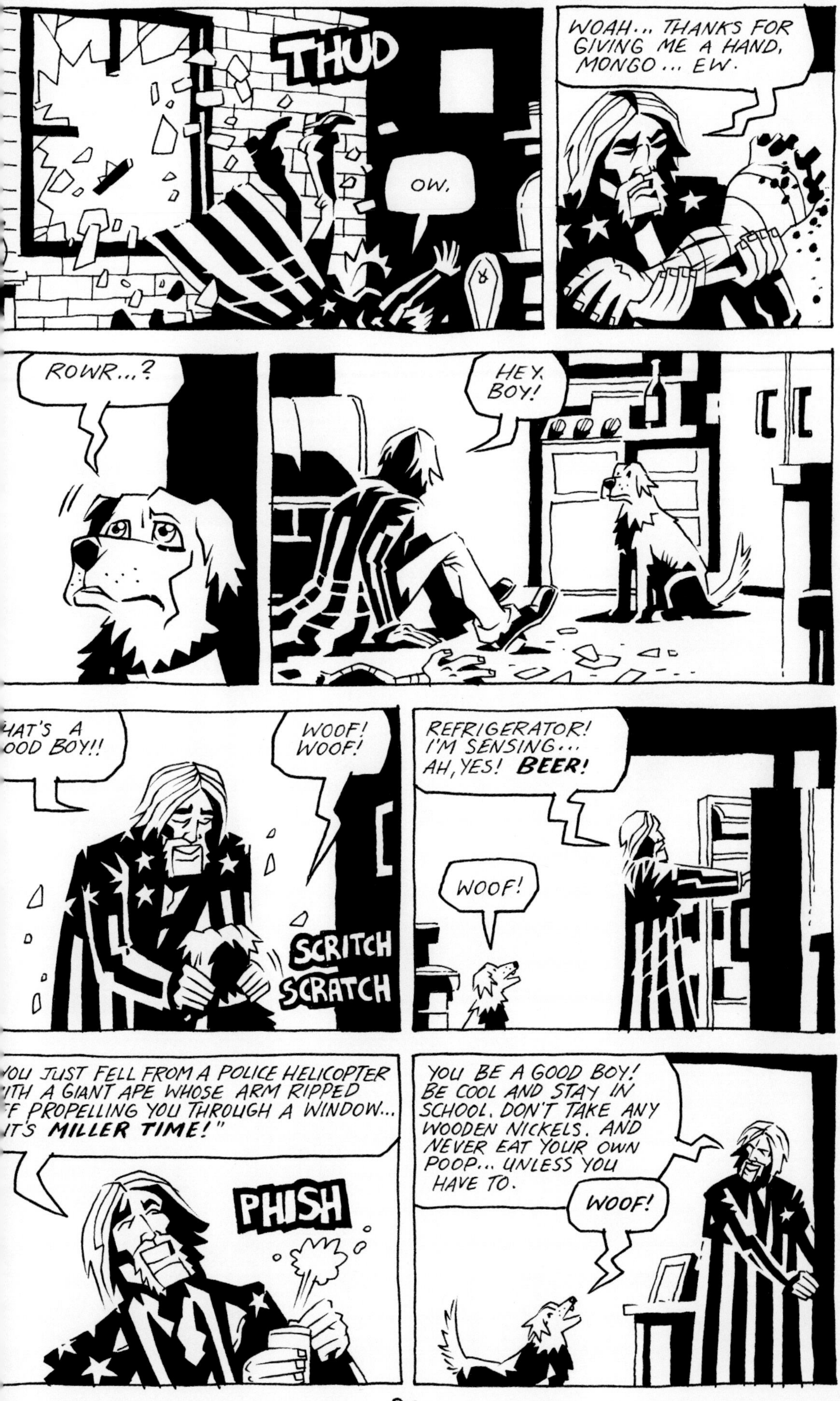
THUD
OW.
WOAH... THANKS FOR GIVING ME A HAND, MONGO... EW.
ROWR...?
HEY. BOY!
HAT'S A OOD BOY!!
WOOF! WOOF!
SCRITCH
SCRATCH
REFRIGERATOR! I'M SENSING... AH, YES! BEER!
WOOF!
YOU JUST FELL FROM A POLICE HELICOPTER ITH A GIANT APE WHOSE ARM RIPPED F PROPELLING YOU THROUGH A WINDOW... IT'S MILLER TIME!"
PHISH
YOU BE A GOOD BOY! BE COOL AND STAY IN SCHOOL. DON'T TAKE ANY WOODEN NICKELS. AND NEVER EAT YOUR OWN POOP... UNLESS YOU HAVE TO.
WOOF!

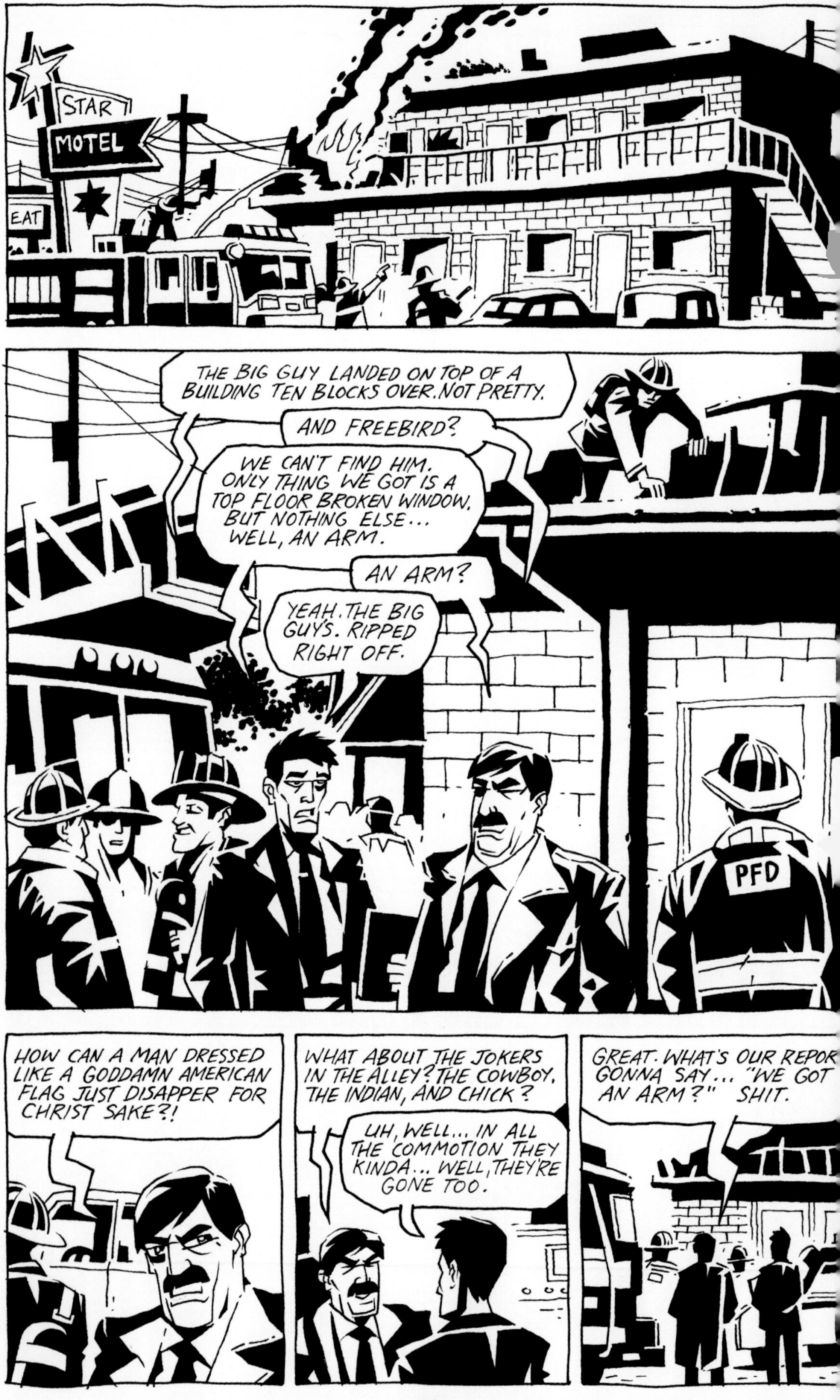
STAR
MOTEL
EAT
THE BIG GUY LANDED ON TOP OF A BUILDING TEN BLOCKS OVER. NOT PRETTY.
AND FREEBIRD?
WE CAN'T FIND HIM. ONLY THING WE GOT IS A TOP FLOOR BROKEN WINDOW. BUT NOTHING ELSE... WELL, AN ARM.
AN ARM?
YEAH. THE BIG GUY'S. RIPPED RIGHT OFF.
PFD
HOW CAN A MAN DRESSED LIKE A GODDAMN AMERICAN FLAG JUST DISAPPER FOR CHRIST SAKE?!
WHAT ABOUT THE JOKERS IN THE ALLEY? THE COWBOY, THE INDIAN, AND CHICK?
UH, WELL... IN ALL THE COMMOTION THEY KINDA... WELL, THEY'RE GONE TOO.
GREAT. WHAT'S OUR REPOR
GONNA SAY... "WE GOT AN ARM?" SHIT.

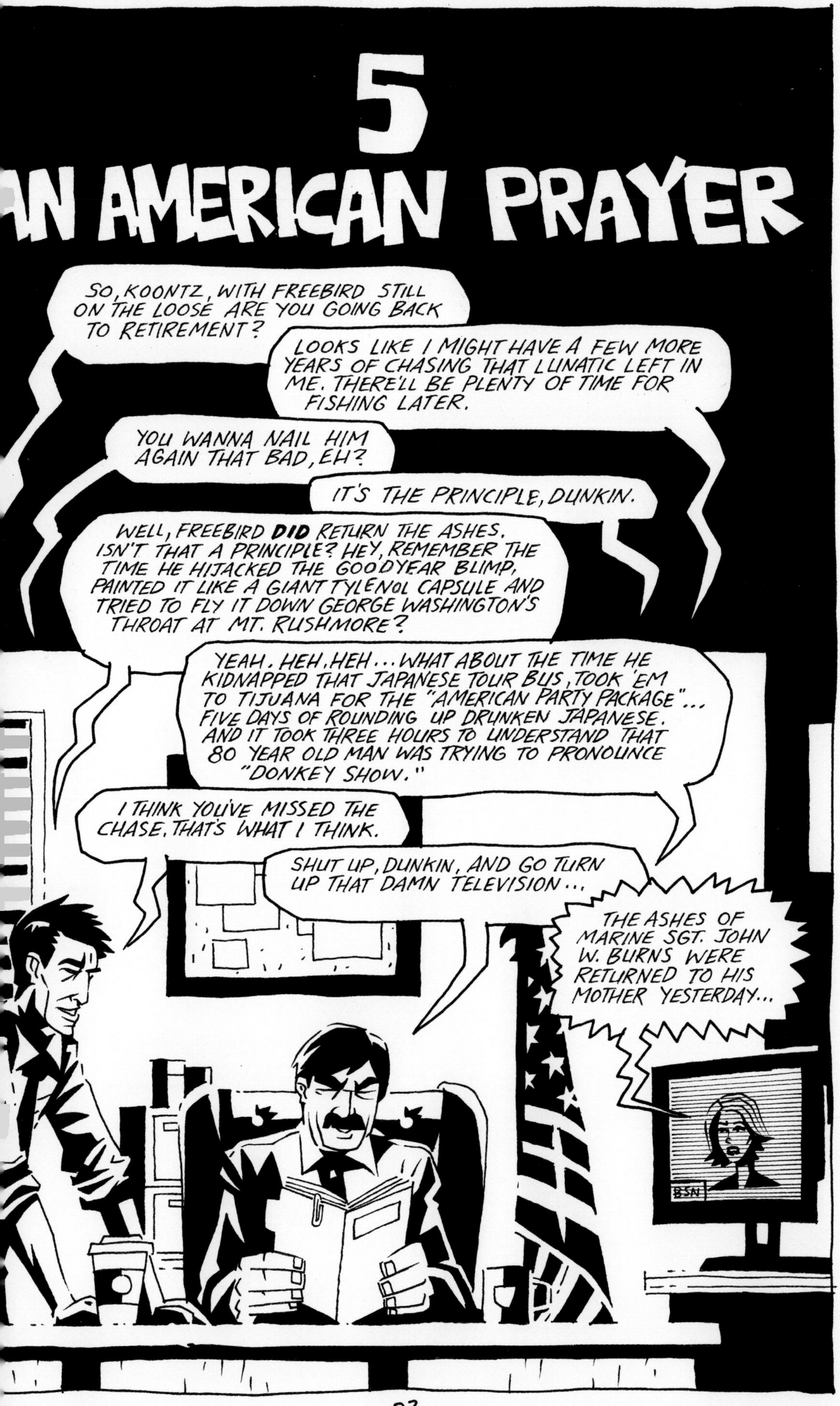
5
AN AMERICAN PRAYER
SO, KOONTZ, WITH FREEBIRD STILL ON THE LOOSE ARE YOU GOING BACK TO RETIREMENT?
LOOKS LIKE I MIGHT HAVE A FEW MORE YEARS OF CHASING THAT LUNATIC LEFT IN ME. THERE'LL BE PLENTY OF TIME FOR FISHING LATER.
YOU WANNA NAIL HIM AGAIN THAT BAD, EH?
IT'S THE PRINCIPLE, DUNKIN.
WELL, FREEBIRD DID RETURN THE ASHES. ISN'T THAT A PRINCIPLE? HEY, REMEMBER THE TIME HE HIJACKED THE GOODYEAR BLIMP, PAINTED IT LIKE A GIANT TYLENOL CAPSULE AND TRIED TO FLY IT DOWN GEORGE WASHINGTON'S THROAT AT MT. RUSHMORE?
YEAH. HEH. HEH... WHAT ABOUT THE TIME HE KIDNAPPED THAT JAPANESE TOUR BUS, TOOK 'EM TO TIJUANA FOR THE "AMERICAN PARTY PACKAGE"... FIVE DAYS OF ROUNDING UP DRUNKEN JAPANESE. AND IT TOOK THREE HOURS TO UNDERSTAND THAT 80 YEAR OLD MAN WAS TRYING TO PRONOUNCE "DONKEY SHOW."
I THINK YOU'VE MISSED THE CHASE. THAT'S WHAT I THINK.
SHUT UP, DUNKIN, AND GO TURN UP THAT DAMN TELEVISION...
THE ASHES OF MARINE SGT. JOHN W. BURNS WERE RETURNED TO HIS MOTHER YESTERDAY...
BSN

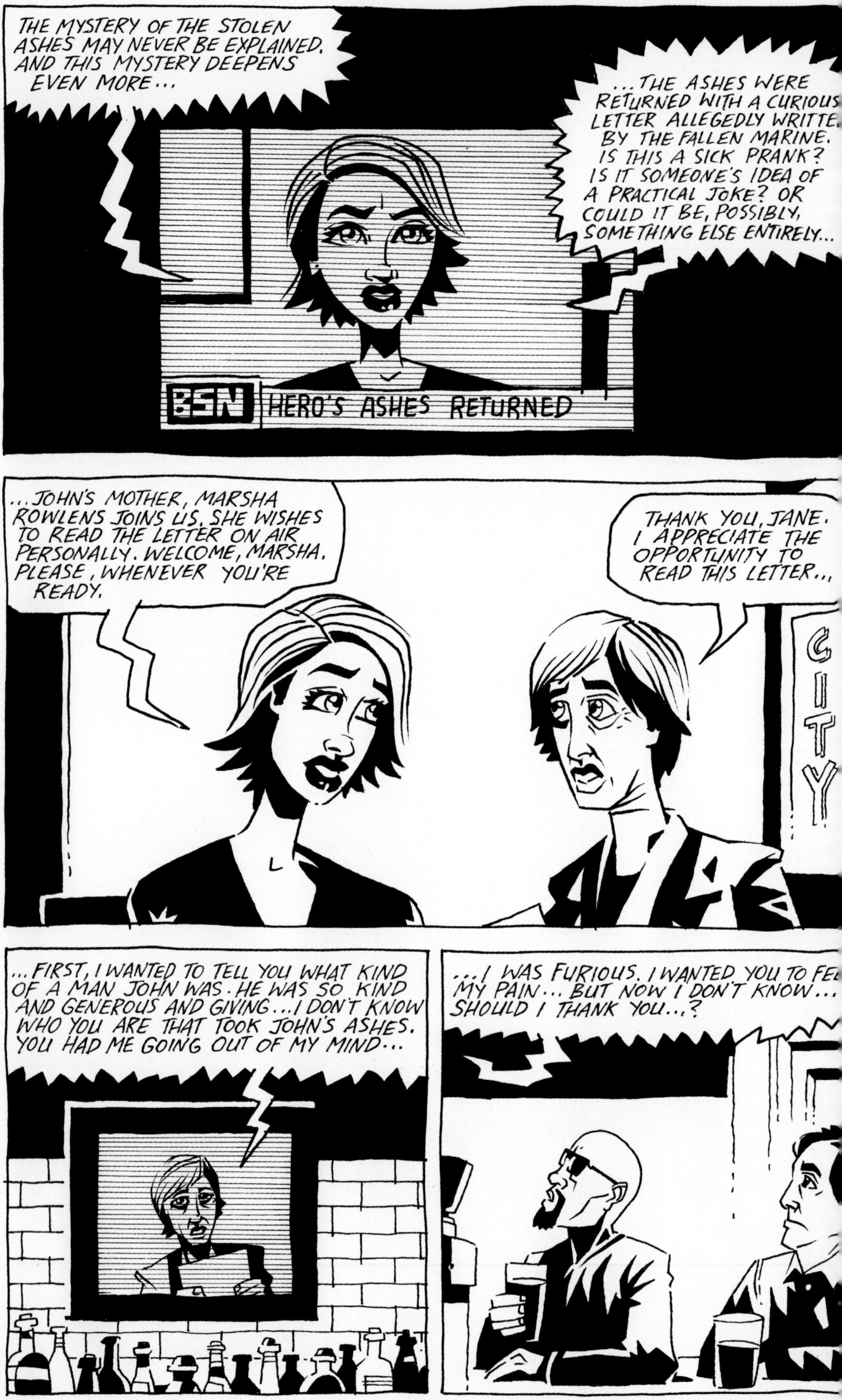
THE MYSTERY OF THE STOLEN ASHES MAY NEVER BE EXPLAINED. AND THIS MYSTERY DEEPENS EVEN MORE...
...THE ASHES WERE RETURNED WITH A CURIOUS LETTER ALLEGEDLY WRITTE BY THE FALLEN MARINE. IS THIS A SICK PRANK? IS IT SOMEONE'S IDEA OF A PRACTICAL JOKE? OR COULD IT BE, POSSIBLY, SOMETHING ELSE ENTIRELY...
BSN
HERO'S ASHES RETURNED
...JOHN'S MOTHER, MARSHA ROWLENS JOINS US. SHE WISHES TO READ THE LETTER ON AIR PERSONALLY. WELCOME, MARSHA. PLEASE, WHENEVER YOU'RE READY.
THANK YOU, JANE. I APPRECIATE THE OPPORTUNITY TO READ THIS LETTER...
CITY
...FIRST, I WANTED TO TELL YOU WHAT KIND OF A MAN JOHN WAS. HE WAS SO KIND AND GENEROUS AND GIVING... I DON'T KNOW WHO YOU ARE THAT TOOK JOHN'S ASHES. YOU HAD ME GOING OUT OF MY MIND...
...I WAS FURIOUS. I WANTED YOU TO FEE MY PAIN... BUT NOW I DON'T KNOW... SHOULD I THANK YOU...?

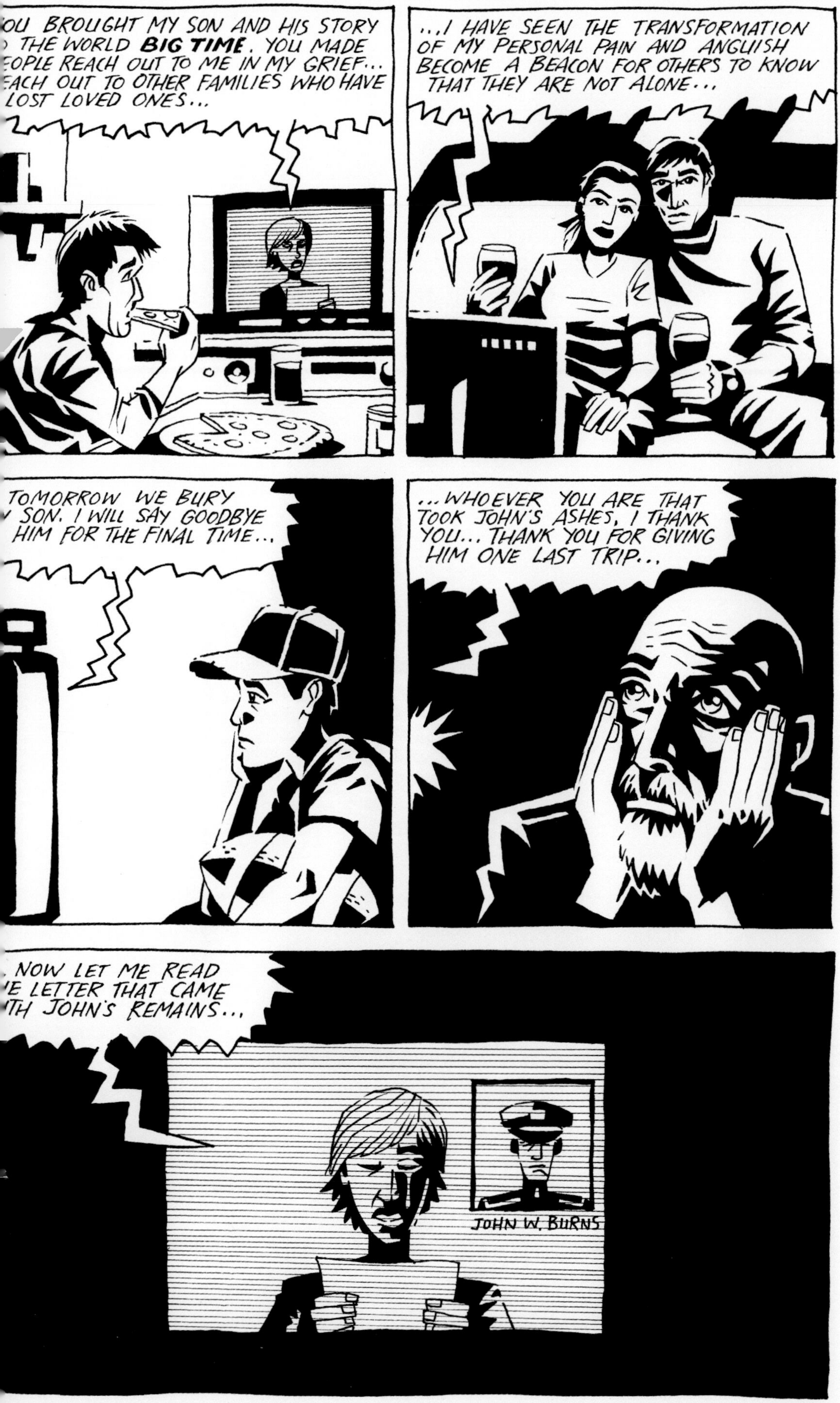
OU BROUGHT MY SON AND HIS STORY
THE WORLD BIG TIME. YOU MADE
EOPLE REACH OUT TO ME IN MY GRIEF...
EACH OUT TO OTHER FAMILIES WHO HAVE
LOST LOVED ONES...
...I HAVE SEEN THE TRANSFORMATION OF MY PERSONAL PAIN AND ANGUISH BECOME A BEACON FOR OTHERS TO KNOW THAT THEY ARE NOT ALONE...
TOMORROW WE BURY
SON. I WILL SAY GOODBYE
HIM FOR THE FINAL TIME...
...WHOEVER YOU ARE THAT TOOK JOHN'S ASHES, I THANK YOU... THANK YOU FOR GIVING HIM ONE LAST TRIP...
NOW LET ME READ
E LETTER THAT CAME
TH JOHN'S REMAINS...
JOHN W. BURNS

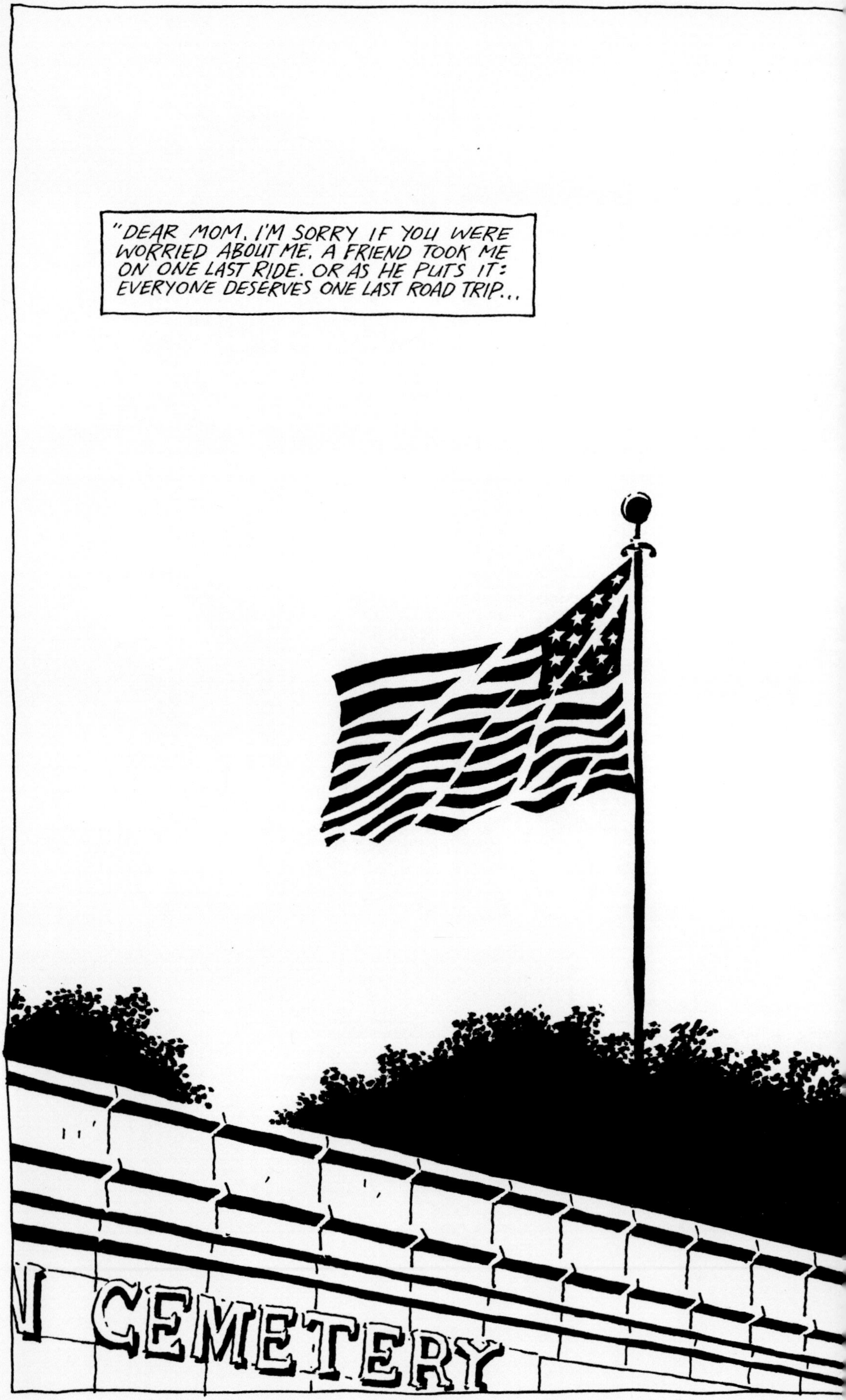
"DEAR MOM. I'M SORRY IF YOU WERE WORRIED ABOUT ME. A FRIEND TOOK ME ON ONE LAST RIDE. OR AS HE PUTS IT: EVERYONE DESERVES ONE LAST ROAD TRIP...
CEMETERY

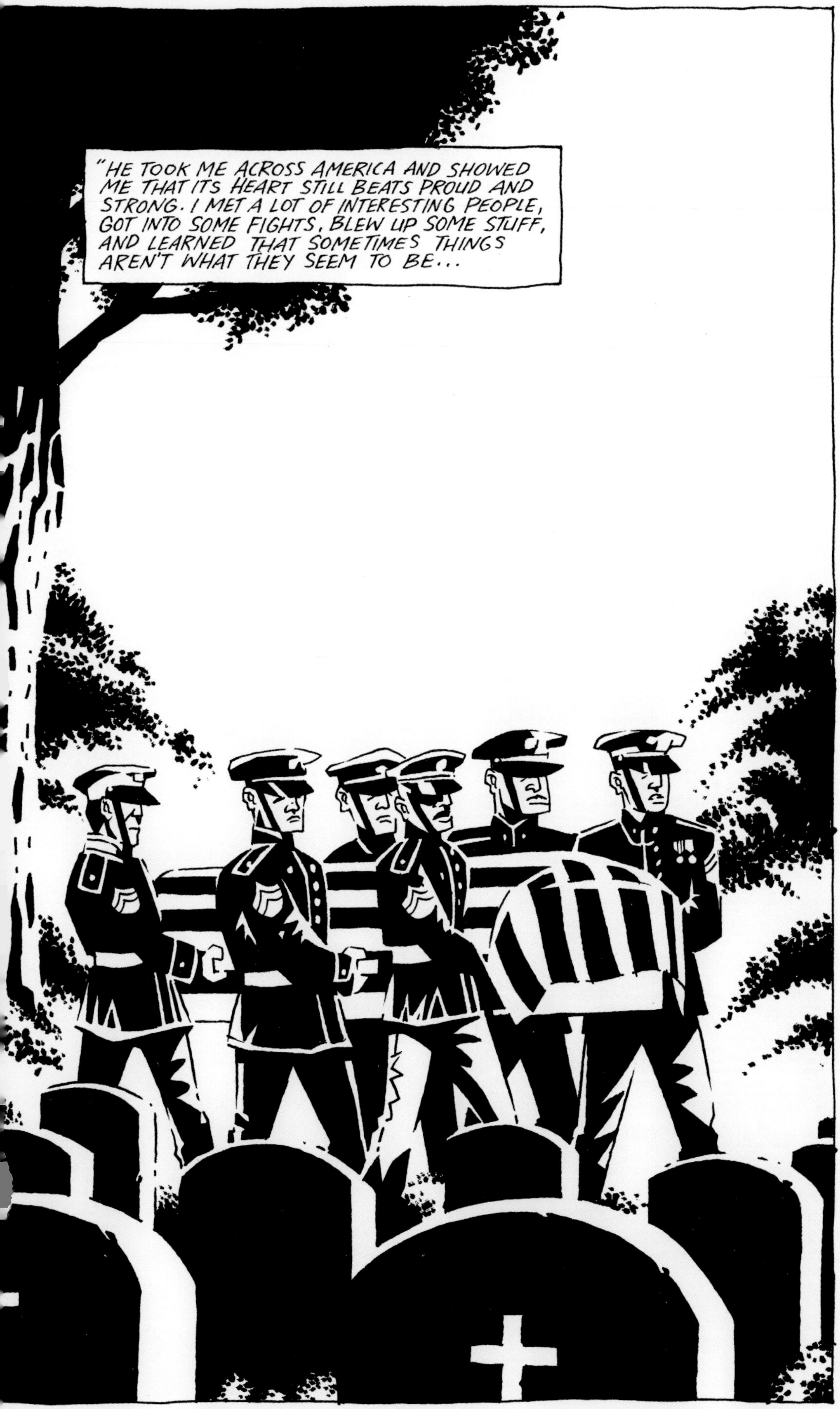
"HE TOOK ME ACROSS AMERICA AND SHOWED ME THAT ITS HEART STILL BEATS PROUD AND STRONG. I MET A LOT OF INTERESTING PEOPLE, GOT INTO SOME FIGHTS, BLEW UP SOME STUFF, AND LEARNED THAT SOMETIMES THINGS AREN'T WHAT THEY SEEM TO BE...

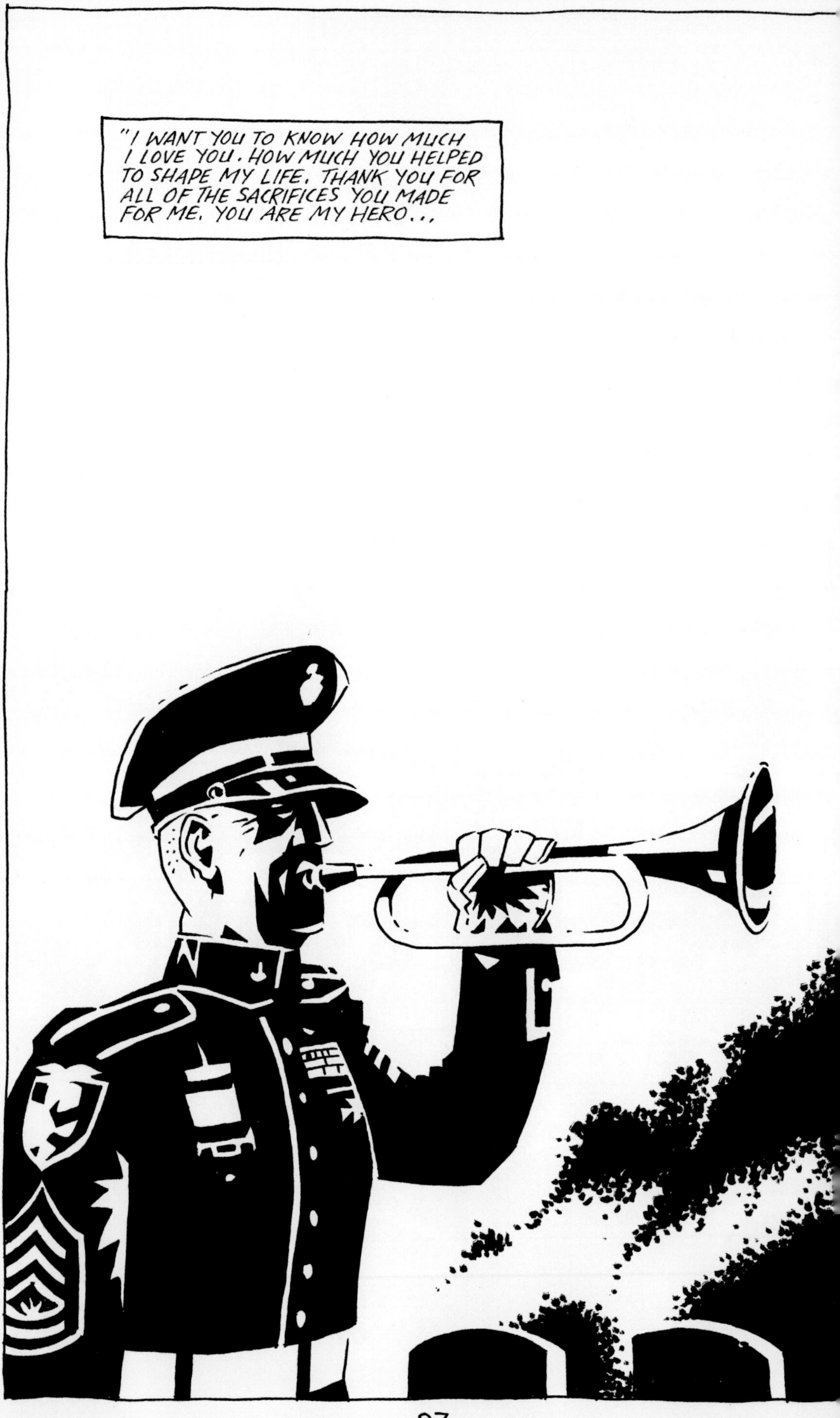
"I WANT YOU TO KNOW HOW MUCH I LOVE YOU. HOW MUCH YOU HELPED TO SHAPE MY LIFE. THANK YOU FOR ALL OF THE SACRIFICES YOU MADE FOR ME. YOU ARE MY HERO...

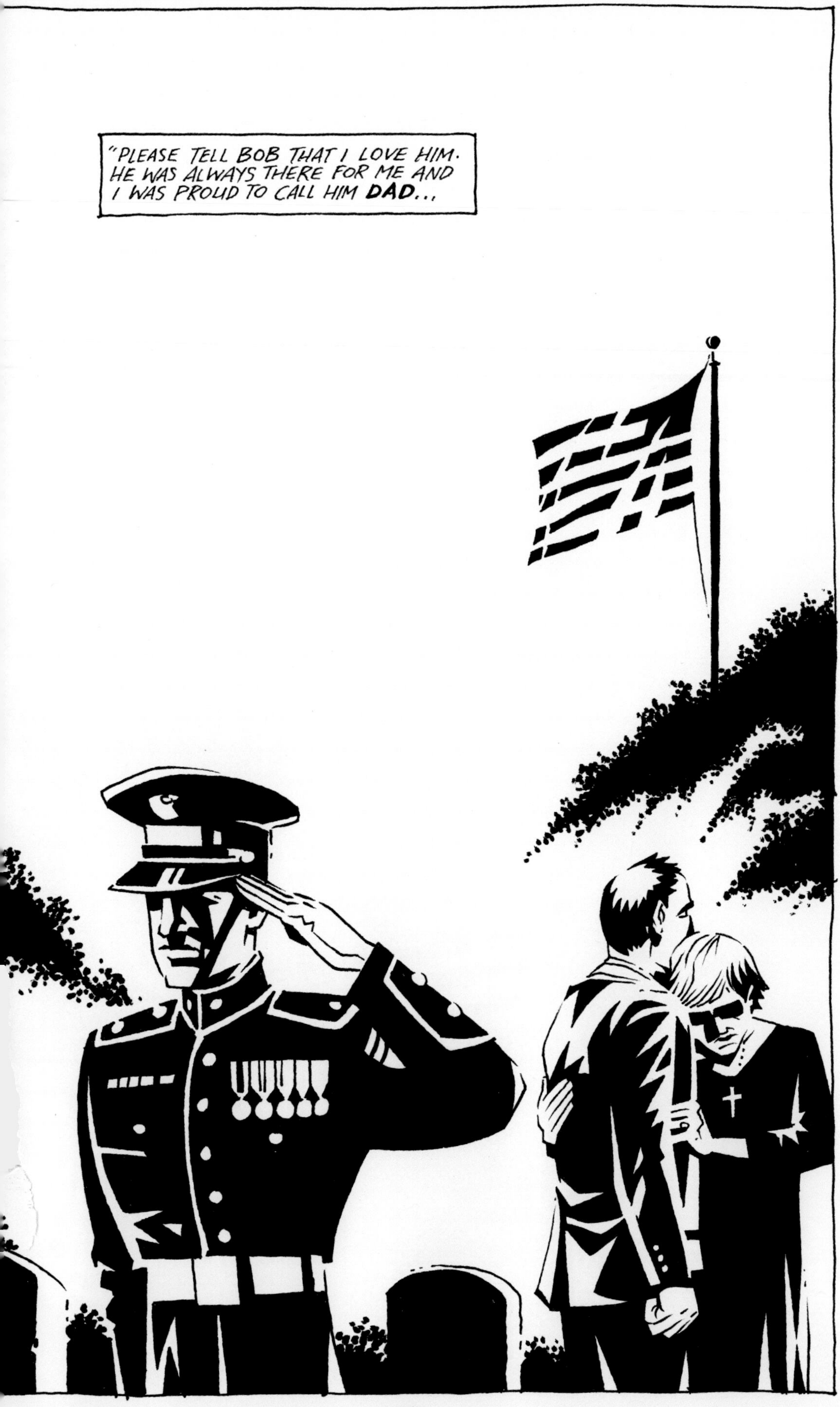
"PLEASE TELL BOB THAT I LOVE HIM. HE WAS ALWAYS THERE FOR ME AND I WAS PROUD TO CALL HIM **DAD**...

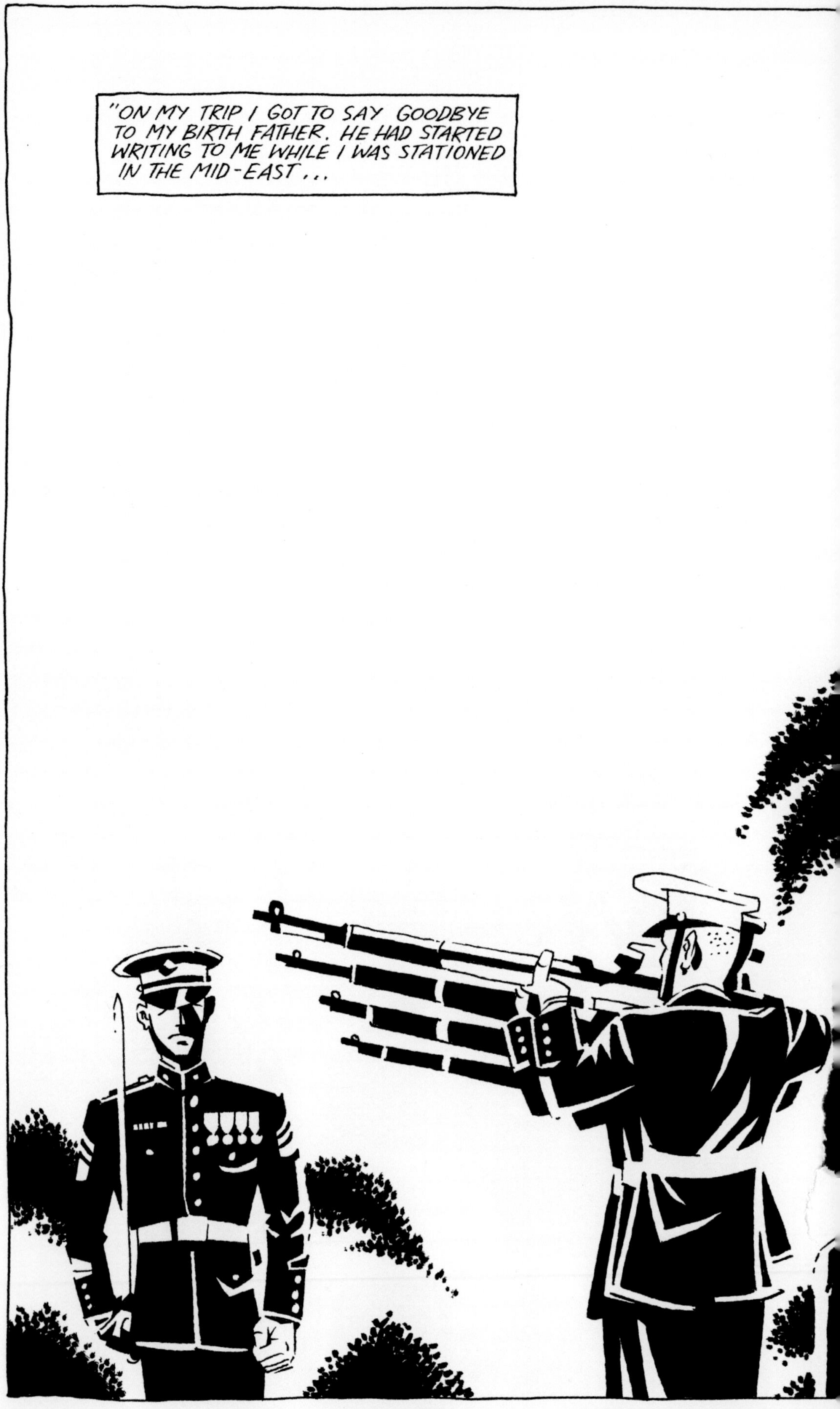
"ON MY TRIP I GOT TO SAY GOODBYE TO MY BIRTH FATHER. HE HAD STARTED WRITING TO ME WHILE I WAS STATIONED IN THE MID-EAST...

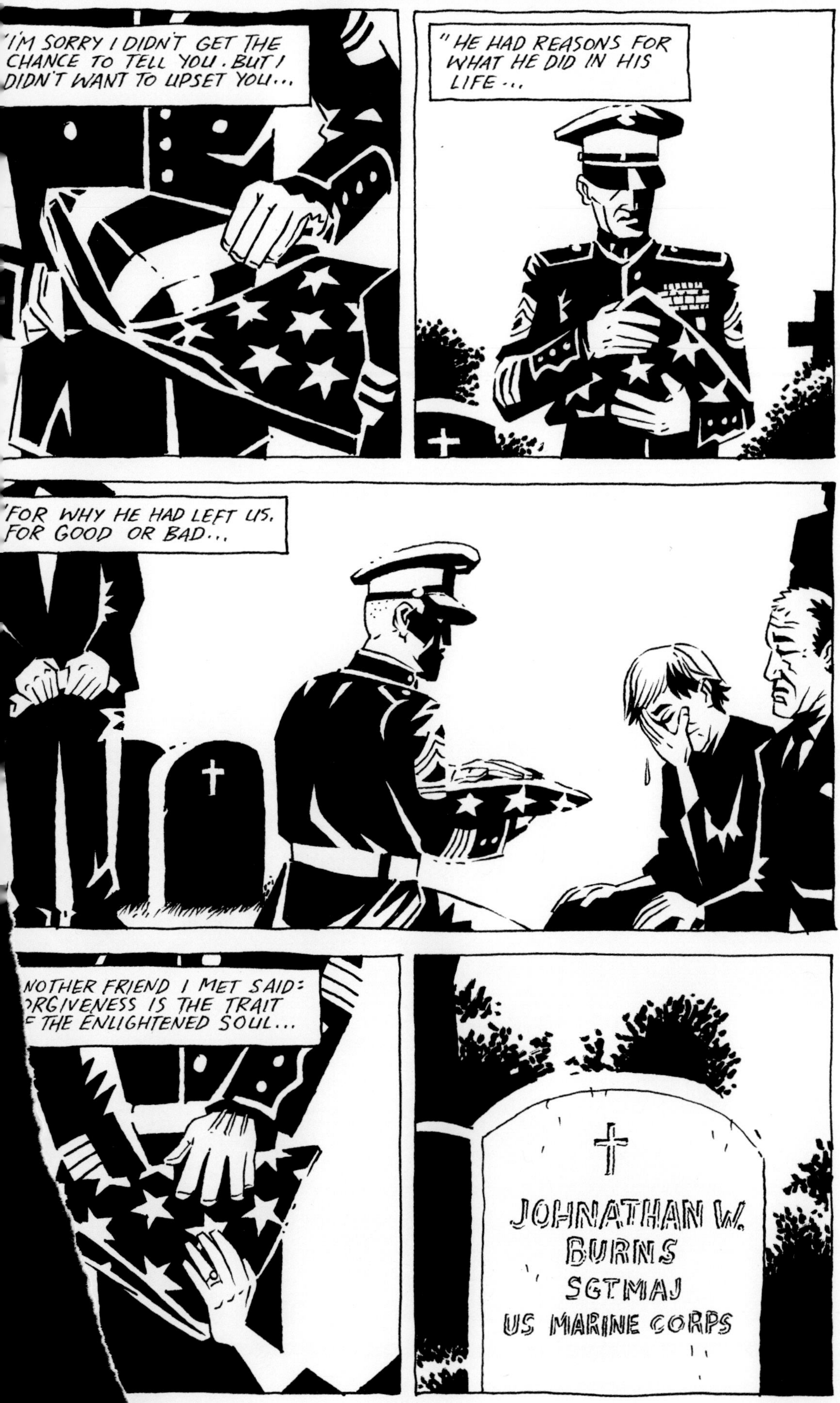

"I'M SORRY I DIDN'T GET THE CHANCE TO TELL YOU. BUT I DIDN'T WANT TO UPSET YOU...
"HE HAD REASONS FOR WHAT HE DID IN HIS LIFE...
"FOR WHY HE HAD LEFT US. FOR GOOD OR BAD...
NOTHER FRIEND I MET SAID: ORGIVENESS IS THE TRAIT F THE ENLIGHTENED SOUL...
JOHNATHAN W. BURNS
SGT MAJ
US MARINE CORPS

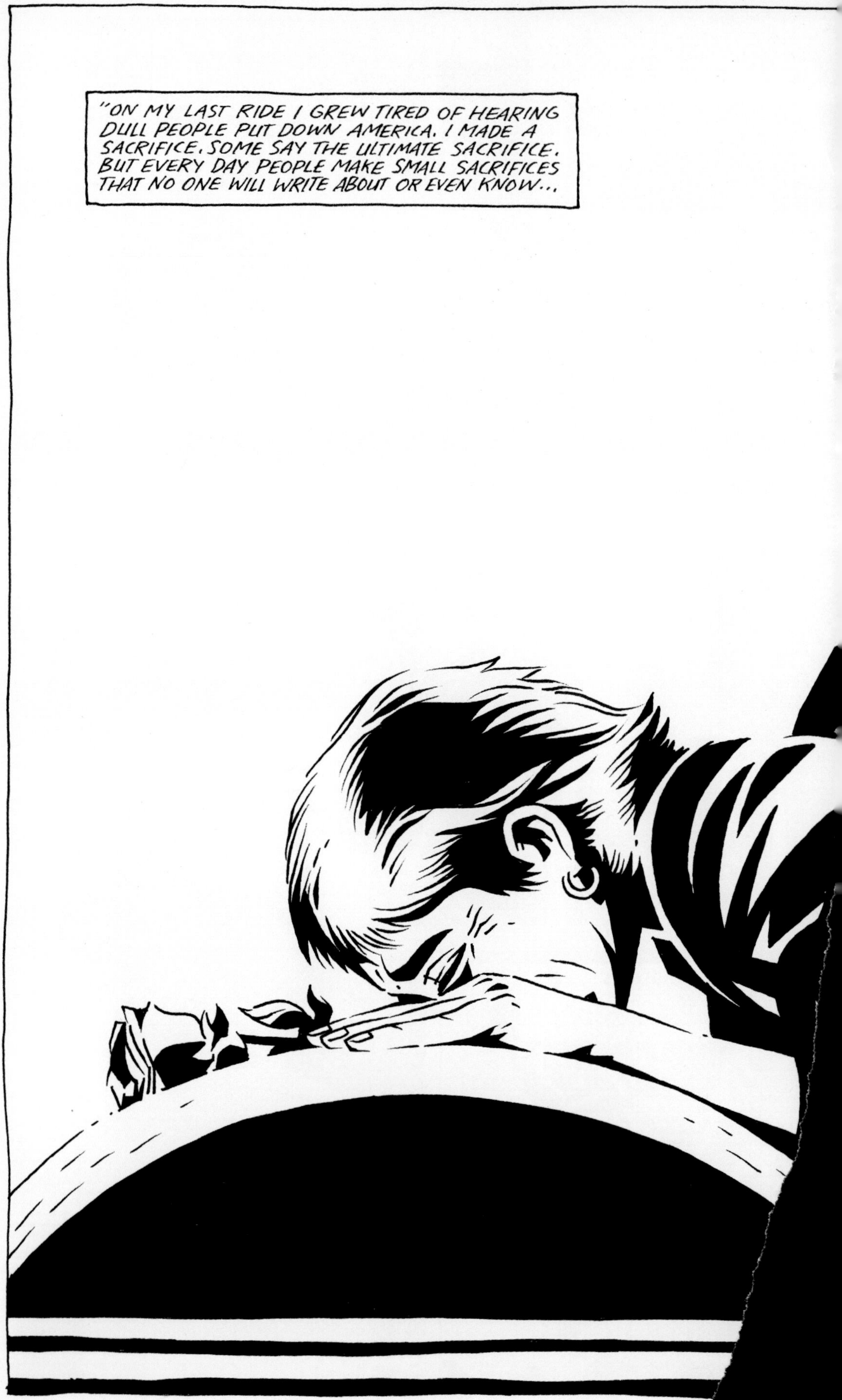
"ON MY LAST RIDE I GREW TIRED OF HEARING DULL PEOPLE PUT DOWN AMERICA. I MADE A SACRIFICE. SOME SAY THE ULTIMATE SACRIFICE. BUT EVERY DAY PEOPLE MAKE SMALL SACRIFICES THAT NO ONE WILL WRITE ABOUT OR EVEN KNOW...

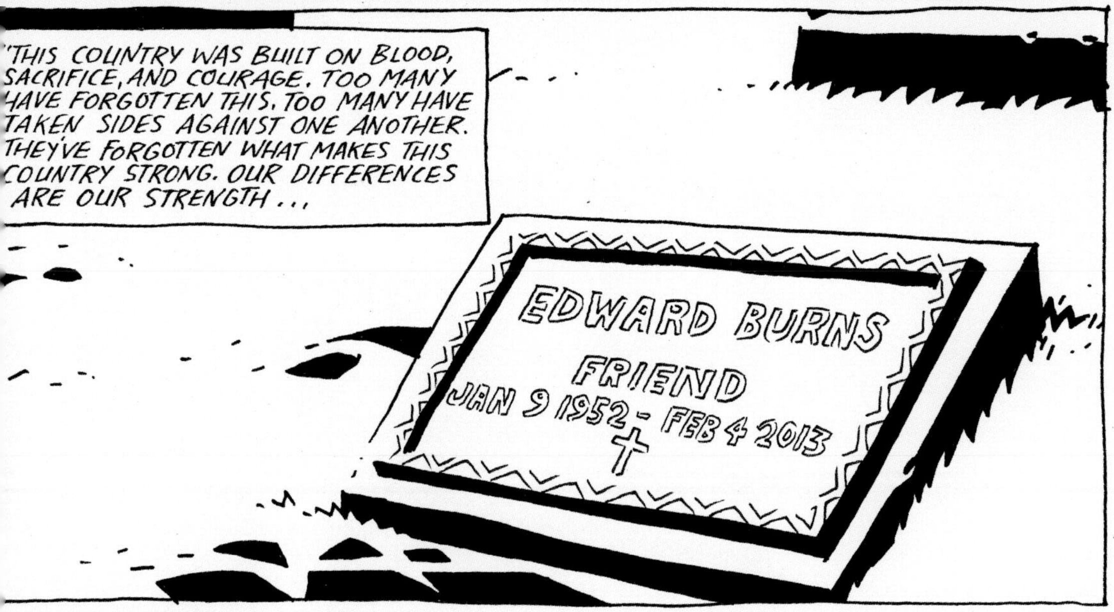
"THIS COUNTRY WAS BUILT ON BLOOD, SACRIFICE, AND COURAGE. TOO MANY HAVE FORGOTTEN THIS. TOO MANY HAVE TAKEN SIDES AGAINST ONE ANOTHER. THEY'VE FORGOTTEN WHAT MAKES THIS COUNTRY STRONG. OUR DIFFERENCES ARE OUR STRENGTH...
EDWARD BURNS
FRIEND
JAN 9 1952 - FEB 4 2013

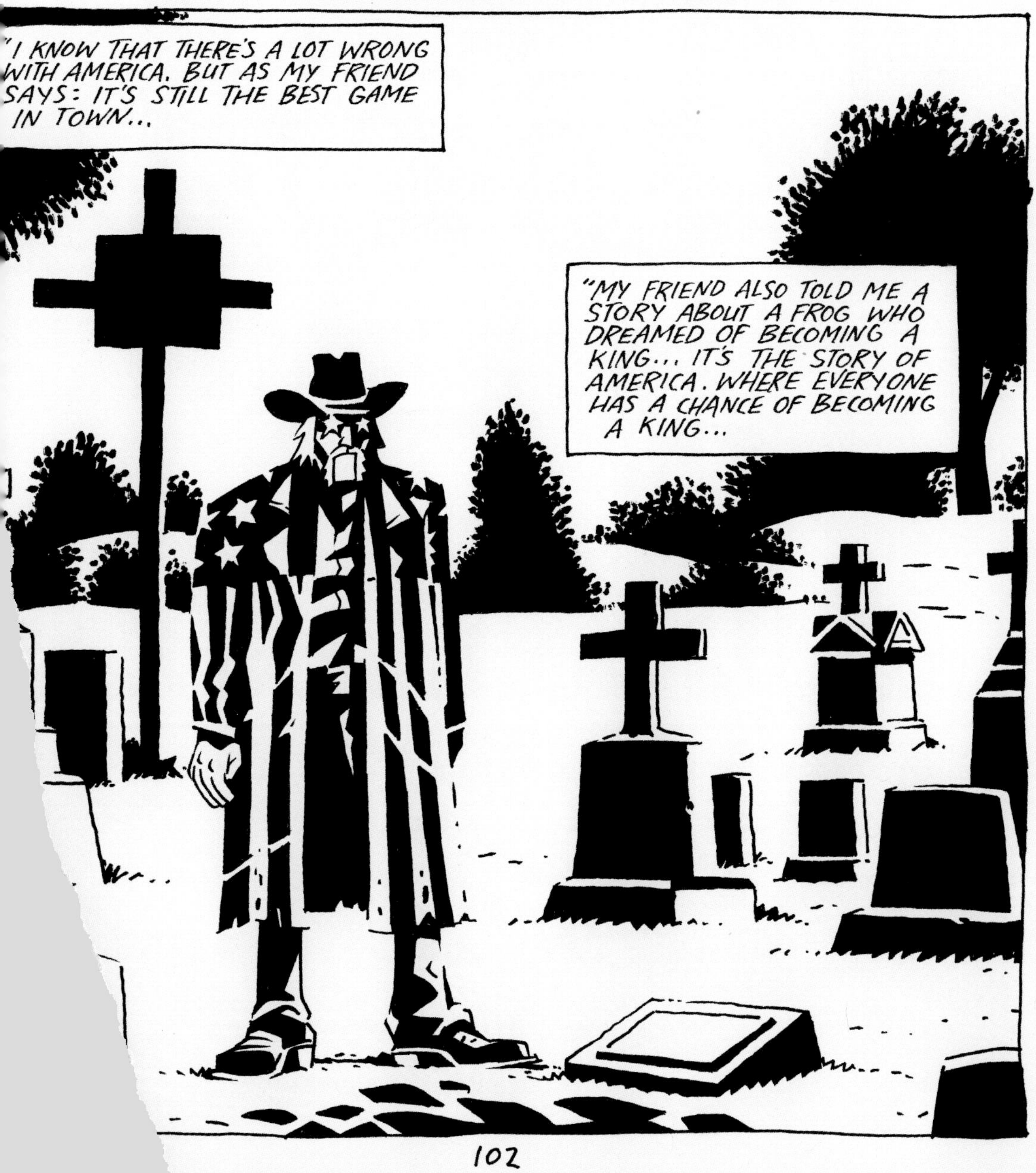
"I KNOW THAT THERE'S A LOT WRONG WITH AMERICA. BUT AS MY FRIEND SAYS: IT'S STILL THE BEST GAME IN TOWN...
"MY FRIEND ALSO TOLD ME A STORY ABOUT A FROG WHO DREAMED OF BECOMING A KING... IT'S THE STORY OF AMERICA. WHERE EVERYONE HAS A CHANCE OF BECOMING A KING...

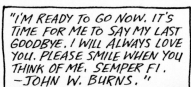
"I'M READY TO GO NOW. IT'S TIME FOR ME TO SAY MY LAST GOODBYE. I WILL ALWAYS LOVE YOU. PLEASE SMILE WHEN YOU THINK OF ME. SEMPER FI. —JOHN W. BURNS."

THANK YOU, MARSHA...

MARSHA ROWLENS

BOUNTY FOR FREEBIRD IS STILL ON. LAUGHING BEAR IS NOT HAPPY.

LAUGHING BEAR CAN BLOW SMOKE OUT HIS ASS. I'LL GET FREEBIRD.

MAYBE YOU WILL. MAYBE YOU WON'T...SO YOU'VE BEEN CHASIN' FREEBIRD FOR A LOOOOONG TIME, EH, SEAGRAVE?

DON'T REMIND ME.

LOOKS LIKE YOU, TONTO AND I ARE THE ONLY BOUNTY HUNTERS LEFT IN THE HUNT.

NEVER CALL ME **TONTO** OR I CUT YOUR THROAT. IT MEANS **DUMB**.

OKAY, SHEESH. TOUCHY.

HE DON'T HAVE MUCH OF A SENSE OF HUMOR.

I PROPOSE A TOAST THE BEST HUNTER WINNING. BUT I DO HAVE ONE QUESTION

...OKAY, IF THE GONZO BROTHERS ARE GONE, WHATEVER HAPPENED TO THE REST OF THE KOIKE KOJIMA CLAN?

CHECK PLEASE!

Red Rooster LOUNGE

COCKTAILS

BIG TV

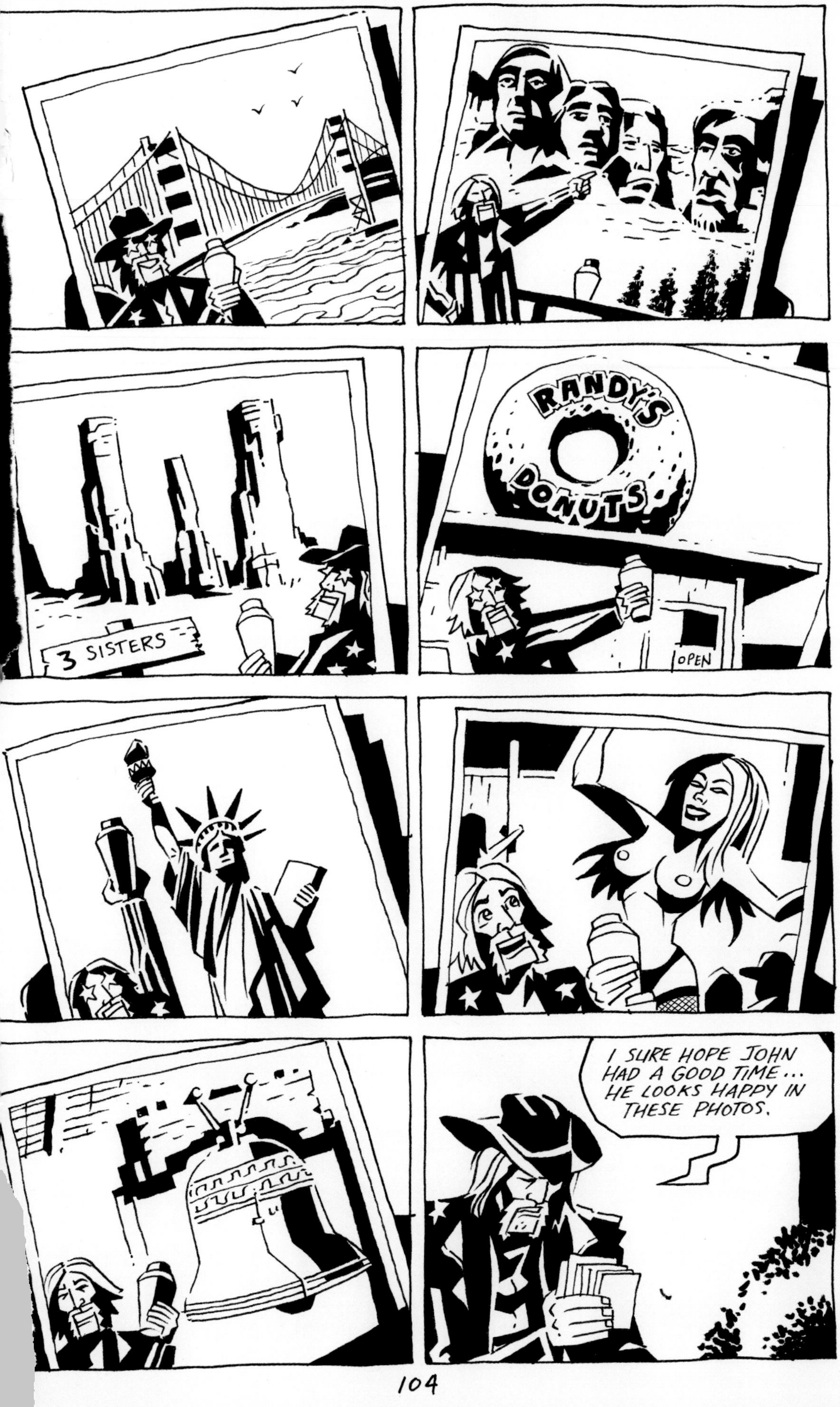
RANDY'S
DONUTS
3 SISTERS
OPEN
I SURE HOPE JOHN HAD A GOOD TIME... HE LOOKS HAPPY IN THESE PHOTOS.

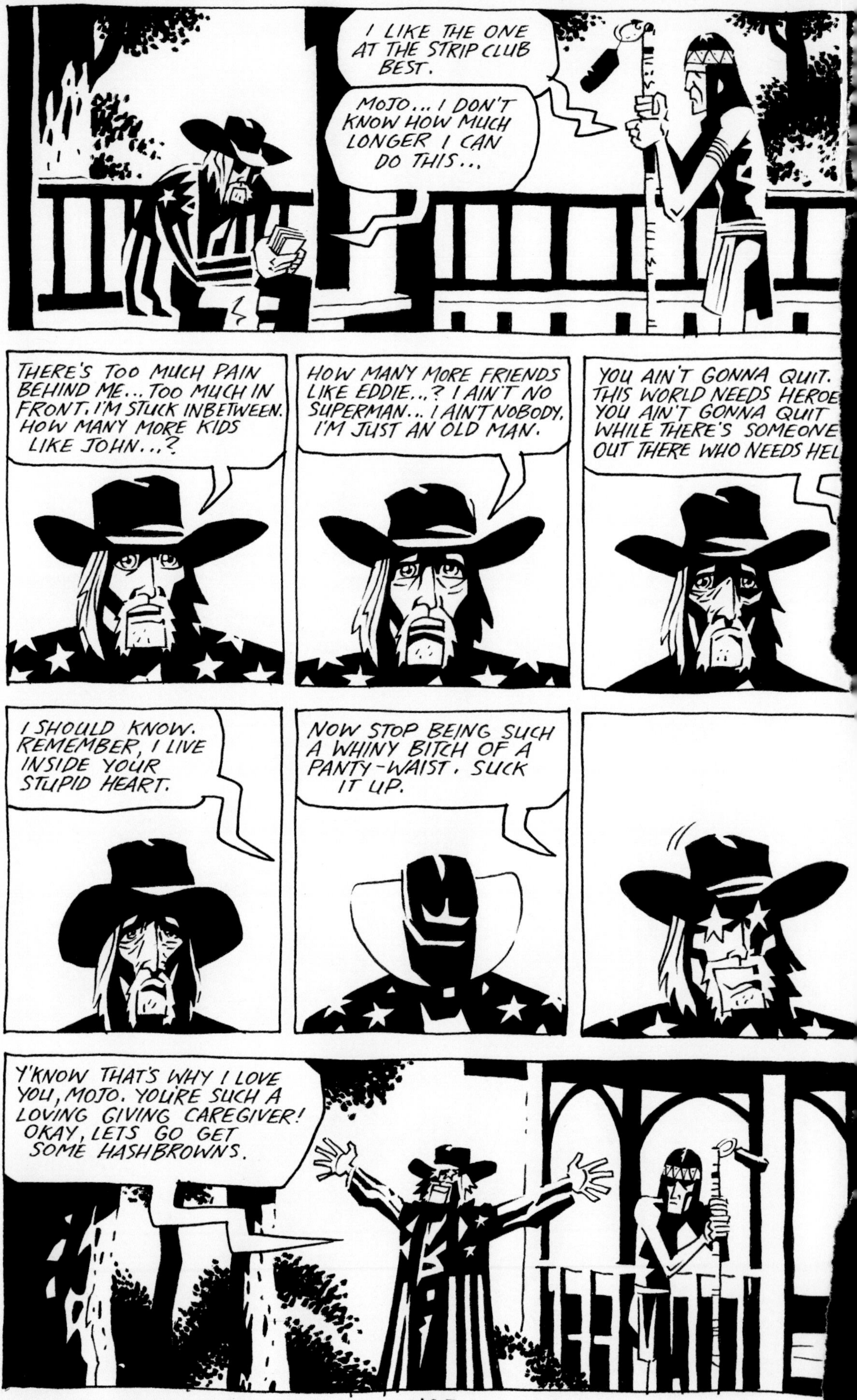

I LIKE THE ONE AT THE STRIP CLUB BEST.
MOJO... I DON'T KNOW HOW MUCH LONGER I CAN DO THIS...
THERE'S TOO MUCH PAIN BEHIND ME... TOO MUCH IN FRONT. I'M STUCK INBETWEEN. HOW MANY MORE KIDS LIKE JOHN...?
HOW MANY MORE FRIENDS LIKE EDDIE...? I AIN'T NO SUPERMAN... I AIN'T NOBODY. I'M JUST AN OLD MAN.
YOU AIN'T GONNA QUIT. THIS WORLD NEEDS HEROE YOU AIN'T GONNA QUIT WHILE THERE'S SOMEONE OUT THERE WHO NEEDS HEL
I SHOULD KNOW. REMEMBER, I LIVE INSIDE YOUR STUPID HEART.
NOW STOP BEING SUCH A WHINY BITCH OF A PANTY-WAIST. SUCK IT UP.
Y'KNOW THAT'S WHY I LOVE YOU, MOJO. YOU'RE SUCH A LOVING GIVING CAREGIVER! OKAY, LETS GO GET SOME HASHBROWNS.

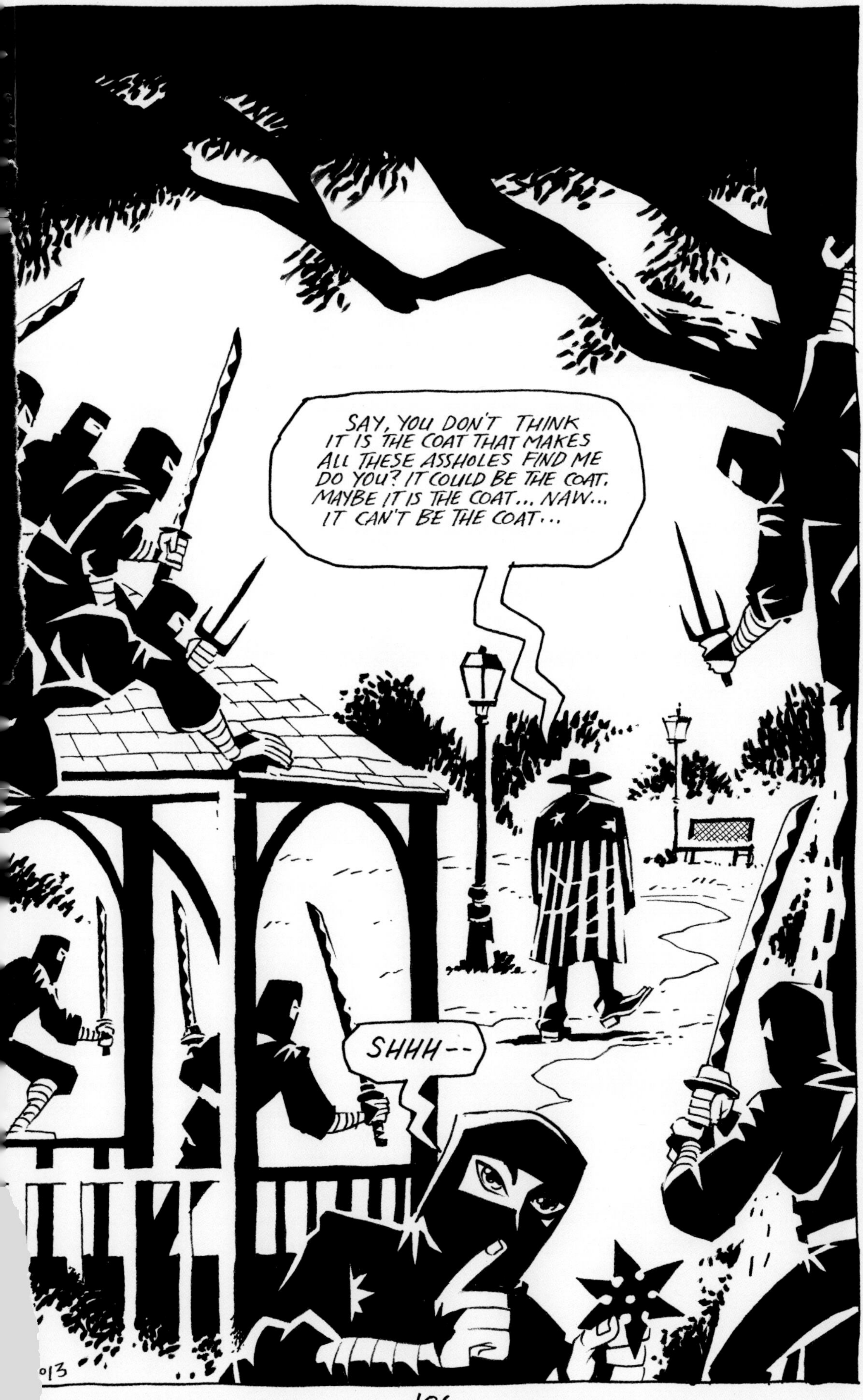
SAY, YOU DON'T THINK IT IS THE COAT THAT MAKES ALL THESE ASSHOLES FIND ME DO YOU? IT COULD BE THE COAT. MAYBE IT IS THE COAT... NAW... IT CAN'T BE THE COAT...
SHHH--
013

Afterword

The Great Mandala

by J. D. Bonaire

Things are in some ways a lot crappier than they were when we were growing up. But in a few ways — a few important ways — they're better.

In the 1960s, the United States was ramping up a military campaign in Viet Nam. A lot of people couldn't understand why that was a good idea: no matter how one looked at it, whether militarily, geopolitically, economically – you name the prism and it still never made any sense. (Except perhaps for the military industrial complex, whose prism was a bank statement, who made huge profits supplying the Pentagon with replacements for the massive amounts of munitions and equipment that were being consumed daily). But despite the lack of sense the whole thing made, the war kept going. Because nobody cared.

Now, when I say *nobody* cared, that's not quite accurate. Rather, *nobody who mattered* cared. When Viet Nam started, our military was a volunteer army, and those who made up its boots on the ground consisted of young men who generally make up our military when its ranks are filled by enlistees and we haven't been attacked. Like Hispanics. And African-Americans. And White Boys from small farm towns. And young people living in poverty. And so on; you know the list. A list which comprises our treasure — our youth — wanting the education benefits they can't get any other way, wanting to get away from a place they can't find any other way of leaving, or wanting to find a place they can't find any other way of getting to, wanting brothers and sisters who have their backs, wanting to feel what it's like to be responsible for somebody else's back. Our treasure that so many politicians seem to be so cavalier about expending. As long as the young people who filled the military's increasing need for replenished treasure came from the nobody who matters coffers, the war went on unabated. Because the part of America that mattered wasn't paying attention.

And then a funny thing happened. The *nobody who matters'* coffins started piling up so fast that the *nobody who matters* coffers began to run dry. So America instituted a draft, and when the draft wasn't sufficient to feed the military war smachine's appetite for boots on the ground, America began to change the rules of the draft. Used to be, as long as you were in college, you were "deferred." Used to be, if your family was even as low down as middle middle class you could get into the Reserves, and the Reserves were ready willing and able but somehow never got called into battle, wink wink (think George W. Bush), or you could find some doctor who wrote that you couldn't serve cause you had a deviated septum, or flat feet, or bad allergies, or wet your bed, or or or. Used to be any grad school enrollment led to deferral automatically too. In fact, you were draft deferred even if your academic journey was sufficiently unfocused that long after your class had graduated you were still on campus, finding your niche. (Or, as Bluto lamented after Dean Wormer expelled the Deltas and notified each of their draft boards, "Christ! Seven years of college down the drain!") That all changed. "Real" kids started to be drafted... the kind that *you actually had heard of*. So-and-so's cousin. The kid down the block you'd seen shooting hoops once in a while. And then, your cousin. And then, your older brother.

You think America is polarized now? A vocal minority of America's being led around by its nose, and they're rabid about things like "immigration" (*really? Please*), and gay rights (we can touch on that another time if you'd like, but the key is it's simply not the result of a choice), and the entitlement of all Americans to own shoulder-mounted anti-aircraft missiles that come out of tubes 'cause the right to bear arms shall not be abridged, and you think America is polarized now? America's not polarized now. Not like it was during Viet Nam. By the late sixties everyone was yelling: you were on one side or the other, but you were on a side, and whichever side you were on, you were passionate and loud and strident, and everyone else you knew was too. When it started it was old white men (don't trust anyone over 30) against everyone who'd stopped going to barbers (are you a boy or are you a girl), but it became about one side yelling "unpatriotic traitor!" at what increasingly were mobs of soccer moms. The Viet Nam war effort was unquestionably crippled by the "Pentagon Papers," *The New York Times'* publication of classified documents that showed the top military command had been knowingly, intentionally and repeatedly lying to the American people about... well, about everything that mattered... How many were being injured. How many were being killed. That we were "winning". What our prospects were for "winning" even more in the future. All lies. But the fatal blow to the Viet Nam war was the saturation point of the immediacy of war dead on the American consciousness. On *moms*. My pastor's kid? My *neighbor's* kid? **My kid?!?** Be the first one.... on your block.... to have your son come home in a box? Hell no they won't go — **I won't let them**. You old men want to continue to run the country? This ends now or your career does. Or our marriage does. Or my love does. If you need this to keep going on, you're not the man I thought you were, and I will

ii

sadly find another one. But by God I will. Not even the war between the North and the South rived families the way the Viet Nam war did.

And in the detritus of the Viet Nam war's collateral damage, unnoticed at first, were all the soldiers. All the young people who'd enlisted or been drafted, who went for God and country, wasn't theirs to question was only theirs to follow orders, and then finally it was over, and those who were still able to draw breath — more than 58,000 no longer could — started coming home.

And we spit on them. We called them baby killers. They had gone to do their patriotic duty, most barely out of high school, and we held them accountable for everything that was wrong with that war and its political process. It was as if America accepted the cavalier way that Washington was willing to waste the treasure of America's youth, and so when they returned we gave them that same disrespect. They weren't looking for parades and medals. But they hadn't expected our enmity. It was, in the lifetime of any living American, our most shameful moment. Explainable? Yes. Understandable? That too. Forgivable? Not ever.

We began this discourse with the happier thought that some things are better today for America than they used to be, and some of those things are important. This is one of them. America has accepted that our treasured youth goes into the military with all of the high-valued idealism we would want them to. America has begun to understand that our military personnel owe their allegiance to their military brothers and sisters and measure their performance by that allegiance and the following of orders from their commanding officers. If we didn't think Iraq One was necessary, if on the eve of Iraq Two we were skeptical there were really Weapons of Mass Destruction, if our cynicism was confirmed when none were found, if we believed Iraq Two was instead all about oil or making a former bloodline commander-in-chief proud or taking out a really bad guy because, well, because we could, we've come to acceptance of the seminal truth that the people to judge and hold accountable are not the noble uniformed marionettes, but the ones who control their strings.

The men and women who did and do and will serve in America's military deserve our utmost respect, and appreciation, and admiration, and support. As do their families. And this is so regardless of the merits of the missions into which our military/political rulers send them. Having made the quantum leap to recognition of that truth, we need to be true to our word. We need to insist our government makes good on its promises: complete medical care; educational and training opportunities; specialized and long-term care for PTSD; a Veterans'

Administration that functions with the efficiency of a state-of-the-art Silicon Valley company rather than like something out of Sgt. Bilko. And if we can't do that, then we ought to change the system over to one of military service for all Americans, for *all* Americans, as Israel does, so that if what our returning Veterans find when they come back is cinders and ashes, at least we'll be providing an equal opportunity disappointment. But we all know — or at least our moms know — that ain't happening.

There is a very concrete list of things that America's politicians shouldn't be allowed to screw with in the country's annual budgets. Kids' educations. Health research. There's others; it turns out there's actually a pretty long list that virtually all Americans agree upon. But morally, ethically, in terms of who we are, and who we want to be, and how we see ourselves, and how we want to be seen, we should now and always treat our returning and returned Veterans as jewels who belong on cushions of our pride and gratitude.

The Great Mandala wheel moves slowly, but sometimes it does move, and of those times, sometimes we actually move forward. This is one of those times. Let's just not forget that. And maybe, each in our own way, give it a little help.[1]

J. D. Bonaire
Butte, Montana
October, 2013

---

[1] Publisher's Note: CAPTAIN FREEBIRD has been a favorite of Veterans since Matt Fillbach and Shawn Fillbach first created the Captain more than a decade ago. If anyone in America knows of a Veteran who would enjoy *CAPTAIN FREEBIRD: AMERICAN PRAYER* but money is an issue, please email us at SupportForVeterans@firstcomicspublishing.com, or write to us at SUPPORT FOR VETERANS, P.O. BOX 609, 2460 Dundee Road, Northbrook IL 60062 with the details. First Comics will get them a copy. For free. And it will be our privilege to do so.

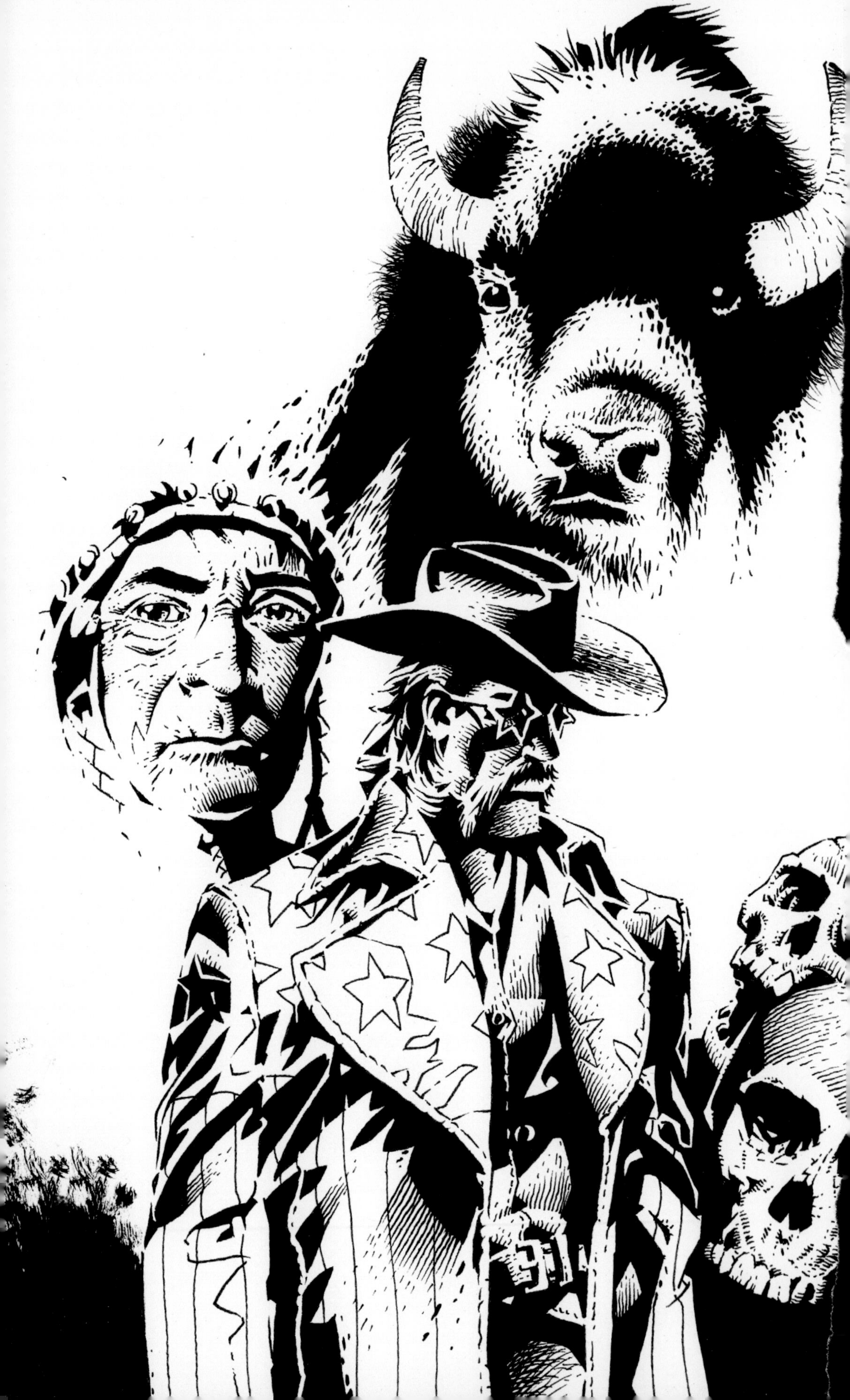